CHINESE MONKS IN INDIA

BUDDHIST TRADITION SERIES

Edited by
ALEX WAYMAN

VOLUME 3

CHINESE MONKS IN INDIA

Biography of Eminent Monks who went to the Western World in Search of the Law during the Great T'ang Dynasty

BY

I-CHING

TRANSLATED BY

LATIKA LAHIRI

MOTILAL BANARSIDASS PUBLISHERS
PRIVATE LIMITED • DELHI

2nd Reprint : 2015
First Edition : Delhi, 1986

ISBN : 978-81-208-0062-5

MOTILAL BANARSIDASS
41 U.A. Bungalow Road, Jawahar Nagar, Delhi 110 007
8 Mahalaxmi Chamber, 22 Bhulabhai Desai Road, Mumbai 400 026
203 Royapettah High Road, Mylapore, Chennai 600 004
236, 9th Main III Block, Jayanagar, Bengaluru 560 011
8 Camac Street, Kolkata 700 017
Ashok Rajpath, Patna 800 004
Chowk, Varanasi 221 001

Printed in India

by RP Jain at NAB Printing Unit,
A-44, Naraina Industrial Area, Phase I, New Delhi–110028
and published by JP Jain for Motilal Banarsidass Publishers (P) Ltd,
41 U.A. Bungalow Road, Jawahar Nagar, Delhi-110007

TO MY LATE LAMENTED

FATHER

FOREWORD

The Chinese are justifiably said to be fond of, and adept at historical records, such as the record here translated by Lahiri. It is frequently claimed that the Indians were neither fond of nor adept at such records. Even so, Chinese monks did not lose sight of India as the spiritual fountain of Buddhism. Certain native Chinese compositions by Buddhists were attributed to Indian authorship to lend the works greater prestige—thus the attributed authorship contradicts correct literary history, despite the fondness of the Chinese for historical records.

As long as the Buddhist institutions of India continued as viable spiritual centres, they inspired visits by intrepid Chinese monks, who braved all sorts of perils to reach 'non-historical' India. And I-Ching wrote up the lives of the eminent Chinese monks who risked their lives to come to India to study, during the Great T'ang Dynasty of China. He modelled his composition called Kao seng-chuan after earlier and a large work of this genre. Latika Lahiri provides the first English translation of I-Ching's treatise. Doubtless, many a scholar will be interested in this translation and the notes thereto, as they previously used the observations of India by the celebrated Hsuan-tsang. Indian scholars also, despite the 'non-historical' label, can be expected to consult and appreciate Lahiri's translation.

New Delhi
August 9, 1986

ALEX WAYMAN

CONTENTS

PROLOGUE

This work was started in 1958 when I was an Indian Government scholar in Peking (Beijing) University. It was through the initiative of Dr. Ji Xianlin, the renowned Buddhist and Sanskrit scholar, now the Vice-Chancellor of Peking University, that I undertook this difficult but interesting task of translating *Kao-Seng Chuan* (Biography of Eminent Monks) by I-ching as there was no complete English translation of the text. Under his able guidance I undertook the work with much hesitation. I am extremely grateful to him.

Here I also record my gratitude to Prof. Feng, "An Old Master", a veteran retired professor of Indian Philosophy, Tokyo University, but for whose active support and generous encouragement I would not have undertaken this work. He helped me in reading the text with all sincerity and patience. Old and traditional China was revealed to me through him. His suggestions and encouragement were very helpful. I remember him today with sorrowful heart when he is no longer in this world.

I brought back the incomplete manuscript to India in 1959.

In India I could not find a bi-lingual scholar (Sanskrit and Chinese)who could help me in completing the work. After joining the University of Delhi I had the opportunity to get help from Mr. Richard Yang who had then joined this University as a visiting professor. The work was practically completed in 1969. But due to various factors such as unavoidable delay in printing, pre-occupations in service life, etc. its publication got delayed.

The object of the present work is to make available the informations relating to historical, geographical and political condition as well as the prevailing condition of Buddhism in East Asian countries in general and in India in particular during the seventh and the eighth centuries. In working on this text, my attention was not exclusively fixed on the specialists and scholars only.

In recent times the Buddhist Studies have become very popular among the educated people not only in India but also in countries other than India. I hope this subject will receive increasing attention and interest from the students of Buddhism.

In the following pages I have transcribed the Chinese words in English phonetics and adopted mostly the Wade-Giles system as used in Mathew's *Dictionary*. Modern China is making frequent changes in the style of transcription of Chinese words in English. I have adopted some important names frequently used in this publication according to Chinese pronunciation such as Fa-hsien, Hsüan-Chuang and I-Ching, etc.

The practice of adopting Sanskrit names on ordination prevailed among the monks in China as well as in the Far Eastern countires. Some of the names of the fifty-six monks of the text are not given in Sanskrit which I have tried to translate into Sanskrit without any corroboration. If these are not correctly translated, it is my shortcoming.

I am greatly indebted to my colleagues and friends Professor Richard Yang, Professor Tan Chung of Jawaharlal Nehru University, and Professor Lokesh Chandra for their very valued help and encouragement.

Lastly I am deeply thankful to Mr. Dwijendra Nandi for his many helpful suggestions and editorial as well as other assistance. I am also indebted to my talented young grand nephew Mr. Angshuman Bagchi for preparing the index, a task of great labour willingly undertaken by him.

This is the very humble result of my hard efforts. If the publication is able to satisfy even partially, the inquisitive readers and receive their critical appreciation, my labour will be more than repaid.

New Delhi LATIKA LAHIRI

ABBREVIATIONS

ARBRPIMA	A Record of Buddhist Religion as Practised in India and Malaya Archipelago
BCC	Buddhist Conquest of China
CTT	Chinese Tripitaka Taishō
HCIP	History and Culture of Indian People
KSC	Kao seng-chuan
NC	Nanjio's Catalogue

CHART OF CHINESE DYNASTIES
UP TO SUNG

The Hsia Dynasty 2205–1818 B.C.
The Shang Dynasty 1766–1154 B.C.
The Chou Dynasty 1122–255 B.C.
The Ch'in Dynasty 255–209 B.C.
The Han Dynasty:
(Also styled Former Han or Western Han) 206 B.C.–A.D. 23
The Later or Eastern Han A.D. 25–220

The Three Kingdoms

The Minor Han Dynasty A.D. 221–263
The Wei Dynasty A.D. 2202–64
The Wu Dynasty A.D. 222–277

The Western Tsin Dynasty A.D. 265–313
The Eastern Tsin Dynasty A.D. 317–419

Division between North and South

The Sung Dynasty A.D. 420–477
The Northern Wei Dynasty A.D. 386–535
The Ch'i Dynasty A.D. 479–501
The Liang Dynasty A.D. 520–556
The Ch'en Dynasty A.D. 557–587
The Sui Dynasty A.D 581–618
The T'ang Dynasty A.D. 618–905
The Liao Dynasty (Khitan Tartar) A.D. 9161–168
The Chin or Kin Dynasty (Tartar) A.D. 1115–1234
The Sung Dynasty A.D. 960–1126
The Southern Sung Dynasty A.D. 1127–1278

INTRODUCTION

The *Kao seng-chuan*, "Biographies of Eminent Monks", written in the third half of the seventh century, by the famous monk-scholar, I-ching, is the prototype of earlier Buddhist compilations. I-ching's *Kao seng-chuan* is undoubtedly an indispensable source of and an outstanding work dealing with the history of Buddhism and Buddhist Church in China, and the socio-political and cultural history of India of the seventh and eighth centuries. It is a brilliant piece of literature of the T'ang period (A.D. 618-907). I-ching's poetic expression at the end of major and minor biographies and his style sometimes excel even the famous writers and secular poets of that period.

The compilation of lives of eminent monks is not an innovation by I-ching. From the very hoary ancient days, the Chinese had shown their eagerness and keen insight to preserve their history. Their love for history and interest in historical records encouraged the Buddhist scholars of China to preserve the valuable biographies of devoted, intrepid, illustrious and worthy monks from India and Central Asia. Their lives are included in *Kao seng-chuan*. I-ching only followed the tradition and time honoured convention, methodology, and more or less the same style as adopted by his predecessors like Hui-chiao 慧皎, Seng-yü 僧祐 and others. The *Kao seng-chuan*[1] (*Chinese Tripiṭaka*, Taisho Ed. Vol. 50, No. 2059 in 14 chapters) of Hui-chiao (A.D. 497-554) contains 257 major and 259 minor biographies of eminent monks, from A.D. 67 to 519, thus covering almost five hundred years. The monk Seng-yü (who lived under the reign of the Emperor Wu of the Liang Dy.—A.D. 502-557), in the last three chapters of *Ch'u-san-tsang Chi-chi*[2] 出三藏記集

1. Arthur F. Wright. *Hui-chiao's Lives of Eminent Monks.* Silver Jubilee volume, Zinbun-Kagaku Kenkyusyo. Tokyo University (Tokyo, 1954), pp. 383-432.

2. The oldest extant catalogue compiled by Seng-yü in A.D. 518.

Collection of notes concerning the translation of Tripiṭaka (T. 2145), gives biographies of 32 famous monks, mainly translators and exegetes.

Tao-hsüan, the most famous Buddhist historian of the T'ang Dynasty (A.D. 618-907), continued the series of eminent monks known as *Hsu-kao seng-chuan*, Further Biographies of Eminent Monks, which contains biographies of 33 monks (CTT 50 No. 2060, pp. 425, 657 c-658a). Not only the biographies of eminent monks have been preserved but also lives of eminent nuns have occupied the same exalted position in the *Kao seng-chuan* (hereafter abbreviated KSC). It records the biographies of 65 Eminent Nuns, *Pi-ch'iu-ni chuan* 比丘尼傳 (CTT 2065) compiled by Pao-ch'ang of the Liang Dynasty. All these intellectual elites' writings of lives of eminent monks, on account of their excellent qualities, both as historical as well as literary works, became the standard to be followed by future biographers. I-ching tried to write within the convention and tradition of Chinese historiographers. The historical biographies of the renowned Indian Ācāryas like Aśvaghoṣa[1], Nāgārjuna[2], Āryadeva[3], and Vasubandhu[4] and the biography of Emperor Aśoka[5] and others are to be found in *KSC*. These biographies are undoubtedly an indispensable source for the history of the early *gentry* Buddhism and Buddhist Church in China and are of immense importance for their literary and social value.

The monk Hui-min 慧民 of the Liang Dynasty (A.D. 502-557), first introduced the title *KSC* and gave the name to his work. Hui-chiao, compiler of *KSC* wrote in his preface "...If men of real achievement conceal their brilliance then they are eminent but not famous; when men of slight virtue happen to be in accord with their times then they are famous but not eminent."[6] Thus Hui-chiao has made a clear-cut distinction

1. Taisho Ed. Vol. 50 No. 2046, p. 183. Translated by Kumārajīva.
2. Ibid. No. 2047, p. 184. Translated by Kumārajīva.
3. Ibid. No. 2048, p. 186. Translaten by Kumārajīva.
4. Ibid. No. 2049, p. 188. Translated by Paramārtha also called Guṇaratna from Ujjain.
5. Ibid. No. 2042, p. 99. Translated by a Parthian (Persian) monk, An Fa-ch' in.
6. Ibid., p. 408.

between an eminent monk and a famous one. A famous monk might be able to glorify his religion during his life time but an eminent monk was able to set open a new vista and was to herald a new epoch in Buddhism by his brilliant scholarship and example, and his life would be the model to future generations.

I-ching undertook the difficult task of collecting and compiling the biographies of fifty-six monks who may not be considered as important as Tao-an, Hui-chiao, Kumārajīva and others but their contribution is equally great in promoting and transmitting the light of Buddhism. From his preface, from his *KSC* as well as from his own biography, we understand his various motives which prompted the writer in compiling the biographies of eminent monks.

His main objective was to immortalise those self-sacrificing monks who made a striking contribution to the propagation and prosperity of Dharma bequeathed by the Buddha. They were the torch-bearers who would illuminate the posterity. I-ching not only tried to establish the religious eminence of the monks but also the prestige and honour they commanded from the people, officials, kings, princes in China as well as in India. The austere lives, self-sacrificing and adventurous spirit, the brilliant scholarship and wonderful accomplishment of the Buddhist monks would inspire the future generations. In this regard I-ching's monks are eminent.

From I-ching's account of these monks, we get a general impression of the immense hardship and perils the pilgrims braved during their travel, their indomitable spirit and desire for learning Buddhism in India. But in spite of these difficulties they never faltered, never wavered. This quest for spiritual knowledge gave them impetus to take up the perilous journey either by land or by sea. It is in fact, a pathetic succession of tales of woes and disappointment. Some of them withered away unrecognised without sharing the benefit of their experience and learning with their compatriots in their own homeland. I-ching in the Preface said, "No doubt, it is great merit and fortune to visit the Western country (India) in search of the Law but at the same time it is an extremely difficult and perilous undertaking." I-ching gave his own experience in the same Preface. "Many days I have passed without food even without a drop of water. I was always worried and no spirit was left in me....If, however, a monk happened to reach India after such perilous journey, he would find no Chinese monastery there. There was no fixed place to settle down. We had to move from place to place like a blade of grass swept by wind. I wish to fulfil my desire so that the future generations may know all about the facts. I had heard with my own ears and seen with my own eyes the difficulties the monks had undergone previously."

He mentioned that on one occasion a monk with a very vague idea of Buddhist establishment in India drew a sketch of Jetavana Vihāra but the sketch was far from reality. I-ching sent a plan of Nālandā to acquaint the Buddhist followers with the real Nālandā of India. I-ching was very much distressed when he found the Chinese government did not appoint any commission to investigate the whereabouts of those missing monks. He thought it reasonable and proper to write a comprehensive and connected account of them.

Sino-Indian relation was established by the selfless Buddhist monks of both India and China who undertook to carry the message of love which Buddha delivered for the suffering mankind. The cultural intercourse between the two great countries was primarily initiated by the Chinese, hence, source materials of its history are to be found in Chinese only. Unfortunately, Indian history has not recorded the great achievements of those noble Indian scholars who went to China with purely missionary spirit and whose names are interwoven with the history of Buddhism in China. They were the torch-bearers of Indian civilisation abroad. The Chinese not only preserved the names of those Indians but also had preserved the record of the Chinese monks who went out to India in search of the Law. These source materials of spiritual and cultural intercourse between the two ancient civilisations have not yet been fully explored.

Politically India was considered weak and feeble, being the prey of frequent foreign invasions in the North, but the spectacular cultural conquest which India had achieved cannot be under-estimated. Indian culture penetrated peacefully and gloriously into various parts of Central Asia and East Asia enriching their political, social and cultural life including art, literature, and architecture. Sir Charles Eliot says, "For the reality of

Indian influence in Asia—from Japan to the frontiers of Persia, from Macedonia to Java, from Burma to Mongolia is undoubted and the influence is one."[1] This idea of 'oneness' removed natural, political, social and religious barriers and united all these countries into one world.

This cultural intercourse between India and China was mainly carried on through important routes : one, over-land route through Central Asia to India; another, sea-route, starting from the port of Kuang-chou through the South China sea into the Indian ocean.

The over-land route was older and the sea-route became popular with the advancement of science and culture during the T'ang Dynasty. The ancient route passed through one of the caravan towns and the Chinese territory of Tun-huang, outside the Great Wall, on the edge of the Gobi desert and then through the province of Kan-su to Ch'ang-an and Lo-yang. This over-land route with its cities and towns was 'terra incognito' to the Chinese till the second century B.C. In the seventh and eighth centuries, navigation became a little easier and safer with China's progress in ship-building and mariners' compass. Such dangerous routes were used by the *Śramaṇas* who built up the cultural relation between India and China. The immense hardship and privation the monks had to face either by ancient over-land or sea-route is still a legend to us, living in the Space Age when the journey to the Moon is no longer a myth. I-ching was the pioneer who first took up the sea voyage from China.

After the introduction of Buddhism, the Buddhist intellectuals faced a serious problem regarding the translation of Buddhist Sūtras with their highly technical terminology. In order to popularise the new Faith and salvage the docrine from initial vagueness and remove doubts, the sacred books had to be made available to the population. People had to be given an opportunity to acquire correct knowledge of the philosophical thoughts of Buddhism and also have an idea of the controversial issues. The main concentration of the Buddhist community in China, therefore, was on the translation and explanation of Indian Buddhist texts. In this matter China was much ahead of time.[2]

1. *Hinduism and Buddhism.* Introduction p. xi.
2. Chao Po-chu: *Buddhism in China*, p. 10. f. n. E. Zürcher—*The Buddhist Conquest of China*, pp. 202-204. E. J. Brill. 1972. Leiden.

Lo-yang, the capital city became an important centre of a highly organised team of translators. In this stupendous task those whose names still shine like bright stars are the bi-lingual scholars like a Parthian monk An Shih-kao[1], Dharmarakṣa[2] and Lokakṣema[3] of Indo-Scythian origin and Kumārajīva[4] of Kucha. They worked with a team of Chinese monk-scholars who helped them in their work. As a result of this joint endeavour about 1153 Buddhist texts were translated into Chinese two and a half centuries after the first introduction of Buddhism in China in A.D. 67. Equally important are the famous Chinese monk-scholars like Tao-an[5], Chih-ch'ien,[6] and Hui-yüan[7] who awakened a new spirit and encouraged the Chinese monks to make pilgrimage to India. Before long missionary activities entered a new phase.

The Chinese Buddhists were greatly confused by multifarious forms of Buddhism introduced in China from India and Central Asia by importation of missionaries belonging to different schools and different countries, by translation of Mahāyāna Sūtras like *Vimalakirtinirdeśa*, *Saddharmapuṇḍarika*, *Mahāparinirvāṇa* and the *Buddha Avataṁsaka nāma Mahāvaipulya Sūtra* of two great Indian schools of Nāgārjuna and Asaṅga and by the translation of some Hīnayāna texts. Amidst this ever growing confusion and uncertainty the Chinese thinkers were groping in the dark for centuries and thus led to the departure of renowned pilgrims like Fa-hsien in A.D. 400, Hsüan-chuang in A.D. 629 and I-ching in A.D. 637 and others for India in search of genuine texts and the true doctrines and to pay homage to the far-famed shrines of their religion. The confusion caused by erroneous translation of the Buddhist texts, the misunderstanding of subtle and mystic ideas of the Buddhist philosophy and lack of disciplinary code for monastic

1. *Chinese Tripiṭaka*. T. Vol. 50, No. 2059, p. 323. Nanjio's Catalogue Appendix ii, No. 4.
2. Ibid. App. II, No. 23.
3. CTT Vol. 50. No. 2059, p. 324, NC ii. 3.
4. Ibid. p. 330. NC ii, No. 59.
5. Ibid. p. 351.
6. NC ii, No. 18.
7. *KSC*, vii. 358. 1. 6.

life prompted the earnest pilgrims to undertake hazardous voyages across the breadth of Asia to procure complete and purer sources. The eternal religious fervour of the monks to make pilgrimage to India, the holy land of the Buddhists, was nonetheless important.

After the death of Tao-an (who was eager to send monks to India) in A.D. 385, a large number of Chinese Śramaṇas was ready to make pilgrimage to India. Fa-hsien, the able disciple of Tao-an, the pioneer of all, started on the adventurous journey to India from the western border of China, with an avowed intention of collecting Buddhist texts on the Vinaya so that he could be able to correct the misrepresentation and irregularities of the Vinaya rules practised there. Fa-hsien left an account of his journey of about sixteen years (A.D. 399-414) in the *Fo-kuo chi*[1] (Record of the Buddhist Country). He knew Sanskrit well and succeeded in translating a voluminous work on the disciplinary code of the Mahāsaṅghika.

The period which intervened between the visits of the two famous missionaries viz. Fa-hsien and Hsüan-chuang (A.D. 629-645) of the Great T'ang period is known for the visits of Sung-yün and Hui-sheng[2] (A.D. 518) who left very short narratives of their travel.

The Sino-Indian cultural intercourse which was built by resolute monks during the five centuries, had a set-back. There was a temporary eclipse of activities of the missionaries nearly for one hundred years. But after this period of inactivity and stagnation, a new era began in the history of Buddhism with the political unification achieved under the Sui (A.D. 590-617) and the T'ang Dynasties (A.D. 618-907). During this new era of rejuvination, Buddhism became more prosperous and flourishing under the Imperial patronage.

1. It was translated into English by S. Beal in 1869, 1884; by H. A. Giles in 1877. A notice by T. Watters was published in the *China Review* 1879 and 1880 and one by Prof. James Legge in 1886 (Clarendon Press). French Translation was done by Re' musat in 1836.

2. CTT 51, No. 2086 p. 866, Vol. These two monks were sent by the Empror of the Northern-Wei Dynasty to visit the relics of the prince Sudāna (*S*udāna Kumārarāja Jātaka) of Dantalokagiri. After their short visit to the holy land (India) they went back to China in the second year of the 正光 Cheng-kuang period (A. D, 519) of the Emperor Hsüan-Wu.

Both the Sui and the T'ang Dynasties made it an Imperial policy to patronise the Buddhist establishment by innumerable donations, by erecting hundreds of Buddhist monuments and temples not only in the Imperial capital but also in provincial cities and towns. By then Buddhism had already acquired a glorious past history of five centuries. Buddhism flourished both in the North and South China. During the first two hundred years of the the T'ang, Buddhism flourished as never before.

In the third year of the 貞觀 Chen-kuan period (A.D. 627-649) of the Emperor T'ai-Tsung, the most renowned traveller, the Great Tripiṭaka-master Hsüan-chuang secretly set out on his long journey to the West in A.D. 629. His travel in the Western regions and in India covered almost seventeen years (A.D. 629-645). When Hsüan-chuang returned from India, the Emperor T'ai-Tsung gave a great ovation and public honour was conferred upon him. He returned with a priceless treasure consisting of 657 sacred books, images of the Lord in gold and silver, 150 relics of the Buddha and good-will from India. Learned monks were employed to assist him in translating the large number of books he had brought. Hsüan-chuang presented to the Emperor the account of his travel known as *Ta-T'ang-hsi-yü chi*[1] (The Buddhist Record of the Western World of the Great T'ang' Dy.). The pilgrim-monk worked tremendously till his end came in A.D. 664, and translated the most difficult Mahāyāna texts—*Vijñaptimātratā Siddhi Śāstra* with sanskrit commentaries, *Mahāprajñā Pāramitā Sūtra, Madhyānta Vibhaṅga Śāstra* etc.

The detailed and romantic accounts of the Buddhist shrines in India and other countries he passed through and his perfect faith, devotion and love for learning became a constant source of inspiration to his contemporaries and posterities. I-ching, the most important Chinese traveller after Hsüan-chuang and a devout Buddhist, was greatly moved and inspired by the life of his illustrious predecessor.

1. It was translated into French by M. Julien, under the title *Memoires sur les Contress occidentales* in 1857; *Histoire de La Vie de Hiouen-Thasang* is another French translation by the same author (1853). Also see the English translation *The Record of the Western Kingdom* by S. Beal and Thomas Watters, 1884; *The Life of Hiuen-Tsang* (abstract) by S. Beal, 1888; *The Life of Hiuen-Tsang* by Chinese Buddhist Accociation, Peking, 1959.

I-ching was born in Fan-yang (near Peking) in 635 A.D. when the Emperor T'ai-Tsung was reigning. At the age of nine he went to his preceptors Shan-yü and Hui-hsi who were living on the mountain at Shan-tung. First he was taught the secular literature and later on, he devoted himself to the Sacred Buddhist Canon. He took his *Pravrajyā* (Order) when he was fourteen years old. He must have witnessed the great ovation extended to the great pilgrim Hsüan-chuang by the Emperor T'ai-Tsung. He entertained the idea of visiting India from early life, but he had to wait till his thirty-seventh year (A.D. 671) when his dream came to be true. He was very energetic, painstaking, persevering and loving to his friends and teachers.

After getting fully ordained by his *Upādhyāya* Hui-hsi, I-ching devoted full five years to the study of the Vinaya, practised some of the 13 *Dhūtāṅgas*. All through his life he never deviated from the teachings of his preceptor.

I-ching had great admiration and love for his predecessors both Fa-hsien and Hsüan-chuang. The former was much interested in the monastic code and the latter in Buddhist philosophy and metaphysics. I-ching belonged to the *Mūla-Sarvāstivāda* School and his primary object was to collect the original texts of the Vinaya like Fa-hsien and to study the Buddhist code of disciplinary rules in India. We get the idea of the prevailing system of discipline in the biography of Shih-lo-po-p'o, Śīlaprabha (One of the 56 monks) of the T'ang period—"Many years had already passed when the great religion (Buddhism) had flooded China in the East but the Institutional School has just started, at the same time the Canonical texts emphasising the importance of monastic discipline are also very rare."

While I-ching was in Ch'ang-an attending religious discourses, he agreed to form with Ch'u-i, a teacher of the Law of Shen-si, Hung-i, a teacher of Śāstra of Lai-chou and two or three other monks and make pilgrimage to the place known as Vulture's Peak (Gṛdhrakūṭa) in Rājagṛha. Ultimately most of his companions backed out for some reason or other. I-ching undertook his projected journey with a solitary young monk Shan-hsing of Shen-si. He embarked on a merchant ship from Canton and proceeded towards the South. "He thus parted with his friends while he did not find a new acquaintance in India". He was very much unhappy in his solitary wandering but the memorable lines of Confucius—"An excellent General can resist the aggressive army but the resolution of a gentleman will never change"—always consoled him, inspired him and kept his spirit high. He took leave from his preceptor Hui-hsi who encouraged him to proceed on the pilgrimage, and blessed him to attain spiritual light. Before his departure, the devout Buddhist neighbours came to say good-bye to him and gave him fine pieces of silk, brocades and thousands of canopies to be offered with devotion to the holy shrines and Buddha images in India, on their behalf.

I-ching reached Śrī-vijaya (Sumatra) and stayed there for a couple of months studying Sanskrit Grammar. Śrī-vijaya became one of the most important centres of learning under the patronage of the Śailendra Kings. There he studied the practices and customs of the Buddhists of Śrī-vijaya and other neighbouring countries. I-ching during his long sojourn of twenty-five years (A.D. 671-695) travelled through more than thirty countries.

In India, this devoted scholar spent ten years learning Sanskrit Grammar and Buddhism from profoundly erudite scholars of the premier University of Nālandā, the *Alma mater* of Hsüan-chuang. Nālandā was then at the zenith of prosperity and fame. I-ching had deep regard and sincere gratitude for his teachers. "I-ching with utmost reverence and undivided mind prostrated before the image of the Buddha and first prayed for China that the four kinds of benefits must prevail in the *Dharmadhātu* (in the realm of Law) among all the living beings there." After visiting the Buddhist shrines he took leave to return home. He sailed from Tāmralipti in A.D. 685 and reached the crowded city of Śrī-vijaya. He stayed there again for four years. From there he sent, through one of his friends, a complete manuscript of *Nan-hai-chi-kuei-nei-fa chuan* ('A Record of The Buddhist Religion as Practised in India and the Malay Archipelago'[1], A.D. 671-695), the *Ta-T'ang-hsi-yü-chiu-kao-seng chuan* (Biographies of Eminent Monks who went to the Western World in Search of the Law During the Great T'ang Dynasty'[2]) in two volumes which is

1. English translation by the learned Japanese scholar J. Takakusu (Munshi Ram Manoharlal, Delhi).

2. French Summary by E. Chavanness—*Memoire compose a l'epoque de la grande dynastie T'ang sur les religieux eminents qui allerent chercher la loi dans les*

translated here, to Ch'ang-an (modern Si-an). During his stay in India, he came across a large number of Chinese monk-pilgrims whose accounts he recorded later. Most of them were contemporaries of I-ching. He at the end has remarked, "My only desire is to receive the light handed down from time to time. I am satisfied that I, having learned the Law in the morning, my doubt like rising dust is dispelled in the morning. I shall not regret dying in the evening."

On his return to the Divine Land, he received official reception in 689 A.D. The later part of the seventh century was dominated by the Dowger Empress Wu, a devout follower of the Faith. Under the patronage of Wu, I-ching spent his busy life in China completing the stupendous task of translating the texts he carried home, with the assistance of some Indian monks like Sikṣānanda, Īśvara and others. He completed the translation of 56 works in 230 volumes and 5 compilations in A.D. 700-712. The Account of The Fifty-six Monks is one of them. He died in A.D. 713 in his seventy-ninth year of age. This devout scholar who braved all the perils of journey to India to collect original *Vinaya text* was one who decided 'not to live but to know'.

These fifty-six monks were all Chinese with a few exceptions of Koreans and one from Sogdiana.[1] They started their travel with the commencement of the glorious reign of the Great T'ang Dynasty (hence the title of the work). They came to India with an insatiable desire to pay respect to the far-famed remains of the Buddha and to learn Buddhism in its birth place. I-ching has described the gifts and honour they received from the Indian rulers, princes and the Buddhist scholars during their sojourn in India.

Dr. Lo says that Prof. Liang Ch'i-ch'ao[2] (1873-1929) after much research had found about 180 monk-pilgrims and mentioned them in his essay on "*Chinese students going abroad* 1500 *years ago and afterwards*". Most of the eminent monks whose lives

pap d'occident, par I-tsing, Paris 1894 (Buddhist Bibliography p. 115), the English excerpt "Indian Travels of Chinese Buddhists" by S. Beal. The *Indian Antiquary* vol 10. 1881. p. 109.

1. Khirgiz S. S. R., Kazak, S. S. R. in U. S. S. R.

2. Chinese Sources for Indian History published by the National Archives of India p.83. Liang Ch'i-Ch'ao, was a great thinker, reformer and literary figure of modern period.

are recorded by I-ching's *KSC* belonged to unknown families living in poverty with an exception of four or five who belonged to the *gentry* family. Their fathers, grandfathers, were holding Imperial posts. In the third and fourth centuries a new type of Buddhism known as *gentry* Buddhism was developed by a group of cultured, intellectual monks who excelled both in secular learning and Buddhist scholarship. But in the sixth-seventh centuries the scene changed and the Buddhism which was confined to the higher strata of the Chinese society became known to the common masses and by the time of the T'ang it was deeply rooted in the society. It is because of this that I-ching did not know the secular surnames of the monks or anything about their family connections. But most of them were well versed both in non-Buddhist and Buddhist literature. Their literary activity is greatly emphasised. Some of them having memorised the Classics[1] at an early age became proficient in writing prose and poetry and in calligraphy.

The lives of those fifty-six monks throw a flood of light on their patriotic zeal, love for their own homeland China, for its old ways of social and domestic life. Wherever they went they always longed to return to China. The Chinese monks all through the history of India-China intercourse never thought of settling down in India. The splendour of India did not shake their love for their own motherland. Their feelings, their subtle emotions are well expressed in the following lines. On one occasion, I-ching along with Prajñādeva was on a visit to Gṛdhrakūṭa. They offered worship there and then ascending to the mountain top cast their glances afar and seemed to see China (on the horizon). Both were sorrowful at heart. I-ching composed a poem expressing the feelings of the moment. Its concluding lines are: "...You go to India not for worldly happiness but for the Life Eternal".

Many of these fifty-six monks after ordination took Indian names. The Chinese transcription of the Sanskrit names of some of them are given against their names. This transcription is not difficult to interpret but in many cases transcriptions of Sanskrit

1. Five classics *viz. Shih-ching, Shu-ching, I-ching, Li-chi* and *Ch'un Ch'iu* (*Book of Songs, Book of History, Book of Change, Book of Rituals, Autumn and Spring*).

names are not given. I have tried to translate those Chinese names into Sanskrit.

Arthur F. Wright has done wonderful and excellent work on Hui-Chiao's Lives of Eminent Monks (*KSE*) and thus set an example for the future scholars to work on the same scientific line (*Silver Jubilee Vol.* Kyoto University).

The long history of Sino-India relation was founded entirely upon Buddhism. This was possible as a result of peaceful penetration by missionaries and traders and not by force of arms. This relation was mainly spiritual and cultural in character carried on by Buddhist monks both from India and China. The Indian religion with its fascinating culture had exercised a profound influence over the countries in the East and the South where it spread.

Biography of Eminent Monks
Who Went to the Western Region
in Search of the Law
During the Great Ta'ng Dynasty

ENGLISH TRANSLATION

CHAPTER I

PREFACE

Biographies Of Eminent Monks Who Went to The Western World[1] In Search Of The Law During The Great T'ang Dynasty.

I, Śramaṇa[2] I-ching returned to Shih-li-fọ-shih, Śrī-vijaya[3] in the South Sea from the Western Country (India), and from

1. The ancient Chinese travellers always mentioned India and neighbouring regions lying to the Western border of China as Hsi-yü, Western World. Hsüan-Chuang's travel is known as *Hsi-yū chi*, 西域記

2. He, who renounces the family, to follow the Law is called *Sha-man* 沙門 He has to observe 250 rules.

3. This name has been mentioned many a time in this text. Śri-vijaya or Sumatra was one of the important islands in the South-China sea or Malay Archipelago. It was for a long time a renowned centre of Indian civilisation. I-Ching who made the voyage to India by sea, stayed in this prosperous and flourishing Kingdom for seven years from A.D. 688-695 both on his outward voyage to India and on his return. The record of his experiences contains more information about South-East Asia than is to be found in the official annals of dynastic history of China. Śrī-vijaya was the meeting place of both Indian and Chinese pilgrim-monks proceeding to opposite directions as the Caravan town like Tun-huang was the resting place for the traveller monks coming and going by the Caravan route. In the 222nd Chüan of the *New T'ang Dynasty Record*, there is a mention of Chih-li-fo-shih. It was commonly called Śrī-Bhoga. From east to west, it was one thousand li and from north to south four thousand li with fourteen cities. Śri-vijaya produced lots of gold and was famous for mineral products. See J. J. Takakusu, *A Record of the Buddhist Religion as practised in India and Malay Archipelago*, p. XI. (hence forth abridged ARBRPIMA); Chang Hsing-lang, Chung-hsi chiao-t'ung Shih-liao (The *Materials for a History of Sino-Foreign Relation*) Vol. VI, p. 374.

C. P. Fitz Gerald, *The Southern Expansion of the Chinese People*, Second Map. S. E. Asia.

there sent back the manuscript of (Nan-hai) *Chei-Kuei* (nei-fa-chuan)[1] and the sketch of the Nālandā, Na-lan-t'a monastery.

Previously there were many noble monks in the Divine Land (China) who had gone to the Western Country (in search of the Law) without caring for their lives. Fa-hsien, the pioneer of all, went forth on difficult and perilous route (to India and the neighbouring countries). Hsüan-Chuang, following his footsteps, opened the regular overland route to India.

The earliest Chinese travellers started their solitary journey either by following high road, crossed the Great Wall (Western frontier) or they took the sea route to reach India. The monk-travellers, while making journey by land or by sea, remembered all along the traces of the Buddha and prostrated before his Law reverentially. They always desired to go back to their mother-land to report their experiences to the Emperors.

However, it was a great luck and fortune (to visit India), but it was extremely difficult and perilous undertaking. None of those who brought leaves, flowers and canopies (to offer), could produce any significant result, and a few of them could complete their mission. This was due to the rugged stony deserts and big rivers of the Land of the Elephants (India), the blaze of the Sun that puts forth scorching heat, or the sky kissing waves swelled by giant whales, the abysses and the waters that reach the heavens. While travelling alone outside the Iron Gate 鐵門 T'ieh-men[2] (between Samarkand and Bactria), one wandered amongst ten thousand mountains, fell into the pit of cliffy mountains or while sailing beyond the Copper Pillar T'ung-chu[3] 銅柱 one had to cross thousand rivers 千江 and, lost one's life.

1. For details Vide I-Ching's own description of Nālandā.

2. Iron Gate was the name of a mountain pass at about ninety miles south-east of Samarkand. The pass was almost inaccessible. In the *Ta-T'ang-hsi-yü chi*, Hsüan-Chuang had mentioned the name of Iron Gate. He described that on both sides of the pass there were precipitous mountains of iron colour. Innumerable iron bells were fixed on the gates which were strong and impregnable. Iron pass is Derbent near Badakshan.

3. During the time of the Eastern Han, A.D. 25-220, Ma-Yüan, the well-known commander was sent to resist the attack by Tibetans. He repelled the

I had passed many days without food, even without a drop of water. I really wonder, how could the travellers, under such difficult conditions, keep up their morale and spirit. Due to this perilous journey, the appearance of the pilgrims would undergo complete change.

When I decided to leave China I had fifty companions, but finally most of them stayed back. If, however, a monk happened to reach India after such perilous journey, he would find no Chinese monastery there. There was no fixed place (for us) to settle down. We had to move from place to place like a blade of grass swept by wind. Under such difficult circumstances, to study Buddhism and the Law was really a very great task. Their sincerity and devotion were praiseworthy indeed !

I wish to fulfil my desire (to write about my experience) so that the future generations may know all about the facts. I had heard with my own ears, and had seen with my own eyes, the difficulties the monks had undergone previously. Hence, I write this book according to the chronological order of the past events. I record first the biographies of those who were still living and afterwards of those who had already passed away.

1. 太州玄照法師 Hsüan-chao Fa-shih of T'ai-chou.
2. 齊州道希法師 Tao-hsi Fa-shih of Ch'i-chou.
3. 齊州師鞭法師 Shih-pien of Ch'i-chou.
4. 新羅阿離耶跋摩法師 A-li-yeh-pa-mo Fa-shih of Hsin-luo.
5. 新羅慧業法師 Hüi-yeh Fa-shih of Hsin-luo.
6. 新羅求本法師 Ch'iu-pen Fa-shih of Hsin-luo.
7. 新羅玄太法師 Hsüan-t'ai Fa-shih of Hsin-luo.
8. 新羅玄恪法師 Hsüan-k'o Fa-shih of Hsin-luo.
9.-10. 新羅復有法師二人 'wo other monks from Hsin-luo.

attack and turned them back to the Western frontier. Later on, he commanded the army to Chiao-chih, modern Tonkin. The people of Chiao-chih tried to overthrow the Chinese supremacy over them. But Ma-Yüan defeated the rebellious people headed by a woman. To commemorate this victory he erected copper pillars on the extensive southern border. These were used as a mark of demarcation between the two countries.

11. 覩貨羅佛陀跋摩師 Fo-t'o-pa-mo-shih of Tu-huo-luo.
12. 並州道方法師 Tao-fang Fa-shih of Ping-chou.
13. 並州道生法師 Tao-sheng Fa-shih of Ping-chou.
14. 並州常慜禪師 Ch'ang-min Ch'an-shih of Ping-chou.
15. 常慜弟子一人 A disciple of Ch'ang-min.
16. 京師末底僧訶師 Mo-ti-seng-he-shih of Ching-shih.
17. 京師玄會法師 Hsüan-hui of Ching-shih.
18. 質多跋摩師 Chih-tuo-pa-mo-shih.
19-20. 吐蕃公嬭母息二人 Two men.
21. 隆法師 Lung Fa-shih.
22. 益州明遠法師 Ming-yüan Fa-shih of I-chou.
23. 益州義朗律師 I-lang Lü-shih of I-chou.
24. 朗律師弟子一人 A disciple of Lü-shih Lang.
25. 益州智岸法師 Chih-an Fa-shih of I-chou.
26. 益州會寧律師 Hui-ning Lü-shih of I-chou.
27. 交州運期法師 Yün-ch'i Fa-shih of Chiao-chou.
28. 交州木叉提婆師 Mu-ch'a-t'i-p'o-shih of Chiao-chou.
29. 交州窺冲法師 K'uei-ch'ung Fa-shih of Chiao-chou.
30. 交州慧琰法師 Hui-yen Fa-shih of Chiao-chou.
31. 信胄法師 Hsin-chou Fa-shih.
32. 愛州智行法師 Chih-hsing Fa-shih of Ai-chou.
33. 愛州大乘燈禪師 Ta-ch'ang-teng ch'en shih of Ai-chou.
34. 唐國僧伽跋摩師 Seng-chia-pa-mo-shih of T'ang-kuo.
35-36. 高昌彼岸智岸 Pi-an and Chih-an of Kao-ch'ang.
37. 洛陽曇潤法師 T'an-jun Fa-shih of Lo-yang.
38. 洛陽義輝論師 I-hui Lun-shih of Lo-yang.
39-40-41. 又大唐三人 Three more men from China.
42. 新羅慧輪法師 Hui-lun Fa-shih of Hsin-luo.
43. 荊州道琳法師 Tao-lin Fa-shih of Ching-chou.
44. 荊州曇光法師 T'an-kuang Fa-shih of Ching-chou.
45. 又大唐一人 One more from China.
46. 荊州慧命禪師 Hui-ming Ch'an-shih of Ching-chou.
47. 潤州玄逵律師 Hsüan-k'uei Lü-shih of Jun-chou.
48. 晉州善行法師 Shan-hsing Fa-shih of Chin-chou.

49. 襄陽靈運法師 Ling-yün Fa-shih of Hsiang-yang.
50. 澧州僧哲禪師 Seng-che Ch'an-shih of Feng-chou.
51. 洛陽智弘律師 Chih-hung Lü-shih of Lo-yang.
52. 荊州無行禪師 Wu-hsing Ch'an-shih of Ching-chou.
53. 荊州法振禪師 Fa-chen Ch'an-shih of Ching-chou.
54. 荊州乘悟禪師 Ch'eng-wu Ch'an-shih of Ching-chou.
55. 梁州乘如律師 Ch'ang-ru Lu-shih of Liang-chou.
56. 澧州大律法師 Ta-chin Fa-shih of Feng-chou.

There were fifty-six monks as mentioned above. The monks whose names are mentioned in the beginning (of the list) were all scattered. I-ching met only five of monks—Wu-hsing, Tao-lin, Hui-lun, Seng-che and Chih-hung mentioned in this note. In the first year of the 垂拱 Ch'ui-Kung[1] period, I-ching with the monk Wu-hsing, the Dhyāna-master, bade farewell to China and embarked on his journey towards Western regions. Even 'to-day' (at the time of I-Ching), no commission had been deputed to find out whether they were living or they were dead.

Śramaṇa Hsüan-chao Fa-shih—the monk Hsüan-chao was a native of Hsien-chang[2] in T'ai-chou. His Sanskrit name was 般迦舍末底 Pan-chia-she-mo-ti, Prakāśamati. He was known as Jñānaprabha in Chinse. His grandfather and father—both were successively holding high posts in the Imperial Services. But at an early age he cut his hair done up in a knob, threw away the hairpins and accepted the tonsure.

As he grew, he desired to pay homage to the sacred places. For this purpose, he went to the capital city to attend discussions and deliberations on Buddhist Sūtras and Śāstras. In the middle of the 貞觀 [3] Chen-Kuan period, in the monastery of

1. In A.D. 685 the Dowger Empress Wu of the T'ang Dynasty dethroned the rightful sovereign and usurped the throne for herself for twenty years. To commemorate this event, she started this era and founded the Dynastic title of Chou instead of the T'ang from this date.

2. In T'ai-chou Fu, modern Che-kiang, or Che-chiang, Lat. 28°52', Long. 120° 46'.

3. T'ai-Tsung the second Emperor of the T'ang Dynasty started this era in A.D. 627.

Ta-hsing-shan[1] 大興善 of Hsien-chang, he first started learning Sanskrit literature with the monk teacher Hsüan-chang. Thereafter, he with a mendicant stick proceeded towards the West as a *Parivrājaka* cherishing the memory of 祇園 Chih-yüan, Jetavana.[2] Leaving behind Chin-chou (Lan-chou) (or the Capital city) he crossed the drifting sands and passing through the Iron gate, ascended the snow-clad mountains. In the fragrant water of the nearby lake he had his wash, bearing in his mind to complete the vow of (acquiring) profund knowledge. He climbed the dangerous 葱阜. Ts'ung-fou[3] Pamir, and kept up his vigour and spirit. He took a vow of achieving San-yu[4], 三有 Trailokya; he crossed 速利

1. 'The Great goodness-promoting' '*Bhadrodaya*' was one of the ten famous T'ang monasteries of the capital Ch'ang-an. According to Ennin's report dated A.D. 775, the capital had three hundred Buddha halls as well as thirty-three small monasteries and an unspecified number of larger ones. Vide The Chinese *Tripiṭaka*, Taisho Ed. (Hence forth C.T.T.) Vol. 51, No. 2093, p. 1022.

2. The founder of the Jetavana-Vihāra, in the vicinity of Śrāvastī, was a famous and wealthy merchant Anāthapiṇḍika (supporter of destitute and orphans) of Śrāvasti. He purchased the pleasure-garden of the prince Jeta by paying a fantastic price for the residence of the Buddha. Anāthapiṇḍika transformed the park into a Saṅghārāma which developed into a large establishment and became a favourite resort of the Buddha and his followers. The legend says that the Buddha had spent nineteen 'Vassa' period in this Jetavana and delivered most of his important sermons here. The early Chinese travellers like Fa-hsien and Hsüan-Chuang visited this place. Fa-hsien recorded that "The Jetavana-Vihāra was originally seven storeyed. The kings and the people of the countries vied with one another in their offerings hanging up about it silken streamers and canopies, scattering flowers, burning incense and lighting lamps, so as to make the night as bright as the day." James Legge: *A Record of the Buddhist Kingdom* (Translation) pp. 56, 57.

In A.D. 636 when Hsüan-Chuang visited this place, he found that most of the buildings had fallen into decay.

3. Pamir or Onion range (Kizil rabat). It was known as the Imaos to ancient Greek geographers. Pamir joins both the mountains, the T'ien-Shan (Celestial Mountain) in the north and the snow clad mountain in the south. It is popularly known as the 'Roof of the World'.

4. *Triloka*. The three kinds of '*bhava*' or existence. The state of mental existence in the realm of *Kāma* or desire, Kāmaloka, the field of five senses of form or *rūpa*—planes of meditation, *rūpaloka* and beyond form, *arūpa*—the formless world corresponding to the higher level of *Dhyāna*.

Su-li[1] to reach 諸貨羅 Tu-ho-luo[2], Tokhara. Then he passed through the countries of the barbarians and reached 吐蕃 T'u-fan.[3] He was very much favoured by the princess Wen-Ch'ang of Tibet who gave him financial help for his journey to North India. He gradually reached 闍蘭陀 Tu-lan-t'a, Jalandhara.[4]

It was an extremely difficult and perilously long journey. Before he could enter the city, he fell in the hands of robbers. There was no place where the merchants and travellers could go and report the crime or could get help. Despairing of human

1. According to Hsüan-Chuang's Travel Su-li (Sogdiana) was the place between the city of Su-she water and the country of Kasanna inhabited by Su-li people. Su-li was not only the name of the place but also the name of the people, their language and literature. The Chinese character 窣利 Su-li used by Hsüan-Chuang differs from 速利 used by I-ching. He has mentioned the Su-li people as a general term for the northern extra-India people. Takakusu thinks Su-li was in the West of Kashgarh peopled by Mongols or Turks. See Dr. P. C. Bagchi: *India and Central Asia*. pp. 43, 44.

2. Tokharestan, the land of Tukhara people was a great centre of Indian culture and religion in Central Asia.

To the ancient Greek it was known by the name of Tochari. In the ancient *Chinese Annals* of the Han Dynasty, it is recorded as Ta-hsia. In the second century B.C. China first established contact with Ta-hsia. In the *Record of the Northern-Wei Dynasty* it is transcribed as T'u-hu-luo 吐呼羅. and in the *T'ang Annals* it T'u-huo-luo 吐火羅, in the *Saṃyuktāgama,* Tou-sha-luo 兜沙羅 and in the *Saddharma Smṛtyupasthāna Sūtra* Tu-Chu. 都佉

During the Mahomedan period Tokharesthan was limited to the territory between Badakshan and Balk. But in the earlier period the geographical boundary of the country was more extensive than in the Mahomedan period. According to Hsüan-Chuang, Tu-huo-luo was extended up to the Onion range (Ts'ung-ling) in the east, to Persia in the west, in the south it touched the snow-capped Hindukush and to Iron Pass (Derbent near Badakshan) in the north. According to Thomas Watters Tu-huo-luo of Hsüan-Chuang was definitely Tukhara of ancient geographers. See Watters—(*On Yuan Chwang's Travel in India*), Vol. I, p. 103.

Aurel Stein. *On Ancient Central Asian Tracks*, p.107; Dr. P.C. Bagchi: *India and Central Asia*. Chapter II; *Feng Ch'eng-Chun*: *The Geographical names of the West.* Hsi-Yü-ti-ming: p. 72.

3. Tibet.

4. Jalandhara in Punjab.

assistance, he chanted some sacred words. In the following night he had a dream that fulfilled his desire. Suddenly he woke up and found that the robbers were all fast asleep. Stealthily he left the place and fled away quickly. Thus he averted the danger.

He lived in Jalandhara for four years. There he was warmly received by the king and all arrangements for his food and stay were made. While he was living in Jalandhara, he practised Sanskrit language and studied the Buddhist *Sūtras* and Vinaya texts, but made little success.

Next he gradually proceeded towards south and reached 莫訶菩提 *Mo-ho-p'u-t'i*, the Mahābodhi saṅghārāma[1] where he spent four years. He felt very much disappointed that he could not see the reverend Ārya but he was lucky enough to pay reverence to the sacred vestiges of the presence of the Buddha. He saw the image of 慈氏 T'zu-shih Maitreya[2] that

1. Mahābodhi Saṅghārāma was situated in the present thriving village of Bodh-Gayā (Lat. 24° 42'N, Long. 85° Ol' E, in the District of Gayā, Bihar). The present Bodh-Gayā grew and developed around the ancient Sambodhi near the sacred village Uruvela, and this Sambodhi later on with the entire Buddhist establishment over there came to be known as Mahābodhi. The Saṅghārāma was erected during the Gupta period at the foot of the Bodhi tree. Hsüan-Chuang had left a vivid description of this great establishment. He saw an image of Avalokiteśvara and Maitreya each made of silver. They were above 10 ft. high.
Vide. Rajendra Lal Mitra: *Buddha Gayā*;
Watters II. pp. 113-136;
Dr. D. Mitra: *Buddhist Monuments*, pp. 60-66.

2. Mention of this *Bodhisattva* has been made in early Buddhist literature like *Lalitavistara, Divyāvadāna, Mahāvastu, Saddharma-Puṇḍarika* and *Vimalakīrtinirdeśa Sūtra*. The popularity of Maitreya Bodhisattva in China was enormous. The Buddhist texts which narrate the story of Maitreya were extensively translated into Chinese. In all these Sūtras, it is said that during the rule of Cakravartī ruler, peace would specially prevail in this world when Maitreya the 'Buddhist Messiah' would descend from the *Tuṣita* heaven, appear in the world and become Buddha under Nāgārjuna tree, open three successive meetings, preach law, and rescue the suffering humanity.

had been carved in perfect likeness; it exhibited the fine and delicate, absolute sincerity and carefulness (of the artist). It created more veneration. Deeply he studied 俱 舍 *Chu-she, Kośa*,[1] *Chieh-tui-fa* i.e. 解 對 法 *Abhidharma*[2] and the Vinayas[3]

See Latika Lahiri: 'Lungmen Cave Inscriptions and the Popularity of Maitreya Bodhisattva', *Proceedings of the International Seminar on Buddhism and Jainism*, (Cuttuck) pp. 75-82.

1. Vasubandhu, one of the three Asaṅga brothers who lived in the fourth century A.D., was one of the most prominent figures in the history of Buddhist literature. An erudite scholar, he was a *Sarvāstivādin* but in late life he was greatly influenced by his elder brother Asaṅga and became a devout Mahāyānist. The chief and the most celebrated work of Vasubandhu is the Abhidharmakośa, a general exposition of *Abhidharma*. The original Sanskrit is lost, but extant in Chinese (*Nanjio's* Cat. No. 1267, 1269, 1270) and Tibetan, Paramārtha, the biographer of Vasubandhu translated the *Abhidharmakośa* into Chinese between A.D. 563-567. In the following century, the renowned Chinese pilgrim scholar Hsüan-Chuang also translated this text into Chinese. According to Paramārtha this work consists of 600 verses (*Kārikās*). It deals with the entire field of Ontology, Psychology, Ethics, Cosmology and the doctrine of Salvation.

See *Encyclopaedia of Religion and Ethics* Vol. I, pp. 19, 20; Winternitz Vol. II, pp. 356-359;

Sir Charles Eliot Vol. II pp. 88, 89.

2. The third section of the *Tripiṭaka*, *Abhidharmapiṭaka*, Buddhist Scholasticism. In the *Aṭṭhasalinī Buddhaghoṣa* defined *Abhidharma* as higher religion or excellent religion. The prefix '*Abhi*' means "excellence and difference" and *Abhidharma* according to him is Dharma which excels and is differentiated from other Dharma (*Suttapiṭaka*). But the Buddhist scholars, at present, do not find much difference between the philosophy and Dharma as taught in the *Suttapiṭaka*. In the nineteenth century Europe there was an idea that the *Abhidharma* is the Buddhist metaphysics but the present scholars differ with the idea. "The only difference between the scriptures of the *Abhidharmapiṭaka* and the *Sūtrapiṭaka* is that these works are more scholastic, drier and mere circumstantial than those of the *Sūtrapiṭaka*."

Abhidharmapiṭaka or *Lun-tsang* is like the *Sūtrapiṭaka*, divided into Mahāyānist and Hīnayānist texts. The books belonging to *Abhidharmapiṭaka* are *Dhammasaṁganī* "Compendium of Dhamma", the *Vibhaṅga* "Classification", *Dhōtukathā* "Discourses on the Elements", *Puggula Paññati*, "Description of Human Individual" and *Kathāvatthu* "Subject of Discourses".

Encyclopaedia of Religion and Ethics; Winternitz Vol.II pp. 165-173.

Prof. G. P. Malalasekera. *Ditcionary of Pāli Proper Names*. Vol. I. p. 138.

3. Discipline of the order, Vinaya is the name given to the system of monastic life, or the disciplinary rule and precepts governing the Monachism. The Vinaya is the fundamental basis for the existence of Buddhist monastic

of the two Schools (Mahāyāna and Hīnayāna) and became very much enlightened.

Next he went to the Nālandā monastery where he remained for three years. There he studied 中論 *Chung-lun*,[1] *Prāṇya-mūla Śāstra* like *Śata Śāstra* etc. with the (Indian) monk 勝光 Sheng-kuang, Vijayaraśmi, and 瑜伽十七地 Yü-chia-shih-ch'i-ti *Saptadaśabhūmiśāstra-Yogācāryabhūmi*[2] with Bhadanta, the virtuous preceptor 寶師子 *Pao-shih-tze, Ratnasiṃha.*

He learned the different degrees of 禪門定 Ch'an-men-ting[3], abstract contemplation (so that mind itself would be free

---

life. Vinaya is the rock bed of Saṅgha-life. It contains the following texts: (1) *Sutta Vibhaṅga* consisting of *Mahāvibhaṅga* and *Bhikkunīvibhaṅga*; (2) The *Khandakas* consisting of *Mahāvagga* and *Cullavagga*; (3) The *Parivāra*. The most essential part of Vinaya is *Pāṭimokkha* the disciplinary code of an Order. *Pāṭimokkha* gives a list of penal consequences of these transgression together with corresponding atonement.

See Winternitz Vol. II, pp. 21-24.

Dr. S. Dutt. *Early Buddhist Monachism.*

1. *Prāṇyamūla Śāstra* or *Prāṇyamūlaśāstra* ṭikā, *Chung-lun* literally means discourse on the *Mādhyamika Śāstra.* The great exponent of the *Mādhyamika* or the Middle School, Bodhisattva Nāgārjuna wrote this Śastra and Nilacakṣus or *Piṅgalanetra* was the compiler. This Work of *Nāgārjuna* was translated by *Kumārajīva* in Chinese in A.D. 409. This book of the Later Chin Dynasty (A.D. 387-417) is now available only in Chinese and Tibetan.

See *N.C.* No. 1179.

2. *Saptadaśabhūmiśāstra-Yogācāryabhūmi* is one of the works of *Asaṅga* of the fourth century A.D. The legend says that *Yogācarabhūmiśāstra* was dictated to him by Maitreya from *Tuṣita heaven.*

This Mahāyānist work has both Chinese and Tibetan versions. It was translated by Hsüan-Chuang in Chinese (NC. No. 1170) in A.D. 646-47. This Chinese version is ascribed to Maitreyanātha and the Tibetan version to Asaṅga. The Sanskrit text of the *Saptadaśabhūmi* consists of 40,000 *ślokas.* It agrees with the Tibetan text.

The Doctrine of Yoga was first propounded by Patañjali, the great grammarian who flourished in the second century B.C. Later on, Asaṅga founded a Yoga School in Buddhism in the fourth century A.D. Hsüan-Chuang was a great patron of Yogācāra system.

The original Sanskrit text of *Yogācārabhūmiśāstra* has been recovered from Tibet by Rāhul Sānkrityayana.

3. In the *Dictionary of Chinese Buddhist Terms* there is mention of Ch'an-men and Ch'an-ting separately. Ch'an is a transliteration of Dhyāna in Sanskrit, Jhāna in Pāli and Zen in Japanese. The basic meaning of Ch'an is

from all subjective and objective bondages), earnestly gazing at the gate of a precipice to get the bottom of the vast principle or law.

Thence he proceeded along the bank of the Gaṅgā. He received hospitality from the King of Shan-pu[1] country, to the north of the *Gaṅgā*. He lived in the monastery of the 信者 Hsin-che—Great Faith and other monasteries for about three years.

The envoy 王玄策 Wang Hsüan-ts'e,[2] from the Court of the T'ang Emperor, on return to China, gave a very good report about the monk Prakāśamati, to the Emperor. Immediately the Emperor sent people to West India in search of the monk and ordered them to escort him back to the Imperial Capital. On their way back, they arrived in 泥波羅 Ni-po-lo, Nepal. The King of Nepal helped the monk Hsüan-chao to proceed towards Tibet. There he called on the Princess 文成 Wen-Ch'ang[3] who helped him with money needed for the journey from Tibet to China, the country of the T'ang rulers.

So after travelling a long distance in Western Tibet he reached China. In September, he left 苫部 Shan-pu and arrived at

---

'meditation' Dhyāna leads to 定 Ting-Samādhi. Ch'an-men-ting is the method of meditation and Samādhi.

1. See Chang Hsing-lang, *Chung-hsi Chiao-t'ung shih-liao* Vol. VI, p. 363, No. 8.

2. He came to the court of Kānyakubja, as an envoy of the Chinese Emperor in A.D. 655. The King Harṣavardhana died by that time and the throne was usurped by A-lao-na-shun—Aruṇāśva. The Chinese envoy Wang Hsüan-ts'e was not received with honour. He went back to Tibet, raised an army and attacked the usurper. Aruṇāśva was taken as a prisoner to China and along with the captive a vast amount of booty.

See R. S. Tripathi: *History of Kanauj* pp. 188-190. *J. R. A. B.* VI, pp. 69-70. Herbert A. Giles, *A Chinese Biography Dictionary* No. 825.

3. The wife of the most powerful ruler Srongstan-Gampo of Tibet. He was so formidable that he compelled the Emperor of China to give him in marriage a lady from the Imperial Court. She was a devout Buddhist and brought with her Buddhist religion and Buddha images to Tibet. The Tibetans say that there were three other great Kings outside China who were the suitors for the princess' hand—the King of Magadha, of Persia and of the Hor (Turki tribes).

洛陽 Lo-yang[1] in January. He travelled more than 10,000 li in five months time. In 麟德 Lin-te[2] period the Emperor gave him a long audience in the Imperial Court and commanded him to go to 羯濕彌囉 Kashmir to escort an old Brahmin named 盧迦溢多 Lu-chia-i-tuo, Lokāditya.

While in Lo-yang he met many venerable monks and discussed mutually the fundamental principles of Buddhism. In Lo-yang he took in hand the translation work of the Vinaya of the 薩婆多部 *Sa-p'o-tuo-pu*[3] *Sarvāstivāda* School with the assistance of the great *Vinayācārya* (Vinaya-master) 道 Tao

---

1. The city of Lo-yang (Lat. 30°, 43′ N, Long. 112° 28′ E.) in Ho-nan witnessed rise and fall of various Imperial Dynasties throughout the historical epoch of China. Lo-yang was a great centre of Buddhist culture. According to the Chinese tradition, the first Buddhist temple (in China) known as White Horse Pagoda (Pai-ma-Ssu) was built in Lo-yang by the Emperor Ming of the Eastern Han Dynasty in A.D. 65-67, in honour of the two Indian monks Kāśyapa Mātaṅga and Dharmāraṇya. The greatest Imperial patron of the new religion (Buddhism) were the Northern-Wei rulers (A.D. 336-534). The Buddhist cave-temples at Lung-men near Lo-yang contain some of the finest artistic remains of early Chinese Buddhism. Under the Emperor Hsüan-wu, some famous temples were constructed in Lo-yang, the Yung-ming temple, the Ching-ming temple and Yao-kuang temple. The most outstanding Buddhist activity carried out by Dowager Empress Ling of the Northern-Wei, was the construction of the Yung-ming temple by spending a fantastic amount of money. It is said that in Lo-yang there were 1367 Buddhist temples.

See, Yang Hsüan-chih. *Lo-yang Chia-lan-chi* (Record of the Monasteries in Lo-yang), C.T.T. Vol. 51, No. 2092, p. 999; J. R. WARE. *Wei-Shu on Buddhism*; Tong Pao. 30, 1933.

2. The Emperor Kao-Tsung of the T'ang Dynasty started this era in A.D 664, fourteen years after his accession to the throne.

3. The *Sarvāstivāda* school is one of the earliest schools of Buddhism. The history of this School begins with the Kathāvatthu of Moggaliputta Tissa in B.C. 240, who presided over the Aśoka's Council. The doctrine of this school is "Sarvam Asṭi" Everything exists.

This materialistic and realistic school appears later on as the Vaibhāṣika. Three hundred years after the Parinirvāṇa of the Buddha, Kātyāyaniputra compiled the *Jñānaprasthāna Sūtra* which is the fundamental work of the *Sarvāstivādins*. The Chinese traveller Fa-hsien (A.D. 399-414) who came to India in search of the Vinaya texts says that this school was followed at Pāṭaliputra as well as in China. Sarvāstivādins were located in Central India, North India, North-Western frontier, Kashgar, Udyāna etc. Kaniṣka was

and Dharmācārya 觀 Kuan etc. of the 敬愛 Ching-ai[1] temple. But after some time he proceeded towards India in obedience to the Emperor's command. His long cherished desire, therefore, was not fulfilled; he had to leave all the Sanskrit manuscripts behind him in the Capital.

He travelled through the drifting sands, passed over steep and precipitous mountains. He trailed down the side-way of a steep mountain path where a plank lay across a dangerous precipitous point, found the trace of the slanting path and was successful to cross through. He came to a river. There was a hanging rope bridge but he swam across the river. Thus he averted the danger from the robbers of Tibet. For the time being he was saved, he was again attacked by the dreadful tribes but fortunately this time also he narrowly escaped. After much travel he reached North India.

On his way, he met a Chinese envoy sent by the T'ang Emperor who had *Lokāditya* already under his escort. The envoy commissioned Hsüan-chao, who directed them to accompany the band of travellers who were going to 羅荼 Luo-ch'a, Lāṭa country[2] in West India, to collect medicinal herbs for longevity. In the course of journey, he reached the 納婆毘訶羅 Na-p'o-p'i-ho-luo, Nava Vihāra. It was known as Hsin-Ssu (Nava Saṅghārāma) 新寺 in Fu-he-luo 縛渴羅 Bukhara.[3] He saw a washing bowl and other relics of 如來

---

a great adherent of this school, who convoked the fourth Buddhist Council. For the *Sarvāstivādin* doctrine see E. J. Thomas: *The History of Buddhist Thought* (London 1933), pp. 164-174; A. C. Bannerjee: *The Sarvāstivāda Literature.* Calcutta.

1. In the period of P'u-t'ung (A.D. 520-527), this temple was built by the Emperor Wu of the Liang Dynasty. Taking as a model of the great Indian Emperor Aśoka, this Buddhist monk-Emperor of the Liang Dynasty ventured upon the plan of constructing Buddhist temples and monasteries. Among the numerous temples he constructed, the most famous was the T'ung-t'ai temple. See: *CTT* Ed. Vol 51, p 1024.

2. Southern Gujarat. I-ching here mentions Lāṭa in West India together with Sindhu. See J. Takakusu: p. 217. Additional Note.

3. According to Hsüan-chuang Nava *Saṅghārāma* of Balhika was the only Buddhist establishment to the north of Hindukush. It was a great centre of

Ju-lai, Tathāgata.[1] Next he reached 迦畢試 Chia-pi-shih Kapiśa[2] and worshipped the *Uṣṇiṣa* of Tathāgata 如來頂骨 Ju-lai-ting-ku. The pilgrim paid reverence to the *Uṣṇiṣa* by offering fragrant flowers, burning incense and there he inscribed *praśasti*.

He again resumed his onward journey towards Lāṭa country in Hsin-tu.[3] He received very warm welcome from the king of the country where he stayed for four years. Then he proceeded towards South India. From there he sent various medicinal herbs to China.

---

original Buddhist Studies. He has given a vivid description of the city of Balkh which was known as little Rājagṛha because to the followers of Buddhist faith over there, Balkh was as important as Rājagṛha in India. The largest monastery was the Nava Saṅghārāma which was situated outside the city, built by a former King. The main hall of the monastery contained the washing basin of the Buddha and a beautiful image of the Buddha. The name of Nava Saṅghārāma is also known from Arabic sources, where it was mentioned as Nawbahar. It was destroyed by the Arabs in the seventh century A.D.

1. It is a very common belief in India that great teachers appear at regular intervals. In Chinese, Ju-lai means 'one who has come thus'. 'The Chinese translation seems to prove that Tathāgata is equivalent to Tathā-āgata and not to Tathā-gata and the meaning must be, he who has come in the proper manner....' It is the highest title of the Buddha.

2. It was known as Ki-pai or Chi-pai (Gandhāra-Kashmir) in Chinese. It was to the south of Pamir and about 12,200 li from the capital of the Chinese Emperor.

The Record says that Kapiśa was 4,000 li in circuit with snow clad mountain on the north and the ranges of the Hindukush on all the other three sides. According to the Record, the modern Kafristan was Kapiśa or Ki-pai or Kipin. In the History of Early Han Dynasty, it was named as Kapiśa and modern Kashmir was described as ancient Kapiśa. The name of Kapiśa underwent many changes during the time of different Dynastic rulers. There is an interesting account of Kapiśa. During the sixteenth regnal year of the T'ang Emperor T'ai-T'sung, the king of Ki-pai presented him a mattress and a mongoose with sharp teeth and a red tail. It could eat snakes and get their smell. It passed urine on the spot where a patient was bitten by a snake and as soon as it passed urine there the patient was cured of snake-bite.

See Chang Hsing-lang, *Chung-hsi chiao-t'ung Shih-liao*. "The Materials for a History of Sino-foreign relation." Vol. VI, p. 93.

N. C. Sen: "Accounts of India and Kashmir in the Dynastic Histories of the T'ang period", *Viśva Bharati*, Santiniketan (1968) pp. 5-8.

3. Sindhu.

While he was touring in the country, he reached the 金剛座 Chin-kang-tsuo, Bodhimanda[1] where he stayed for some time. In the Nālandā monastery I-ching and this pilgrim met each other. The long cherished desire of such a meeting was fulfilled. They made an agreement to meet again in China.

The road from Nepal to Tibet and the road through the country of Kapiśa to Tuo-tie[2] remained blocked; travel was extremely difficult. So to take rest he proceeded further towards the *Gṛdhrakūṭa* mountain[3] 鷲峯 *Chiu-feng* (Vulture's Peak) and the Veṇuvana (Bamboo grove)[4] for which he had great respect and attachment. Though he had an insatiable desire, yet all his hopes were shattered. Alas ! he faced immense hardship but he could not fulfil his vow. How he wished to ride on cloud and to descend to Mid-India with wings of birds ! At the age of sixty he fell sick and died at A-mo-luo-p'o (bha-va) in Mid-India.

1. Diamond seat where Buddha attained Buddha-hood under the Bodhi-Tree on the bank of the river Lilajan (ancient Nairañjanā). This ground is said to be as hard as diamond. It is believed that the Emperor Aśoka made a gift of the polished sand stone seat, Vajrāsana under the Bodhi-Tree during his pilgrimage to Bodh-Gaya.

2. Tajiks, Tumasik. Tuo-ti is Ta-shih, 大食 大石

3. Gṛdhrakūṭa (Vulture's Peak) mountain was much associated with the life of the Buddha. Gṛdhrakūṭa is on the Chhahata hill at Rājagṛha (modern Rājgir in the Patna district of Bihar). It was one of the favourite resorts of the Buddha and is one of the five sacred hills surrounding the city of Rājagṛha, the capital of the powerful state of Magadha. From the foot of the Gṛdhrakūṭa to the top there is a road supposed to be constructed by the King Bimbisāra, in order to reach the Buddha and listen to his preachings. It was here when Devadatta, the cousin of the Buddha attempted on his life by hurling a rock at him. The hill has many natural caves where the Buddha lived and delivered the *Fa-hua-ching, Saddharmapuṇḍarika Sūtra* according to the Record of Hsüan-Chuang.

According to the legends, the Buddha lived in one of these caves and another was occupied by his disciple Ānanda. Māra taking the form of a vulture appeared before Ānanda and tried to disturb his meditation. When Fa-hsien visited this place, he says that the foot prints of the vulture were still visible.

4. Veṇuvana (Bamboo-grove) at Rājagṛha, modern Rājgir, Lat. 20° 2 'N, Long. 85° 26-E., was one of the favourite resorts of the Buddha. He once went to Magadha when he was received with highest honour by the King Bimbisāra. The King then made a present of his favourite park Veṇuvana (Bamboo-grove) to the Buddha.

To mourn his death, I-ching composed the verse.

'What a towering aspiration he had ! A man of great intellect and wisdom, travelled far and wide, much beyond the boundary of his own motherland. He stayed in the Veṇuvana and constantly enjoyed the sight of fluttering bamboo leaves. He had a great passion for studying Buddhism, and an insatiable desire for searching the "Law". He constantly bore in his mind the desire to return to China. He remained virtuous to the end. To raise the moral standard of the people of his land, he wanted to propagate the *Dhamma*. But alas ! he failed to fulfil his life's ambition, as his life was cut short. His bones were immersed in two big rivers there. The river Pa-shui remains famous and celebrated. How peacefully he held on even to death.'

道希法師 Tao-hsi Fa-shih. The Dharmācārya Tao-hsi belonged to the city of 齊州 Ch'i-chou (Shan-tung). His Sanskrit name was 室利提婆 Shih-li-t'i- p'o, Śrīdeva. He came from an aristocratic family. They were traditionally holding official posts in the Imperial Court.

From his childhood he was virtuous and kind. He studied metaphysics and was greatly influenced by the Buddha's religion. At the same time he had an indomitable spirit of adventure and a longing to visit Mid-India.

In the course of his travel, he had to climb lofty mountains but he never cared for his life. He proceeded towards Tibet but he found the road very dangerous. He was afraid to follow that route to Tibet. He diverted his route and proceeded towards west where he had to face many more difficulties. After passing through many countries he reached the Mahābodhi Saṅghārāma. He spent a couple of years there in search of the Buddhist Sūtras and worshipped the sacred relics of the Buddha. He spent some time at Nālandā and 俱尸 Chū-shih[1], Kāśī. The king of An-mo-luo p'o welcomed him with great respect. He seriously engaged himself in the study of the Mahāyāna,

1. Vārāṇasī in Uttar Pradesh, is a very ancient city where the Buddha was born many a times in his previous births.

Ta-ch'ang 大乘 Sūtras[1] at the Nālandā monastery. He lived in the monastery of 輸婆伴娜 Shu-p'o-pan-na or Nirvāna, the monastery of Great Salvation, where he studied deeply and thoroughly the *Vinayapiṭaka* and the *Śabda-vidyāshatra* 聲明 Sheng-ming.[2] He was a renowned calligraphist, and a man of literary genius. On a slab of stone in the monastery of Great Enlightenment, he inscribed memorial tablet in Chinese language and in the monastery of Nālandā he left more than four hundred volumes of old and new Chinese Sūtras and Śāstras.

I-ching could not meet him in India.

Śrīdeva was living at An-mo-luo-p'o where he fell sick and died at the age of fifty or so. After his death, I-ching came to Āmraka and paid respects to the room where Śrīdeva had lived. He was greatly moved by seeing the room and felt very sad for the monk. There he composed a verse containing seven words. "This monk encountering much hardship reached India alone. He was honest at heart—his only ambition was to propagate Dhamma

1. It is difficult to ascertain who first started this late form of Buddhist dogma and it is equally hard to arrive at any certain opinion as to the exact date. But after the reign of Aśoka, a great change came in Indian Buddhism. The new form of Buddhism is called Mahayāna or Great Vehicle in contrast with Hīnayāna or Small Vehicle. Mahāyāna Buddhism has a conception of Eternal Buddha or Buddhahood as eternal (Ādi Buddha). Its main doctrine is not concerned with personal perfection or individual salvation but the happiness and salvation of all creatures. A great man who strives for this may become a Buddha in some future birth and such a man is called Bodhisattva, P'u-sa 菩薩. According to this *Mahāyāna* Buddhism, Buddha and some Bodhisattvas are supermundane. It believes that faith in a Buddha, especially in Amitābha can secure rebirth in the Western Paradise. Hinayāna is sometimes described as self-benefiting whereas Mahāyāna is said to work for the benefit of others.

Mahāyāna is generally known as Northern Buddhism in contrast with Southern Buddhism. The former system is prevalent in Nepal, Tibet, China, Japan, Korea and the latter in Burma, Ceylon, Laos, Cambodia, Thailand.

For details vide N. Dutt, *Aspects of Mahāyāna Buddhism and its relation to Hīnayāna* (Calcutta Oriental Series 23. Luzac & Co. London. 1930).

2. The science of grammar; it is one of the five sciences taught in ancient India. The science of grammar explains words and their meanings.

but he could not lit the light (of Buddhism). He never reached back home. He died on the way"

師鞭法師者 Shih-Pien Fa-shih, Śrī Kaśa. The Dharmācārya Pien was a native of Ch'i-chou (Shan-tung). He thoroughly studied the Sanskrit language and *Vidyāmantra* 呪禁閑 *Chu-chin-hsien.*[1] He followed the previous monk Hsüan-chao to North India and then from there proceeded towards West. They reached the city of An-mo-luo-p'o, Āmraka and received warm hospitality from the king. While living in the 王寺 Wang-Ssu, Rāja Vihāra, he met the Dharmācārya Tao-hsi. They belonged to the same place in their country. They became very close and intimate friends. The monk Pien could stay only one year together with Tao-hsi. At the age of thirty-five he got ill and passed away while he was living with him (Tao-hsi).

阿難耶跋摩者 A-nan yeh-po-mo, Ānandavarman was a native of 新羅 Hsin-luo.[2] During the time of 貞觀 Chen-kuan period (of the T'ang Emperor) he began his journey from 廣脇 Kuang-hsieh (a small Rājagṛha) of the capital city of 長安 Ch'ang-an[3] in search of the Truth

1. Protective magical charms, *Dhāraṇī*—a collection of *mantras*. In the *Bodhisattvabhūmi* (Chapter XVIII, p. 185) Asaṅga explains the term *Dhāraṇī*. It means that a Bodhisattva must preserve in his memory Dharma, its artha and the mantras for all the time to come.

2. Ancient name of Korea.

3. Ch'ang-an (modern city of Hsi-an in Shen-si. (Lat 34° 17'N, Long. 108° 58'E) like an ancient capital city of Lo-yang witnessed rise and fall of many Empires. It was the capital city of the Earlier Han, Later Ch'in and Northern Chou Dynasties. Ch'ang-an, the capital of the largest Empire of the world, under the T'ang, was the greatest centre of Buddhism in China. The city was teeming with people from all over Asia. The glory of Lo-yang, the ancient stronghold of Buddhism in North, China, was overshadowed by Ch'ang-an when it entered into a period of unprecedented development. The population of the capital city during the Dynastic rule of the T'ang rose to 1,960,186. The city was studded with Buddnist temples, monasteries, pagodas constructed by the devout rulers of the T'ang Dynasty.

The great Chinese traveller Hsüan-Chuang started on his Indiaward journey from Ch'ang-an in 629 A.D. The great Tzu-en monastery was built there in A.D. 648, where the *Tripiṭaka-Āchārya* Hsüan-Chuang translated Buddhist scriptures into Chinese after his return from India. The Ta-yen Pagoda

of Buddhism and to pay respect to the sacred relics of the Buddha. While staying at the Nālandā monastery he took much care in studying the Vinayas and he copied a large number of Sūtras. It is a tragedy that he could not fulfil his heart's desire.

He started his journey from the eastern border of 雞貴 Chi-kuei[1] and died in the west of the 龍泉 Lung-ch'üan[2] or Dragon lake or spring (at Nālandā) at the age of more than seventy. His mortal remains rested in peace in that monastery. 慧業法師者 Hui-yeh Fa-shih. The Dharmācārya Hüi-yeh, Jñānasampada also belonged to Korea. In the Chen-kuan period, he travelled in Western regions. He lived in the Bodhi monastery and paid great homage to the sacred relics of the Buddha. He spent some years in the Nālandā monastery where he studied Buddhism and devoted much time listening to the religious discourses.

While I-ching was reading and checking up the Chinese manuscripts he suddenly discovered the manuscript of 梁論 Liang-lun.[3] At the end, it is said that the Korean monk (Jñānasampada) Hui-yeh recorded it, sitting under the shade of the 佛齒木樹 Fo-ch'ih-mu-shu, the Buddha's Tooth-stick tree.[4] After making inquiries from the monks living in that

was constructed in A.D. 652, which was designed by the venerable monk Hsüan-Chuang himself to store up the Buddhist scriptures in Ch'ang-an. From the last part of the fourth century, the Indian monks like Saṅghabhūti, Gautama Saṅghadeva, Kumārajiva, Yaśa all lived at Ch'ang-an and contributed a great deal for the propagation of Buddha's teachings. In the seventh century there were three Indian astronomical schools in the capital city.

1. Korea. Kao-mei was the ancient name of Chi-kuei. Chi in Chinese means chicken or fowl and 'Kuei' honourable. Chicken is worshipped in that country and people used to put its feathers on their hats for decoration. In Sanskrit it is 'Kukkuṭeśvara. So the name of the country was given Chi-kuei.

2. Dragon spring, according to Hsüan-Chuang, was in the Mango grove to the south of the Nālandā monastery.

3. Articles belonging to the Liang Dynasty (A.D. 502-557), ruled fifty-five years at Nan-ching (Nanking).

4. According to Hsüan-Chuang, there was a marvellous tree near Ch'io-li Tope near the Dragon lake at Nālandā Establishment. Nālandā is associated with the small incidents of the life of the Buddha. This marvellous tree which has been referred to by the Chinese pilgrim monk, had grown out of the twig

(Nālandā) monastery, it was known that he died here at the age of more than sixty. Whatever Sanskrit texts he copied, he left behind in that monastery.

玄太法師者 Hsüan-t'ai Fa-shih. He was also a native of Korea. His Sanskrit name was 薩婆愼若提婆 Sa-p'o-shen-jo-t'i-p'o, Sarvajñadeva. (He was known as I-ch'ieh-chih-t'ien 一切知天 in Chinese.) During the 永徽 Yung-hui[1] period, he reached Tibet and from there he came to Mid-India via Nepal. He made pilgrimage to the Bodhi-Tree, the Wisdom Tree[2] and studied the Buddhist *Sūtras* and *Śāstras* with great pains. He visited many places in the eastern region. On his return journey, he reached 土谷渾 T'u-ku-hun,[3] turbid valley where he met the monk 道希 Tao-hsi. Both of them continued their journey together. They proceeded towards the monastery of Great Enlightenment and from there to China. Nobody knows where and how his (Hsüan-t'ai) life ended.

玄恪法師者 **Hsüan-k'o Fa-shih,** ***Paramapūjya.*** **The monk Hsüan-k'o belonged to Korea. In the Chen-kuan period,**

---

thrown on the ground by the Buddha after using it as brush to clean his teeth. Hsüan-Chuang also mentioned about another Buddha's Tooth-stick tree at Pi-sho-ka or Viśoka. He described the tree, he saw at Nālandā as Yang-chih or "Willow branch". The next pilgrim I-ching found the same tree and considered it not to be Willow.

1. The third T'ang Emperor Kao-Tsung started this era in A.D. 650.

2. The Pipal tree (*aśvattha*, Ficus religiosa) under which Gautama achieved Enlightenment or Bodhi. Afterwards it came to be known as Bodhi tree. The area around the tree later on became famous as Bodh-Gayā, a famous Buddhist place of pilgrimage. A cutting of the Bodhi tree was even carried to and planted in as far as Ceylon.

The present Bodhi tree which we find now at the back of the Mahābodhi temple, has grown out of the root or seed of the original one. It sprang up in A.D. 1876.

Tiṣyarakṣitā, the queen of Aśoka, it is said, attempted to destroy the tree out of jealousy of her husband being deeply associated with the tree. In the beginning of the seventh century Śaśāṅka, the King of Bengal and a follower of *Śiva* cult according to Hsüan-chuang, almost destroyed the tree.

3. Lob Nor, Lap Nor or Lou-lan is one of the fertile oasis in the Southern states of Tarim basin. Under the former Hans, this region was known as Lou-lan. Lob Nor was situated on the oldest route linking Central Asia with China.

he, along with the Dharmâcārya Hsüan-chao, left for pilgrimage. They reached the monastery of Great Enlightenment. He paid great reverence to the vestiges of the Buddha but some days after-wards he fell sick and died at the age of fifty.

There were two other monks from Hsin-luo (Korea). No one knows their origin and names. They left the Capital city of Ch'ang-an and reached the South Sea. They started their voyage to Śrīvijaya and 婆魯師國 P'o-lu-shih[1], the country on the west of Śrībhoga, fell ill and died there.

佛陀達摩者 Fo-t'o-ta-mo, Bodhidharma belonged to 覩貨速利 Tu-huo-shu-li. He was very big-built, and strong enough to undertake the journey for the pilgrimage. He studied the Hīnayāna Buddhism. Sometimes he begged his food. He was a light eater and it helped him to move easily. He reached Shen-chou, Divine Land (China) and, it is said, entered into a monastic life in I-fu. He was very fond of long journey. He travelled a lot in Chiu-chou[2] (China) and visited many places.

He went to India; there he met I-ching in the Nālandā monastery. After some time at the age of fifty he left for North India. He was little more than fifty.

道方法師者 Tao-fang Fa-shih. The Law Master Dharmādeśa was a native of Ping-chou.[3] He left home, crossed

1. Prof. Chavannes, on the report in the *T'ang Dynasty Annals* (Chap. CC.xxiiC), identified the island of P'o-lu-shih and Marcopolo's Ferlec (=Parlak) with a country called Lang-po-lou-se, the western part of Śribhoga as mentioned in the *Annals*. Marcopolo in his account mentioned the eight kingdoms of "Java the less"; out of these he has given graphic descriptions of the six Kingdoms. Dr. R. C. Mazumdar is of opinion (*Hindu Colonies*). Firma. K. L. Mukhopadhyay, Calcutta, 1974) that Ferlec (=Parlak), one of these six Kingdoms mentioned by Marcopolo, must be on the north-east of "Java the less"

I-ching also narrates the story of two Korean monks who went to the island of P'o-lu-shih, west of Śribhoga. P'o-lu-shih or Ferlec is one of the islands mentioned by I-ching, in the south China sea.

2. The Nine divisions of China under the Emperor Yü, the Great.

3. It was one of the twelve ancient Provinces of China. The area varied from time to time under different Dynastic rules. This place was also known as T'ai-yüan Fu. It was in Shen-si.

deserts and mountains; then reached Nepal. He reached and remained in the monastery of Great Enlightenment for a couple of years as the head of the temple. Later on, he again went back to Nepal where he stayed on till the time of I-ching. This monk was very much indisciplined and seldom studied the Buddhist *Sūtras*. He was quite old.

道生法師者 Tao-sheng Fa-shih. He was also a native of Ping-chou. His Sanskrit name was 栴達羅提婆 Chan-ta-luo-t'i-p'o, Candradeva. He was known as 月天 Yüeh-t'ien in Chinese.

In the last year of the Chen-kuan period, he followed the route to Tibet. He went to Mid-India. Thereafter, he reached the Bodhi monastery where he worshipped 制底訖 *Chih-ti-ch'i*, *Caitagṛha*[1] with great reverence. In the Nālandā monastery he was the youngest student. So he was very courteously treated and honoured by the king. After going twelve yojanas to the east from this place, he got the 王寺 Wang-Ssu Rājavihāra.[2] Every resident of the monastery was the follower of the Hīnayāna faith. He lived in the monastery for a couple of years where he studied the principles of Hīnayāna Buddhism and the essence of the *Tripiṭaka* 三藏 *San-ts'ang*.[3]

1. In Chinese the Sanskrit word *Caitya*, Pāli *Cetiya* has been transcribed as 制底 Chih-ti, 制多 Chih-tuo or 支提 Chih-t'i. The term *Caitya* is derived from the word '*Citā*', funeral pyre. It was generally used by the Buddhist in the sense of '*stūpa*', a mound or timuli. A *Caitya* or stūpa is a mausoleum where the relics of the Buddha *Śurīra* (*Dhātu-garbha*, 'structure containing within its womb, *garbha*, corporal relics') were kept. In Pāli it is Dhātugabbha and in Ceylon it is known as dagaba. In these Cetiya gharas, congregational prayers and worships were conducted before a *stūpa* or a Buddha image. *Caityas* or *stūpas* with their surrounding passages for circumambulation became an object of supreme veneration to the Buddhists.
For details see Dr. D. Mitra, *Buddhist Monuments*, pp. 21-30.

2. We find a mention of a Rāja-Vihāra, evidently established by a King, in south-eastern Bengal (present Bangladesha), in the Gunaighar plate inscription (18 miles to the north-west of Comilla, district Tipper) of the Gupta ruler Vinayagupta dated A.D. 507.

3. *Tripiṭaka*, literally means 'Three Baskets". The three divisions of the Buddhist canon: (i) *Sūtrapiṭaka* basket of the *sūtras* or doctrine, (ii) *Vinayapiṭaka* or basket of discipline or system to be followed by the monks or by the Saṅghas, (iii) *Abhidharmapiṭaka* or basket of the higher subtleties of the doctrine.

He carried with him many Buddhist texts, Buddha's images and his teachings to his own country. When he reached Nepal on his way back home, he got ill and died at the age of fifty. There is the decree of Heaven at the age of fifty.[1]

常愍禪師者 Ch'ang-min Ch'an-shih, Nityadakṣa Dhyānācārya. The monk 常愍 Ch'ang-min came from Ping-chou. In his childhood, he cut his hair, threw away the hairpins and (accepted the tonsure) wore Buddhist robes. He was very diligent. He had an insatiable zeal for studying Buddhism and reciting the Sūtras. The Ācārya yearned for the joy of the Western Paradise. With a view of being born there he devoted himself to a life of purity and religion and used to chant the name of the Buddha always. He had a very strong religious foundation. He was born with many good and auspicious signs which are simply difficult to describe.

He visited the capital city of Lo-yang and devotedly enhanced the cause of Buddhism. For the propagation of these venerable ideas he was determined to write the whole of the 般若經 *Pan-jo-ching*, *Prajñā Sūtras*[2] in 10,000 chüan. He was desiring to

1. Confucius said, "At 15 my mind is bent on learning, at 30 I stood firm, at 40 I had no doubt, at 50 I know the decree of Heaven...."

Lun yü Book II, Chap. IV.

2. A corpus of 16 *Prajña Sūtras* with anonymous authorship is known as *Mahāprajñāpāramitāsūtra*. It is believed that in the *Mahāyāna Sūtra* like *Saddharmapuṇḍarīka*, *Laṅkāvatāra* and the *Prajña Sūtra* higher spiritual teachings are explained. The rich collection of *Mahāyāna Sūtra* which contains *Prajñāpāramitāsūtra* were greatly esteemed by the Chinese. All the Sūtras belonging to the *Prajñā* school were translated into Chinese several times, both in a complete form and in extracts. The longest sūtra of *Mahāprajñā pāramitā* in 600 fasciculi equivalent to 200,000 *ślokas* (*Karikās*) was first translated into Chinese. Lokakṣema, an Indo-Scythian monk was credited to introduce the *Mahāyāna* Buddhism in China. His partial translation of *Aṣṭasāhasrikā Prajñā-Pāramitā*, based on manuscript from India by Chu Shuo-fu, started a new epoch in the history of Buddhism in China, Then followed various translations of shorter version like *Prajñā Pāramitā Hṛdaya Sūtra* etc. There are six translations of the *Vajracchedikā Prajñā Pāramitā Sūtra* (Diamond Sūtra) by celebrated Kumārajiva and Hsüan-Chuang (in 600 chüan in A.D. 659). It is said that when Kumārajiva was living in the New monastery at Kucha, he discovered a manuscript of the *Pancaviṃśatisāhasrikā Prajñā Pāramita* from the adjoining old palace of Kucha. The Diamond Sūtra was so popular in China

go on a pilgrimage to India and offer his devotional homage to the sacred vestiges and the relics of Tathāgata; thus to secure for himself the greater merit with a view to a birth in heaven. That opportune moment came, when he went to the palace and submitted his humble petition requesting the Emperor's permission to visit the nine states to propagate Dharma and write *Prajñā Sūtras*. By the grace of God, he was permitted to undertake the journey. He crossed many rivers, travelled all over south China. During his stay in the south, he copied the same Sūtra with sincere devotion. He expressed his gratitude to God who had so kindly fulfilled his long-cherished desire.

Thereafter, he went to the sea coast, embarked on a ship and, sailed for 訶陵國 Ho-ling-kuo, Kaliṅga.[1] From there he again sailed for 末羅瑜國 Mo-luo-yü-kuo.[2] His aim

---

that the entire text had been carved on a stone slab by Sung Hsiao-erh during the reign of Wu-chou (A.D. 684-705) in Fang-shan county. Prajñā is the sixth of the Six Pāramitas with the help of which one reaches the other shore of the Saṃsāra.

See N. C. *Prajñāpāramitā Lit.*, 1-22.

J. Matsumoto. *Die Prajñāpāramita Literature. J.R.A.S.* 1933. p. 178.

E Zürcher *The Buddhist Conquest of China* (Leiden E. J. Brill 1972.) pp. 124-126.

C.T.T. Vols, 5, 6, 7,8.

1. It is one of the islands in the South sea mentioned by I-ching. The Indian name Ho-ling is Kaliṅga on the coast of Bay of Bengal. According to the *The New Annals of the T'ang* (A.D. 618-907), Book 222, Part ii, Ho-ling is another name for Java. In the Chinese Annals of the 2nd century A.D. it was also mentioned as Yeh-tiao.

While Fa-hsien was returning to China after his pilgrimage to India, he passed through Java which was a great centre of Hindu religion and culture in the first half of the fifth century A.D. In the seventh century Buddhism also flourished there.

According to Chinese History, Ho-ling or a part of Java had trade relation with the southern coast of India and Ceylon.

Prof. Chavannes placed it (Ho-ling) on the Western Part of Java and according to R. C. Mazumdar it is in Central Java. See C. P. Fitzgerald, *The Southern Expansion of Chinese People*, Second Map (at the back).

2. The Indian name of Malayu is Suvarṇadvīpa, Dr. R. C. Mazumdar, in his work bearing the title Suvarṇadvīpa, shows that it was the general term for Sumatra, Java and other islands of the Eastern Archipelago.

was to reach Mid-India. Accordingly, he boarded a cargo vessel carrying heavy merchandise. The ship left the shore but could not make any headway due to a sudden typhoon that lashed the region and made the sea very rough and turbulent. Within a few hours, the ship started sinking. In great confusion and panic, the sailors, the merchants on the ship began scrambling for getting accommodation in a small junk for safety. The captain of the ship was a follower of the Buddha. He himself boarded the junk, loudly called the monk to join them for safety. But the monk Ch'ang-min refused to go. He said "you may take someone else in my place. I will not go." He did not join them for the cause of others. He remained silently absorbed as if his short span of life was agreeable to one possessed of the 菩提心 *P'o-t'i-hsin*, *Bodhicitta*.[1] Forget yourself, do good to others. This is the true spirit of a greatman.

Then facing towards west, clasping his hands in adoration, he kept fervently praying and chanting the name of 阿彌陀佛

Malayu, one of the islands of South sea mentioned by I-ching, was an independent kingdom in Sumatra till the seventh century when it was conquered by Śrivijaya and formed a part of the kingdom. The modern name of Malayu in Sumatra is Jambi. The name of Malayu was changed to Bhoga or Śrībhoga just before I-ching's time or during his stay over there. I-ching has mentioned many a times the change of an independent Kingdom's name of Malayu to Bhoga.

In the C.P. Fitzgerald's map (*Burma, Indo-China and the Malay Peninsula*) Malayu is located to the South of Sumatra.

For details see J. Takakusu, *ARPIMA*. xxxix-xlvi.

1. The mind of the Buddha. The *Mahāyāna* Buddhism in China, Japan, Korea makes use of such terms as the Buddha in the heart, the Buddha mind and the Buddha nature. *Bodhicaryāvatāra*, a work of Śāntideva extant in original Sanskrit (Chapt. I called praise of the Bodhicitta), describes Bodhicitta as "the initial impulse and motive Power of the religious life combining intellectual illumination and unselfish devotion to the good of others." According to the Mahāyānist view every man and woman, whether a monk or a layman who cultivates the *Bodhicitta* (Direction towards Bodhi) has the potentiality to attain Buddhahood. By developing *Bodhicitta*, one can be free from his *Pṛthagjanahood*.

See Sāntideva's *Bodhicaryāvatāra*. Chapter one.

N. Dutt.—*Aspects of Mahāyāna Buddhism and its Relation to Hinayān a* pp. 246-7.

A-mi-t'o-fo Amitābha.[1] While he was still chanting the great name, the ship sank quietly. He was more than fifty when he died.

He had only one disciple with him, about whom very little was known. He wept bitterly, invoked with tears and also chanted the name of the West. Without him everything was empty and meaningless. He received help from his companions. This story was narrated by the survivors of the wrecked ship.

It was lamentable that such a great man (like Ch'ang-min) passed away so early ! He sacrificed his life for the good of others. He was pure like a mirror—he was priceless like a jade of 和 闐 玉 Ho-ti'en-yü, Khotan.[2] He would be steeped in a dark fluid without becoming dark. He might be rubbed without getting thin. He devoted his whole life for acquiring the

1. There are variations of the name of Amitābha. They are Amida, Amita, Amitāyus, Amitāyur. Amitabha means boundless light.

There is controversy among the Indian scholars over the time when worship of Amitābha Buddha was first introduced in India. Some are of opinion that Aśvaghoṣa was the first exponent of Amitābha cult; others believe it was Nāgārjuna. There is no authentic information about the origin of this dogma. Sir C. Eliot and E. J. Eitel contend that without any clear antecedent in India it may be supposed that it originated in Zoroastrian mythology. This idea of Amitābha had greatly influenced Buddhism in Kashmir and Nepal and the dogma reached China from one of these countries when a Tukharian prince took the first *Amitābha Sūtra* to China.

Amitābha, the saviour of all, is most popular in China. The principal doctrine of the faith is that salvation is achieved only by absolute trust in invoking the name of Amitābha.

A new school started in China which was known as Sukhāvatī or Ching-t'u, the Pure Land, the home of Amitābha. It is situated to the West of our world where spring is eternal and rebirth takes place in lotus. The followers of the Pure Land school chant the name of Amitābha many a time, desiring to be born again in the Western Paradise. The venerble Hui-yüan of the fifth century was the founder of this school in China. The venerable Tao-luan of the sixth century and Shan-tao of the seventh century were the important propagators of this school. *Sukhāvatī-Vyuha Sūtra* was translated into Chinese by Kumārajiva in A.D. 402, by Guṇabhadra in A.D. 420-429 and by Hsüan-Chuang in A.D. 650. The popularity of Amitābha in China was due to prolific translations of *Amitāyus Sūtras* or the Sūtra of Infinite age.

2. Shih-chi Chüan 81, *Biography of Lin Shiang-ju. Ssu ma-Ch'ien.* (Record of Great Historians—Watson).

highest Prajñā. He channelised his wisdom for a noble cause. In his own land he sowed the seed of good Karma and outside his country he achieved the reward. He voluntarily went forward in the face of a very dangerous situation in which death by drowning in the sea was imminent. He immediately made up his mind and sacrificed himself for others. Ch'ang-min's disciple became friendless.

His filthy, useless body was disintegrated in the sea. By pure meditation he reached the heaven. Dhamma would never be impaired and the flow of virtue could not be restrained. He displayed the brilliance of charity, compassion. Finally the Kalpa[1] of continued mortal existence came to an end for a new one.

末底僧訶 Mo-ṭi-seng-ho. Matisiṃha. He was known as Shih-hui, Prajñāsiṃha in Chinese. He came from 京兆 Ching-chao.[2] His family name was 皇甫 Hsing-fu. His personal name was not known. He travelled far and wide with the monk Pien.

They reached Mid-India and lived in the monastery of Great Faith 信者寺 Hsin-che-Ssu. He had some knowledge of Sanskrit but did not learn the Buddhist *Sūtras* and *Śāstras* in detail. He decided to go back to his own land but on his way back he breathed his last in Nepal at the age of forty only.

玄會法師者 Hsüan-hui Fa-shih. He belonged to the Capital City of China. He was said to be the son of the General An 安

Following the overland route to Northern India he entered into 羯濕彌羅 K'e-hsi-mi-lo[3] Kashmir. He was assig-

1. An aeon of incalculable time. Four Kalpas constitute a Mahā Kalpa. According to Hindu mythology a Kalpa consists of one thousand mahāyugas—a mahāyuga being a period of four yugas viz., Satya, Tretā, Dvāpara and Kali.

2. A district of Ch'ang-an, modern Hsi-an in Shen-si province under the Han Dynasty. Peking was also known as Ching-Chao under the Republic.

3. Kashmir was one of the most important centres of Buddhist Sanskrit learning and the Centre of the most powerful Buddhist sect, *Sarvāstivāda*. Kashmir played an important role in the transmission of Buddhism to China. The Chinese traveller Ou-K'ang or Wu-K'ong while visiting Kashmir (A.D. 759-763) had seen about three hundred monasteries. (CTT vol. 51: No. 2089. II, p. 979).

ned a job to look after the royal elephants by the King of Kashmir. He rode on a royal elephant accompanied by royal music. Everyday the King sent food to the Nāgahrada Parvata Vihāra 龍池山寺 Lung-ch'ih-shan-Ssu[1], where the monk Hsüan-hui was residing. Five hundred 羅漢 Luo-han[2], Arhats received royal hospitality regularly here. This was the place where the venerable Madhyāntika, the disciple of Ārya 尊者 Ānanda, converted the dragon-king. The King of Kashmir was so much impressed by the pilgrim monk that he reverentially proclaimed gracious pardon inside the country. There were more than a thousand convicts who were condemned to death but by royal clemancy the convicts were set free. He had free access to the royal palace where he spent some years as a

1. According to the local reports, Kashmir was originally a dragon-lake. Madhyāntika, an Arhat and a disciple of Ānanda, was perfect in six spiritual attainments (六神 Liu-shen) and achieved Aṣṭa-vimokṣa. Madhyāntika heard Buddha's prediction that he would build a new city. He was very happy, came here and took his seat in a forest on a high mountain where he performed a series of miracles. A dragon appeared before him and wanted to know his desire. The *Arhat* wanted a place to put his knees in the lake where he wanted to sit cross-legged. The dragon granted his request by removing water but Madhyāntika, by super-natural power enlarged his body till the lake was completely dried up. He lived in north-west of this place near the lake.

In the Chien-shih mi-chuan 簡矢密傳 of the *New T'ang shu*, there is a reference of Mahāpadma lake, the present Volur. The Nāga-hrada-parvata vihāra might be very close to this lake.

See Chang Hsing-lang, *Chung-hsi Chiao-t'ung shih-liao*, (The Materials for a History of Sino-Foreign Relation). Vol. 6, p. 375.

2. A saint, a perfect man of Hīnayāna. The Sanskrit technical term Arhat, Chinese Lo-han or A-lo-han is applied to those who have reacned the Eight-fold path and enjoy the fruits of it.

The first Buddhist Sūtra 'The *Sūtra in 42 articles*' translated by Kāśyapa-mātaṅga and Dharmāraṇya into Chinese in the beginning of Christian era, has defined the term Lo-han (Arhat). Thus, he who has left the world in pursuit of the Law is Śramaṇa. He has to follow 250 rules. By various endeavours and efforts he will acquire the purity and will attain four degrees (*Ārya*). The highest degree that of Lo-han confers the power of flying in the air and of transforming one's self at will.

See *Encyclopaedia of Religion and Ethics*. Vol. I. pp. 774-5.

See Zurcher. *BCC* (Notes) Vol.II Nos. 62, 63.

royal guest. But after some time he was very much disappointed and left for South.

In the monastery of Great Englightenment he worshipped the Bodhi Tree and spent hours gazing at 木真池 Mu-chen-ch'ih[1], Muchalinda lake. While he was residing there, he often climbed the Gṛdhrakūṭa mountain, took stroll on the 尊足山 Tsun-tsu-shan Kukkuṭapādagiri[2] (Cock-Foot mountain or Sage's Foot mountain). His knowledge was very deep and penetrating. He had divine sagacity of a sage, and had skill and dexterity. Despite the many difficulties he had to encounter, he mastered Sanskrit pronunciation in a short time. He acquired very little knowledge in Sanskrit Sūtras and religious thoughts. So he decided to go back to his own native country. On his way back to China, he reached Nepal where he unfortunately died at the age of thirty odd years. Nepal had some poisonous herbs. Many people who arrived there died due to those herbs.

There was a man who along with the Chinese envoy went to 縛渴羅 Fu-k'o-luo, Bukhara[3] by the northern route. In

1. Hsüan-chuang has mentioned the Muchalinda lake which was near the Bodhi tree to the east of the Indra tank at Bodh-Gayā. The lake belonged to the Dragon King Muchalinda.

After attaining Enlightenment, the Buddha sat near the Bodhi tree in blissful contemplation for four weeks. On the sixth week he went to Machalinda where he was protected from showers of rain with seven coils of his body and with several extended hoods.

2. Kukkuṭapādagiri-Vihāra named after Kukkuṭapāda-giri, a hill of great purity, mentioned both by Fa-hsien and Hsüan-chuang, has been identified by A. Cunninghum with the modern village of Kurkihar (Lat 24° 49'N; Long 85° 15'E, District Gaya, Bihar) 3 miles to the north-east of Wazirganj and 16 miles to the north-east of Gaya. He is of opinion that the present Kurkihar both in name and position is the famous Cock's Foot hill of the Buddhists. This sacred hill, with three peaks, was the abode of the venerable Mahākāśyapa who was entrusted with the duty and responsibility of protecting the canons by the Buddha. The triple peaked mountain is also known as Gurupādagiri.

3. There is a difference in Chinese transcription of Balkh. Hsüan-Chuang's transcription is Fu-ho (縛喝) whereas I-ching has transcribed as Fu-k'o-luo (縛渴羅) Bukhara. In Balkh or Bukhara, one of the states of Tokharestan, Buddhism was the predominant religion. Hsüan-Chuang has given a graphic description of the flourishing condition of

the 新寺 Hsin-Ssu Navasaṅghārāma where the principles of little vehicle were taught, he became a monk under the name of 質多跋摩 Chih-tuo-po-mo, Cittavarman. Having received the precept, he declined to eat the three kinds of pure food.

The master of the Navāsaṅghārāma said, "the Great Lord Tathāgata himself took five kinds of food considered proper for a monk (五正 Wu-chang).[1] It is not a crime. Why should you not eat?" asked the abbot. "It is not the rule observed by the Hīnayānist. Therefore, I cannot change the old habits now", replied the monk. The abbot said, "I have established a practice here in agreement with the three piṭakas; I have never read such a rule. If you so please you may find out a suitable preceptor. I can no longer be your preceptor".

Cittavarman was thus reluctantly compelled to eat the food. He broke his vow and took food in tears. He conveniently followed the commandments of the monastery. He knew very little Sanskrit. He followed the northern route on his way back (to China). No one knew where he went. His story was narrated by Indian monks from North India.

There were other two monks in Nepal. They were the children of the wet nurse of the princess of Tibet. At a very early age, they left home and became monks. One of them later on, entered

---

Buddhism there. He has mentioned that there were about 100 Vihāras with more than 3000 monks. This city was known as Little Rājagṛha with the largest monastery Nava Saṅghārāma. During Hsüan-Chuang's travel, Balkh was under the Turkish rule. The Turks were the followers of Buddhism. They built a huge Vihāra close to the Sogdh river. In their language Vihāra was known as Bukhar. So the name of the place was Bukhara.

See Sir Aurel Stein, *On Central Asian Tracks*. pp. 321-330; P. C. Bagchi, *India and Central Asia*. pp. 34-35; Rahul Sankrityāyana, *History of Central Asia*. p. 71.

1. Pañcabhojaniyam—the five kinds of food considered proper for monks. These are often mentioned in the Vinaya. *Pātimokkha* or the *Sikṣāsamuccaya* deals with the rules regulating eating and drinking of a monk. 五正 Wu-Chang is an old translation. A comparatively recent translation is 五噉食 Wu-tan-shih. The chapter on Mendicaments says, "O Bhikkhus, do not knowingly eat meat of an animal killed for that purpose. Whosoever does so, is guilty of a dukkhata offence." See—*Pātimokkha*, Pāk 37.

See Sacred Books of the East. Vol. xvii, p. 81. f.n. 117; Vol. xiii p. 40.

the family life again. They lived at the great Rājavihāra (Royal monastery). They mastered Sanskrit language and Sanskrit texts. One of them was thirty-five and the other twentiy-five.

隆法師者 Lung-Fa shih Gauravadharma. The native place of the monk Lung was not known. During the Chen-kuan period, he left home and followed the northern route (to reach India). As soon as he arrived in North India, he wanted to witness the transforming influence (of the Doctrine) in Mid-India. He had a wonderful style of reciting the 法華經 Fa-hua-ching,[1] *Saddharmapuṇḍarika Sūtra* in Sanskrit. He reached 建陀羅 Chien-t'a-luo, Gandhāra[2] where he fell sick and died. This information was gathered from the monks coming from North India.

1. The *Lotus Sūtra*, one of the earliest *Mahāyāna Sūtras*, is composed of both prose and verses—the prose is in pure Sanskrit and verses in mixed Sanskrit. This Sūtra contains twenty-seven chapters.

Winternitz says (*A History of Indian Literature* Vol. II, p. 302) that it is difficult to ascertain the date of the composition of this text. Its sections belonged to various epochs. Dr. P. V. Bapat has placed the work in the first-century A.D., a little later than *Mahāvastu* and *Lalita-Vistara.*

Saddharmapuṇḍarika was very much popularised in China and Japan. The T'ien-t'ai school in China and the Tendai, Nitchiren Sect in Japan consider the Lotus Sūtras as the most important Buddhist text. It has made great contribution to Buddhist art and sculpture in China and Japan.

It was translated into Chinese several times . The earliest translation was done by Fa-hu Dharmarakṣa of the Western Chin Dynasty in A.D. 286, in 28 Chapters, then by Kumārajīva and by Jñānagupta and Dharmagupta of the Sui Dynasty (A.D. 589-618) NC Nos. 134-139.

The title of the *Lotus Sūtra* (in Chinese) according to Dharmarakṣa is Cheng-fa-hua Ching, and according to Kumārajīva Miao-fa-lien-hua ching. Kumārajiva's version contains 28 chapters and agrees with the Tibetan version. See E. Zürcher The *BCC* Chap. II.

2. According to early foreign writers, Gandhāra was the territory between modern Lamghan and Jalalabad on the west, the Swat hill on the north, the Indus on the east and the hills of Kalabag on the south. But according to Indian literary sources, the term Gandhāra denotes an area that included Puṣkalāvati and Takṣaśilā. Puṣkalāvati has been identified with Charsadda (about 16 miles north-east of Peshawar) in Peshawar district and Takṣaśilā in Rawalpindi district in Pakistan.

These places were visited by early Chinese travellers like Fa-hsien, Hsüan-Chuang. Gandhāra was a second holy land of Buddhism where art had flourished contributing a great deal to the history of World art.

明遠法師者 Ming-yüan Fa-shih. The monk belonged to the city of 清 Ch'ing in 益州 I-chou.[1] His Sanskrit name was Cintādeva, Chan-to-t'i-p'o 振多提婆 He was also known as 思天 Szu-t'ian in Chinese language. From childhood he received religious education and as he grew up he became very virtuous. He was handsome, respectful, dignified, courteous and was fond of ceremonics. He was greatly respected in China. He was conversant in 中 Chung[2], 百 Pai,[3] *Mādhyamika* and *Śataśāstra* respectively. He had the mastery to expound the discourses of Chuang-chou,[4] (the great Chinese 莊周 philosopher).

When he was young, he travelled many places in Hū-nan

1. During the time of the Western Hans, I-chou was comprised of some parts of Szu-ch'uan and Yün-nan.

2. The *Mahāyāna* system of thought is divided into *Mādhyamika* and *Yogācārā*. The founder of the *Mādhyamika* school was Bodhisattva Nāgārjuna who lived probably in the 2nd century A.D. The most famous work of Nāgārjuna is *Mādhyamika-Kārika*. He was followed by many Mādhyamika scholars such as Āryadeva (Third century A.D.), Buddhapālita (Fifth century A.D.) and Candrakīrti (Sixth century A.D.).

The "Tri Śāstra" sect in China was formed on the basis of the *Mādhyamika-Śāstra*, *Śata-śāstra* and the *Dvādaśanikāya-śāstra* which were translated by Kumārajiva.

3. One of the three Śāstras of the *Mādhyamika* school. In Chinese 'Pai' means hundred. This Śāstra contains one hundred verses with each one composed of 32 words. So the name *Śata Śāstra* is given. It was written by Vasubandhu in Sanskrit and translated by Kumārajiva in Chinese. But this version differs from the original Sanskrit.

4. D.T. Suzuki, in the Introduction of "*The Text of Taoism*" (translated by James Legge) says: "....Chuang-Tze was the greatest of the philosophers, poets, and literary essayists in the entire history of the Taoist School—more than that, perhaps in all fields of Chinese literature." (p. 3).

Chuang-Tze belonged to the feudal age of China when China was disintegrated into a number of small states. The great historian Ssu-ma Ch'ien in the second century B.C., notes that Chuang-Tze came from An-hui. His personal name was Chou. He was a sincere devotee of Lao-Tze, the great philosopher of the sixth century B.C. Chuang-Tze propagated and expounded the "way of life" or "the Tao" against the materialistic, ethical concept of life propagated by Confucius and his followers.

(七 澤 Ch'i-che)[1] and in the area (三 吳 San-wu[2]) east of Yang-tze river valley, in search of knowledge. Later on, he studied seriously the Buddhist sūtras and śāstras and practised meditation. Consequently, he spent the summer retreat in a lonely, quiet top of the mountain Lu.[3]

Since the magnanimous sacred religion (Buddhism) was already in decadent state, he (with an idea of restoring it) became a mendicant and arrived at extreme south. From here he sailed and reached 交 阯 Chiao-chih.[4] He crossed the vast sea to reach 訶 陵 K'o-ling. From there he went to 師 州 Shih-tzu-chou,[5] Siṃhala. While the King of the country was worshipping, the monk concealing himself in a private chamber, tried to rob the Tooth-relic with the intention of carrying it back to his own country and worshipping with great reverence. He concealed it in his hand and was taking it away when it was detected. The Tooth-relic was then snatched away from him. This was a great humiliation for him.

According to the Ceylonese story, the Chinese pilgrim went to South India and it was related that while he was proceeding towards the monastery of Great Enlightenment, he passed away on the way. How old he was, is not known.

1. Present Hu-nan province. See *Ch'u-T'zu-yüan*, Vol. I, p. 10, folio 3.

2. Area extending over the east of Yang-tze valley. The three places, Su-chou, Ch'ang-chou, Hu-chou are known as San-wu. *Ibid.* Vol. I, p. 15, folio 1.

3. One of the sacred mountains (for the Buddhists) of China in northern Chiang-si. From very ancient times the mountain 'Lu' was hallowed by Taoist and Buddhist traditions. Many miraculous and supernatural events are associated with the mount 'Lu'. The famous Chinese monk Hüi-yuan (A.D. 380) stayed on that beautiful mountain. He left adetailed description of the mountain known as Lu-shan-chi. This mountain has been compared with Gṛdhrakūṭa mountain near Rājagṛha in India. See CTT Vol. 51. No. 209, p. 1024.

4. The frontier of China today is not the same as it was during the time of the T'ang and the Sung. Chiao-chih, the modern Hanoi near Tonkin, the heart of North Vietnam was a Chinese province for about nine centuries from B.C. 111 to A.D. 939. This area became part of the Han Empire and was known as commandery of Jihnan.

5. Siṃhala—Ceylon or present Sri Lanka. It was also known as Ratnadvipa, Isle of Jewels.

After this incident, the King of Ceylon kept the Tooth-relic in a safer place. It was carefully guarded in a very lofty tower, the doors of which were very firmly closed. This room had many sets of heavy doors. The locks of the doors were covered and sealed tightly with mud by five officers. Opening of the doors (of that particular room) would start the automatic alarm in the town and outside the city gate.

Everyday offerings were made and incense was burnt. Flowers were offered all the time. When taken out, the Tooth was placed on a golden flower and its sparkling glow everywhere diffused. The tradition goes that if this country loses the Tooth-relic, the country would be devoured by 羅刹 Luo-sho, Rākṣasas.[1] On account of that, the Tooth was very carefully guarded and protected to avoid such a calamity. It is also said that this Tooth-relic could be taken to China only by the Divine Power; and not by human contrivance.

義朗律師者 I-lang Lü-shih Arthadīpta. The Vinaya-master I-lang belonged to 成都 Ch'eng-tu[2] in 益州 I-chou. He was well versed in 律典 Lü-tian[3] and in interpretation of 瑜伽 Yü-ga, Yoga System.[4] He set forth from Ch'ang-an with the monk 智岸 Chih-an from his own native place and an eminent man I-hsüan, for pilgrimage. 義玄 While he was about twenty years old, he realised the Truth from the teacher. He studied the Buddhist scripture and he himself was a good writer. He desired to pay a visit to the sacred shrines of the Lord Buddha with his disciples. They were like his own brothers taking care of each other. Soon, they develop ed

1. The demons with terrifying looks, with black bodies, red hair and green eyes are supposed to be the original inhabitants of Sri Lanka.

2. The capital of modern Szu-ch'uan province. (Lat. 20° 34'N, Long. 103°-11'E).

3. The Vinaya Canon.

4. The principle of Yoga (the ecstatic union of individual soul with Divine soul) was first propounded by Patañjali in the second century B.C. Asaṅga in the fourth century A.D. founded a similar school of Yoga in Buddhism. Hsuan-Chuang was a follower of this school.

very deep attachment for each other in the course of their journey.

They reached the country 烏 雷 Wu-lei[1], and embarked on a merchant ship. Tossing over thousands of high waves, the ship passed through 扶 南 Fu-nan[2], anchored at 郎 迦 Lang-chia[3] where he was entertained with valuable gifts by the king. The fellow monk 智岸 Chih-an fell sick and breathed his last there. Lang was very much grieved at his death. He along with his fellow companions sailed for Ceylon where they secured new religious texts and worshipped Lord Buddha's Tooth-relic.

Gradually he reached the Western country. I-ching collected this information. No one knew his whereabouts. The people of Ceylon also did not see him again. The people of Mid-India

1. Present Ch'in-hsien, north-south of Kuang-tung island. During the T'ang period this region was known as Wu-lei.

2. The original name of this country is not known. It was known to the Chinese as Fu-nan upto the early period of the T'ang. Fu-nan, the precurser of Cambodia was colonised by the Indian settlers and along with their immigration the Indian culture and religion also spread.

During the period of the Three Kingdoms, Fu-nan or Cambodia was visited by Chinese envoys and in the subsequent years there were several Chinese embassies to Fu-nan. We can get details and full account of Fu-nan only from Chinese sources. In the third century A.D. the southern most part of later Cochin-China was Fu-nan territory. In the early T'ang period a great change took place in Fu-nan, when the name Fu-nan disappeared from the Chinese record and thenceforward it was known as Chen-La. Chen-La had very cordial and close relation with the T'ang rulers. Watters has identified I-shen-na-pu-luo, Iśāṇapura of Hsüan-chuang with Fu-nan.

I-Ching in the late seventh century said that though Buddhism was established in Chen-La, the founder King of the place persecuted the Buddhist in favour of the *Śaivite* sect of Hinduism which had firmly prospered there.

3. Hsüan-chuang in his account has given the names of six countries beyond Samataṭa (Lower Bengal). One of these six countries is Kāmalaṅka which in all probability is Lang-Chia or Lankasu mentioned by I-ching. It is said to be identical with Pegu and the delta of Irawadi. Dr. R. C. Mazumdar also thinks Langkasu of I-ching to be the Mon country in Lower Burma and it may be the same as Tenasserim. In the Historical Records of the Liang Dynasty (A.D. 502-557) a country is mentioned as Lang-kasu. (Book 54). See C.P. Fitzgerald. *The Southern Expansion of the Chinese people*. Maps. 1, 2.

did not hear anything about him. Most probably he died in a foreign land. He was more than forty when he died.

會寧律師者 Hui-ning Lü-shih, Mahābhiśayanavinayācārya, also belonged to Ch'eng-tu in I-chou. He was a very precocious and intelligent child. As a young boy he visited temples and monasteries in pursuit of knowledge. At an early age he renounced the pleasures of the world and was admitted to the Order (*Pravrajyā*). He studied profoundly the Buddhist Sūtras, Śāstras and the Vinaya canons. His desire to know the Buddhist Law inspired him to visit the Western country.

In Lin-te period[1], (A.D. 665) he with a mendicant stick Hsi-chang[2] reached the South Sea from where he sailed for K'o-ling. There he lived for three years with a well reputed monk 若那跋陀羅 Ju-na-p'o-t'o-luo Jñānabhadra. The pilgrim then translated a portion of the *Āgama Sūtra*[3], with Jñānabhadra, concerning the last ceremony held after the *Mahāparinirvāṇa*[4]

1. Started by the third Emperor Kao-Tsung of Ta'ng Dynasty in A.D. 664.

2. A monk's stick partly made of metal with metal rings. They announce their arrival for begging by shaking these rings.

3. The general term *Āgama* has been used for a collection of *Hīnayāna* texts. There are four *Āgamas*, viz. *Dīrghāgama* (*Ch'ang-a-han*), *Madhyamāgama* (*Chung-a-han*), *Saṃyuktāgama* (*Tze-a-han*) and *Ekottarāgama* (*Tseng-a-han*). Each of these *Āgamas* has its corresponding Sūtras in Pāli canon such as *Dīgha-nikāya, Majjhima-nikāya, Saṃyuttanikāya* and *Aṅguttara-nikāya.*

A Parthian monk An-shih-kao arrived at Lo-yang in A.D. 148 and first translated the *Dīrghāgama* into Chinese during the time of the Eastern Han (A.D. 25-220) in 2 fasciculi. *Ekottarāgama* was translated into Chinese by *Dharmanandi* in A.D. 384-385, and *Madhyamāgama* by Saṅghadeva in A.D. 397-398.

See Nanjio's Cat. Nos. 542, 543, 545, G. P. Malalasekera pp. 244-248 *Encyclopaedia of Buddhism* (Ed.) Vol. I, 2. Nos. 542-678. CTT Vol. 1, 2, No. 542-678.

4. Dharmarakṣa of the Northern Liang Kingdom, at the beginning of the fifth century translated the *Sūtra* on the great demise of the Lord or the *Mahāparinirvāṇa Sūtra* into Chinese in A.D. 423. The monk Hui-ning of the T'ang Dynasty with the help of Jñānabhadra translated the *Sūtra* again in 2 fasciculi—(NC Nos. 113-125). The *Mahāparinirvāṇa* of the Hīnayānist was first translated into Chinese by Po Fa-tsu in A.D. 290-360, and by Fa-hsien between A.D. 417-420 in the famous monastery Tao-Ch'ang.

The Chinese *Tripiṭaka* contains three translations of the *Mahāparinirvāṇa* of the Hīnayāna and seven translations of the Mahāyāna.

of Lord Tathāgata. This work does not agree with the Nirvāṇa of the Mahāyana Sūtra. But the venerable I-ching could find the *Nirvāṇa Sūtra* of the Mahāyāna consisting of about 25,000 *ślokas*. There were more than sixty chüan translated into Chinese. He wanted to collect the entire Sūtra but could not succeed; he got a collection of the first 4,000 *ślokas* of the *Mahāsāṅghika* 大衆部 *Ta-chung-pu.*[1]

Hui-ning translated the *Āgama Sūtra* only. He then ordered his disciple monk 運期 Yün-ch'i to go immediately to China and present the Sūtra with respect and honour; he returned to Chiao-fu[2] from where it was taken by horses assigned by the Government. Yün-ch'i then presented the book to the Emperor in the royal palace and requested him to propagate this book among the people of Tung-hsia[3] (China). Yün-ch'i left the capital and reached Chiao-chih 交阯. He told the

After Dharmarakṣa's translation of the *Mahāparinirvāṇa Sūtra*, the Buddhist world in China became very much interested in this text which stresses the eternal, joyous, personal and pure nature of Nirvāṇa. The *Nirvāṇa* school in China is based on the doctrines of the *Mahāparinirvāṇa Sūtra.*

See CTT Vol. 12, No. 374;

Winternitz. *History of Indian Literature*. Vol. II, p. 235.

1. According to the Buddhist canonical tradition, a sharp difference broke out among the monks regarding the observing of certain Vinaya rules, just hundred years after the "Great Demise". The two different groups placed their demands for clarification before the second Council at Vaiśālī. A section of the orthodox monks regarded the Vinaya rules as the very foundation, the rockbed of the monastic life. The rules must be entirely preserved and followed. There were some liberal monks who opposed this view. According to the Ceylonese Chronicles this dispute was not solved in the Council; instead, it was followed by 'Great Schism' (Mahābheda) which split the order into two schools —the *Theravāda* and the *Mahāsāṅghika.*

"The *Mahāsāṅghika* became the starting point of the development of the Mahāyāna by their more liberal attitude and by some of their special theories" (Edward Conze, *Buddhism: Its Essence and Development*, Oxford, 1951, p. 121). At its inception, this school had an important centre at Vaiśālī. Later, Amarāvatī and Nāgārjunakoṇḍā became the important and popular centres of the *Mahāsāṅghikas.*

2. The region of modern Kuang-tung, Kuang-si and An-nan.

3. The Chinese writers sometimes call whole China as Tung-hsia and sometimes only the eastern part of China. Tung-hsia is modern Yen-an. During the Northern-Wei period it was Tung-hsia or Chin-ming.

believers and non-believers of the Faith that he got a gift of hundred pieces of fine shining silk from the Court.

When he returned to K'o-ling he reported to 德智賢 Te-chih-hsien, also known as Jñānabhadra, that the monk Hui-ning wanted to meet him. Just then Hui-ning left for Western country. Yün-ch'i stayed there for some time anxiously waiting to know the whereabouts of the monk Hui-ning. He looked forward to meet him, made inquiries about him. He sent messengers to five Indies 五天 Wu-t'ien[1] in search of him, but no information was available. He had probably died by then. It was really a matter of great regret.

Hui-ning travelled all alone in search of Dharma. His heart's desire was to pay a visit to the land of Buddhism; he just completed the first leg of his travel. Finally, he reached 寶渚 Pao-chu[2] and temporarily lived in 化城 Hua-ch'eng.[3]

He died but his Dharma still survives. He is immortal and his name would be remembered by future generations.

He propagated the Will of Bodhisattva and thus his name imprinted will last for ever. He died at the age of thirty-four or five.

運期師者 Yün-ch'i, Kālacakra. The monk Yün-ch'i was a native of 交州 Chiao-chou. He all along travelled with 曇潤 T'an-rung. He was ordained by 伏智賢 Fu-chih-hsien. He returned to the South Sea 南海 Nan-hai, where he spent more than ten years. He was well acquainted with the language of the people of 崑崙 K'un-lun[4] and

1. India was known as Shen-tu-koa or P'o-luo-men-kuo (Land of Brāhmins) to the Chinese during the time of the Han rulers. The name of India as T'ien-chu became popular during the time of the T'ang Dynasty (A.D. 618-907). India had five distinct divisions viz., Eastern India. West India, South India, North India and Mid India.

See CTT Vol. 51. No. 2087, p. 875, IInd folio. P.C. Bagchi *Monumenta Senica* Vol. XIII 1948 (Peking) *Ancient Chinese names of India*. pp. 366-375.

2. Ratnadvipa.

3. The magic city in the 'Lotus Sūtra'. It means temporary Nirvāṇa or imperfect Nirvāṇa of the Hīnayānists.

4. The Chinese name of Polo Condore is K'un-lun. It is identical with K'u-lun, Ku-lun. The Arab travellers of the ninth century called a group of

acquired some knowledge of Sanskrit language. Later on, he retired to lay life and lived in Śrī-vijaya up to the time of I-ching.

A sudden change took place in him; he was greatly moved by the Law of the Buddha and again he travelled over the island preaching the religion in the city. He propagated the religion among non-believers. He breathed his last when he was forty.

窺冲法師者K'uei-ch'ung Fa-shih. The monk K'uei-ch'ung also came from Chiao-chou. He was a disciple of 明遠 Ming-yüan. His Sanskrit name was 質怛囉 Chih-ta-lo-t'i-p'o, Citradeva.[1] The monk with Ming-yüan embarked 提婆 upon a ship, crossed the South Sea and reached Ceylon and thereafter proceeded towards Western India. There he met the venerable monk Hsüan-chao and with him reached Mid-India

He was very honest, sincere and intelligent. He was good in reciting Sanskrit Sūtras. Wherever he went he collected Sanskrit Sūtras and recited them with tunes and actions. He offered his sincere devotion to the Bodhi tree 菩提樹 P'o-t'i-shu. He reached the Bamboo Grove 竹園 Chü-yüan in Rājagṛha and stayed there long. There he fell sick and died at the age of thirty odd years.

Hui-yen Fa-shih. The monk Hui-yen, 慧琰法師者Prajñāratna was a native of Chiao-chou. He was the disciple of 行公 Hsing-kung. Accompanied by his teacher he reached 僧訶羅國 Seng-ho-luo-kuo (Siṃhala). He stayed there. It was not known whether he died or he was still living.

信胄法師Hsin-chou Fa-shih. No one knows the native place of the Dharmācārya Hsin-chou. His Sanskrit name was

---

small and big islands by the name Sundar or Sondor and Marco Polo by Sundur and Condur. He has not said much of them. The people belonging to the place were of dark complexion with wooly hair. I-ching has said that the country with peculiar inhabitants accepted Buddhism to some extent and he has mentioned a monastery over there.

See J. Takakusu: '*ARBRPIMA* (Munshi Ram Manohar Lal, Delhi) pp. xlix-1. *The Travels of Marco-Polo* (Translated by Manuel Komroff) p. 272.

1. In the text the character is 呾 But I think 怛 is better reading.

設喇陀跋摩 She-li-t'o-p'a-mo, Śraddhāvarman. In Chinese he was known as Hsin-chou, Śraddhāvarman.

Following the northern route, he reached the Western country. He lived in the Monastery of Faith and made offerings there. On the top of the monastery he built a brick chamber and donated it for the use of all who retired from the cares of public life. After some time he fell sick and before his death, one night he suddenly shouted saying that *Bodhisattva* with outstretched hands was beaconing him to his beautiful abode. He received the offer, standing with folded hands, breathed a deep sigh and passed away at the age of thirty-five.

智行法師 Chih-hsing Fa-shih. The Dharmācārya Chih-hsing was a native of 愛州 Ai-chou.[1] His Sanskrit name was 般若提婆 Pan-jo-t'i-p'o, Prajñādeva. In Chinese he was known by the name of 慧天 Hui-t'ien which means Prajñādeva. Sailing from the South Sea,he reached West India, where he worshipped the sacred relics of the Honourable One. He then proceeded to the north of the river 殑迦 Ch'iang-chia[2] the Gaṅgā (the Ganges). He lived in the Monastery of Faith and died there at the age of fifty.

大乘燈禪師者 Ta-ch'eng-teng Ch'an-shih. *Dharmācārya* also came from Ai-chou. His Sanskrit name was 莫訶夜那鉢地已波 Mo-ho-yeh-na-po-ti-i-po, Mahāyānapradīpa. In Chinese he was known by the name of Ta-ch'angteng which means Mahāyānapradīpa. While still young, he sailed for 杜和羅鉢底 Tu-ho-luo-po-ti[3] with his parents. Here he renounced the world and became a monk.

1. It was Ai-chou during the time of the Liang Dynasty. Modern Tungching chou.

2. One of the longest rivers in the world. Rising from the Śivālika mountain of the Himālaya, this river meets the Bay of Bengal in the east covering about 1500 miles. Gaṅgā is the most sacred river of the Hindus.

3. T'o-lo-po-ti has been restored as Dvārāvati. Dvārāvatī in West Thailand (Siam) is identical with Ayuthya (or Ayudhya), the ancient capital of Siam. According to Prof. Chavannes Dvārāvatī is the Sanskrit name of Ayudhya and according to Reginald Le May Dvārāvatī is situated between modern Burma and Cambodia. See *A Concise History of Buddhist Art in Siam*, p. 25.

After that, he followed 郯緒 T'an-sü, the envoy from the Imperial Court and reached the capital. He lived in the monastery of 慈恩 Tz'u-en[1], Mahākaruṇā, the great compassion monastery where the venerble Tripiṭaka master Hsüan-chuang lived, here he (Mahāyāṇa-pradīpa) was ordained to the Buddhist faith. He stayed in the capital for a couple of years, studying the sacred Buddhist Sūtras. He always thought of the sacred vintages of Buddhism and cherished the great desire to visit the Western country. His love for the Faith and magnanimity was inherent in him. At the same time he kept his moral principles high.

He carried Buddhist images, Buddhist *Sūtras* and *Śāstras*, crossed the South Sea and reached Ceylon. He had a glimpse of the Buddha's Tooth and made his offerings to that sacred relic. He passed through South India and then reached Eastern India. From there he proceeded towards 耽摩立底國 Ta-mo-li-ti-kuo, Tāmralipti.[2] As he reached the firth of the river, his boat and other valuables were robbed and destroyed. Only his life was spared by the pirates.

He landed there (Tāmralipti) and spent about twelve years having perfected himself in Sanskrit Sūtras. In the course of his studying and reciting, he read the 緣生等經 Lū-

---

Dr. R. C. Mazumdar thinks that the kingdom of Dvārāvati mentioned by Hsüan-chuang comprises the lower valley of the Menam river and is probably located near Nakon Pathom, 40 miles to the west of Bangkok. (R. C. Mazumdar, *Hindu Colonies*, p. 226)

In the map by C. P. Fitzgerald (*The Southern Expansion of the Chinese People*) Ayudhya (Dvārāvati) has been placed in the north-west of Bangkok.

1. This monastery was built in A.D. 648 at Ch'ang-an, modern Hsi-an in Shen-si province, on the 22nd year of the Chen-kuan period of the great T'ang Emperor T'ai-Tsung. In this monastery of Mahākaruṇā, Hsüan-chuang translated Buddhist scriptures into Chinese, after his return from the Western world.

2. Tāmralipti is modern Tamluk in the district of Midnapur in West Bengal. An ancient port, Tāmralipti situated on the mouth of the Rupnārāyan, was known as Tamalites to the Greek sailors. It was an important port on the east and played a very important part in the economic history of Bengal.

sheng-teng ching *Nidāna Sūtra*[1] and other important texts relating to Buddhism, and entered into an ecclesiastical life.

He joined the company of merchants and with the venerable monk I-ching reached Mid-India. They first visited Nālandā; next proceeded towards 金剛座 Chin-kang-tso Bodhimaṇḍa and moved towards 薛舍離 Hsieh-su-li Vaiśālī[2] and lastly they visited Kuśīnagara Chu-shih-na.[3] The

1. Lu in Chinese means *Pratyaya* — Conviction. But according to the Buddhist specially, it means "a co-operating cause, the concurent occasion of event as distinguished from its proximate cause" M.W.

Nidāna can be explained by 十二因緣 Shih-erh yin-lū, 12 causes of existence. This is the fundamental and admirable principle of Buddhist thought which explains the 12 chains of causation. The formula of 12 Nidānas explains origination and cessation.

The fundamental dogma is "of all the objects which proceed from a cause, the Tathāgata has explained the cause and he has explained their cessation also; this is the doctrine of the Great Śramaṇa." (Translated by Prof. Oldenberg and Rhys Davids.)

The Buddha has explained the origin of life's sufferings by natural causation known as *Pratīlyasamutpāda*. If there are sufferings there must be some causes. Suffereing in life is due to (1) Wu-ming-Avidyā, ignorance, (2) Hsing—*Saṃskāra*, conception, (3) Shih—*Vijñāna*, consciousness, (4) Ming-yi, *Nāmarūpa*, name and form, (5) Liu-ju *Ṣaḍāyatana*, six sense organs, (6) Shou-*Vedanā*, feeling, (7) Ai—*Tṛṣṇā*, desire, (8) Yu—*bhava*, being, (9) Ch'u-*Upādāna*, grasping, (10) Sheng—*Jāti*, birth, (11) Lau-szu—*Jarā maraṇa*, infirmities and death.

This *Nidāna* Śāstra of Ullaṅghana was translated into Chinese by Dharmagupta in A.D. 607 and *Pratītyasamutpāda* of Śuddhamati by Bodhiruci in A.D. 508-534.

See *An Introduction to Indian Philosophy*, pp. 122, 124; N. Dutt, *Early Monastic Buddhism*, p. 215.

2. Modern Basarh (Lat. 25° 59' N, Long. 85° 7'E, District Muzaffarpur, Bihar). 22 miles south-west of Muzaffarpur in north Bihar is the ancient Vaiśālī, the capital of Lichhavis. The Buddha visited this place many times. See Dr. D. Mitra, *Buddhist Monuments*, pp. 73-75.

3. The name Kuśīnagāra or Kuśinārā has been transcribed differently in Chinese. It is either Ku-shih-na or Chu-shih-na or Chiu-shih etc. The name Kuśinagara has been associated with the gospel of the Buddha. The Mahāparinirvāna of the Loıd took place here between the two Śāla trees on the bank of the ancient Hiraṇyavatī.

Tradition says that Kuśinārā was built on the ruins of the ancient city of Kuśāvatī. Kuśinārā, the capital city of the Malla tribes, is identified with the

Dhyāna master Wu-hsing together with them visited all these places.

The pilgrim always remarked with sigh and expressed his desire to achieve Dharma and to propagate it in his own land, China. While he was nearing his end, he expressed that if he could not achieve it in this life, he would then accomplish the same in his next life.

He studied history seriously that would help him to visit the home of 慈氏 Tz'u-ti, Maitreya. Everyday he drew the picture of one or two branches of 龍華 Lung-hua, *Nāgapuṣpa* (dragon flower) to express his sincerity.

He lived in the same old room where the monk Tao-hsi lived before. When he reached there, the monk Tao-hsi had already died. The Chinese and Sanskrit texts (on Buddhist Sūtras and Śāstras) the monk Tao-hsi studied, were still seen there. With a very heavy heart he looked at these books, shed tears and lamented for him. Previously they always moved together, discussed Dharma together at Ch'ang-an, but he could no longer see him in this foreign land. The room was vacant (he was no longer living).

The Dhyāna master died in the Parinirvāṇa-vihāra, Pen-ni-fan 般涅槃 in Kuśīnagara.

Seng-chia -p'a-mo 僧迦跋摩 Saṅghavarman was a native of 康國 K'ang-kuo, Sogdiana.[1] From childhood

---

modern town of Kasia (Lat. 26° 44'N; Long. 83° 55'E) in Deoria district of Uttar Pradesh; 22 miles north-east of Deoria and 34 miles east of Gorakhpur and 180 miles north-west of Patna (Bihar).

1. Prior to the sixth century A.D., Sogdiana was a kingdom which is now known as the Kirghiz S.S.R., and the Kazak S.S.R. covering the regions of present Samarkand and Bokhara.

Ancient Sugdik, Sulik was situated in the north of Tokharestan and T'ien-shan mountain. Gradually the Sogdians moved towards eastern Turkistan. They were originally a branch of Iranian people; their language was also Iranian. The people and their language have long disappeared; but some of the Sogdian translations of Buddhist texts have been unearthed from Eastern Turkistan by archaeologists.

he was a wanderer; he travelled through drifting sand on foot, then reached the Imperial city. His passion for religion was inborn.

During the 顯慶 Hsien-ch'ing[1] period, he was ordered by the Emperor to go for a pilgrimage to the Western country along with the Imperial envoy. He reached the monastery of 大覺 Ta-chüeh, Great Enlightenment. In India he paid offerings to Bodhimaṇḍa. The monk lighted the lamp for seven days and seven nights as offerings to the Council of discourses on Dharma. Again under the Aśoka tree 憂樹 Yu-shu[2] in the courtyard of Bodhimaṇḍa he carved out the image of the Buddha and Kuan-tze-tsai, Bodhisattva Avalokiteśvara.

Thereafter he went back to China. He received an Imperial order again to go to Chiao-chih to collect the medicinal herbs. That was the time when Chiao-chih was under the grip of a severe famine; people were dying in large numbers without food. He prepared food and drinks everyday for the famine-stricken people and distributed them in the afternoon. The pilgrim was very much grieved at heart and shed tears profusely at the sight of this miserable plight of the distressed people. Therefore, he was known by the people of that country as 'Weeping Bodhisattva

---

The Sogdians had close contact with other parts of Central Asia and India. Buddhism spread there from Tokharestan. Sogdian monks played a great part in the transmission of Buddhist culture in China. The two important monks from Sogdiana translated the Buddhist Sūtras into Chinese. They are known by the names of Saṅghavarman and Saṅghabhadra in the second and third-century A.D.

Seng-hui an illustrious monk from Sogdiana worked in South China in the third century A.D. In Chinese Sogdiana is K'eng-chu. Their names are distinguished in Chinese by adding prefix K'eng. Sogdiana has been identified with Śakadvipa by S.C. Vidyābhūṣan. (*J.R.A.B.*, Part I 1902, p. 154).

See Rahul Sankrityayana—*History of Central Asia*, p. 137; Luce Boulnois (Tr. by Dennis Chamberlain), *The Silk Road*, Chap. on Sogdiana, p. 149; P.C. Bagchi—*India and Central Asia*, pp. 36-40.

1. Introduced by the 3rd Emperor Kao-Tsung of the T'ang Dynasty in A.D 656, six years after his accession to the throne.

2. Jonesia Asoka Roxb Gautama Buddha was born under this tree at Lumbini. It is very much associated with Sanskrit literature of India

incarnate'. Some time afterwards, he got slightly indisposed and died immediately at the age of sixty.

彼岸法師智岸法師 Pi-an Fa-shih, Dharmācārya Nirvāṇa, Chih-an Fa-shih. Jñānapārin. Both[1] these monks were the natives of Kao-ch'ang, Turfan.[2] They went to the capital city cherishing the idea of becoming monk. They were anxious to visit Mid-India and to witness with their own eyes the transforming influence (of the Doctrine) that had taken place there.

Then, Pi-an and Chih-an with the Chinese envoy 王玄廓 Wang Hsüan-k'uo boarded the ship. On board they fell sick and died. Many copies of Buddhist Sūtras and Śāstras in Chinese translation, texts on 瑜迦 Yü-chia, Yoga belonging to them were left in the country of Śrīvijaya.

曇潤師 T'an-jun Fa-shih, Meghasikta. He came from Lo-yang. He had profound knowledge of the art of exorcism 咒術 Chu-shu[3] and of metaphysics. Thoroughly

1. Pi-an Fa-shih, 'Pi' in Chinese means "that" in contrast with "this". Pi-an means that world beyond this world, Yondershore. I have translated as *Nirvāṇa* master and Chih-an as Jñānapārin.

2. Turfan was situated in the east of the T'ien shan ranges, in the north of Karashar or Agnidesh in Central Asia. It was closer to the Chinese periphery. It was on the overland route to India. Turfan, though a small oasis state in Central Asia and a resting place for the monk travellers, was not as important as Tun-huang.

In the beginning of the fourth century A.D. the name of the southern part of the territory was changed into Kao-ch'ang by the Chinese. By the middle of the sixth century Western Turks occupied the entire region of Central Asia, dominated previously by the Epthalite or White Huns. Turfan also came under the ascendency of the Western Turks. It was wrested away from the Western Turks by the T'ang Emperor Kao-Tsung. This place was under the Vigurs and next under the Mongols in the thirteenth century.

Wang Yen-te, the Imperial envoy of China left an account of the flourishing condition of Buddhism there. Buddhism was prevalent in Turfan till the first half of the fifteenth century. Several Buddhist manuscript fragments in various languages—Sanskrit, Iranian, Chinese, Tokharian, Sogdian were discovered here.

See—Stein *CAT*, pp. 256-265; Chun Heng-wang, *Simple Geography of China* (Physical Map of China)

3. Art of exorcism including mystical and magical formulae used in Yoga system. Different types of exorcism have been described in the Dhāranis or "Protective spells".

he studied the Vinaya texts and practised 醫明 *I-ming, Cikitsā Śāstra* (science of medicine). He was perfect in manners and bearings, thorough and careful in judgement. He demonstrated his keen desire of serving all the living creatures.

Next, he gradually started his voyage in the South Sea and reached Chiao-chih where he stayed one full year, leading very simple and admirable life. He again embarked on a ship from the South, sailing for West India. On his voyage to India, he reached K'o-ling, fell sick and died at the age of thirty at 渤盆 Po-p'en[1] to the north of K'o-ling, Yavadvīpa.

義輝論師 I-hui Lun-shih. Artharaśmi Śāstrācārya. He was also a native of Lo-yang. He was extra-ordinarily brilliant, reserved and a man of profound thinking. His main ambition was to attain scholarship and Truth. He listened to the discourses on 攝論 She-lun *Samparigraha Śāstra,*[2] 俱舍 *Chu-su, Kośa* etc. and acquired profound knowledge. But the monk had found much discrepancy in those texts. Consequently, he longed to see those original Sanskrit texts and hear personally the discussions. Thereupon, he arrived in Mid-India with the hope of returning to China. But, alas ! like a tender plant, he withered away before he could attain his maturity. When he arrived at 郎迦 Lang-chia he suffered from minor ailments and died at the age of thirty odd years.

There were three other monks in China. Following the northern route[3] they arrived at 烏長那 Wu-ch'ang, Udyāna

1. According to Takakusu modern Pembuan is P'o-p'en situated on the south coast of Borneo.

See *ARBRIMA.*, p. xlix.

2. It must be the *Mahāyāna Samparigraha* or the *Mahāyāna Saṁgraha* (Compendium of philosophical treatises on the Mahāyāna system). This was written by Asaṅga and was translated into Chinese by an Indian monk Paramārtha in A.D., 563, during the time of the Liang Dynasty. The same Śāstra with the same title was translated into Chinese by Buddhaśānta in A.D. 531 during the Dynastic period of the Northern-Wei.

See *NC* Nos. 1183, 1184.

3. The principal overland route that passed through Central Asia is known as "Ser India".

country.[1] They heard that in Udyāna the relics of the Buddha's skull were kept. They worshipped the relics. Whether they were living or not was not known thereafter. I-ching gathered this information from the monks who came from Udyāna.

慧輪師者 Hui-lun-shih.[2] He was a native of 新羅 Hsin-luo. His Sanskrit name was Pen-jo-p'o-mo Prajñāvarman. In Chinese it is known as 慧甲 Hui-chia which means "armour of wisdom". He renounced the world while he was in his own motherland and inflamed with desire, left his country to make a pilgrimage to the far-famed shrines of his religion.

He started his voyage and arrived at 閩越 Min-yeh[3] in China. He travelled a long distance to reach Ch'ang-an. The Ācārya then received an Imperial order to follow the steps of 玄照 Hsüan-chao who had gone to the Western countries and having found him to assist him there. Thereupon, he left for India to pay homage to the sacred places of his religion. He lived in the Monastery of Faith in the city of 菴摩羅跋 An-mo-luo-pa[4] for about ten years. Next, going to east he visited the nearby Tukhara Saṅghārāma 覩貨羅僧寺 Tu-ho-luo-seng belonging to North India. This Saṅghārāma had originally been built long before by the people of that country for the accommodation of the Buddhist monks from Tukhara. The Saṅghārāma was very rich and had an abundant supply of all necessaries and also comfort of life. No other monasteries could surpass it in this respect. The name of the monastery was

1. Udyāna means garden or park in Sanskrit. Fa-hsien visited this place and mentioned that Buddhism was in flourishing condition, where 500 monks were living in Saṅghārāma. Hsüan-chuang's transcription of Udyāna is Wu-chang-na. Wu-ch'ang or Udāyāna comprises "the four districts of Punjkora, Bijawar, Swat and Bunir of present day."

See Watters Vol. I, pp. 225-227; Cunningham, *Ancient Geography of India*, p. 93; James Legge's (Translation) *A Record of Buddhist Kindgdoms*, pp. 28-29.

2. S. Beal has translated (extract) the lives of two monks in *Indian Antiquary*, p. 109, 1881. I noticed some lines are missing in his translation.

3. Modern Fu-Kien or Fu-chien and part of Che-kiang or Che-chiang.

4. S. Beal has rendered this word as Amrāvat (or Amarābād?). *Indian Antiquary* Vol. X, p. 110, 1881.

健陀羅山荼 Gandhāra Sanda, Chien-t'o-luo-shan-t'u.[1] The pilgrim Hui-lun remained there for the purpose of studying Sanskrit language and became well versed in *Kośa*. When the author came there, the monk Hui-lun was forty years old.

The monks coming from north and living in that monastery were the masters of that place. To the west of the monastery of the Great Enlightenment, there was another monastery for the people of 迦畢試 Chia-pi-shih. This monastery rose even to greater prosperity and celebrity for its moral virtues and high standard of learning. The brethren living in that monastery were all Hīnayānists; the traveller monks coming from north also lived there. The name of the monastery was 窶拏折里多 Guṇacarita, Chü-na-che-li-to.[2] In Chinese that was known as 德行 Te-hsing the meaning of which is Puṇyagati.

To the north-east of the monastery of Great Enlightenment, there was another monastery at an interval of two yojanas known 屈錄迦 as Ch'u-lu-ke[3] (chia) Cālukya. This monastery had been built by the King of Cālukya Dynasty of South India. Though the monastery was poor and simple, yet it was famous for a highly disciplined and religious life of its inmates. Recently the King 日軍 Jih-chün, Ādityasena[4] built again

1. Gandhāra Saṅghārāma. Beal has translated this as 'Gandhāra Sand', *Ibid*, p. 110.

2. Chü is 'Ku' or 'Gu'. It is Guṇacarita but the meaning of the Chinese name is Puṇyagati.

3. The Cālukya Dynasty was founded by Pulakeśin I at Badami or Vatapi (Bijapur district, Mysore), in the middle of the sixth century A.D. The Cālukya rulers like other Hindu rulers of India were tolerant to all religions, though they were Brahmanical Hindus. They erected many beautiful temples and excavated many cave-temples like those of the Buddhist rulers. This Saṅghārāma was donated by the ruler of the Cālukya Dynasty for the Buddhist monks of South India.

4. The death of Harṣavardhana of Kanauj in the beginning of A.D. 647 was immediately followed by great political upheaval and chaos in North India and Magadha. But in the last quarter of the seventh century and in the first half of the eighth century A.D. Magadha again rose to a position of Imperial greatness under the later Guptas of Magadha. The Aphsaḍ inscription (near, Bihar) gives a geneaology of the Later Guptas. In the genealogy, the

by the side of that monastery, a new one which was just completed. The monks from south generally stayed there. Everywhere there were monasteries. So the monks could communicate with their own countries. But Shan-chou[1] did not have a single monastery in India to live in. This caused a great hardship for the traveller monks from China.

About forty yojanas to the east of the Nālandā Vihāra along the down stream of the Gaṅgā, there was another Vihāra known as 蜜栗伽悉他鉢娜 Mi-li-chia-hsi-t'a-po-no Mṛgasthāpana.[2] In Chinese it is known as Lü-yüan which means the Deer Park (monastery). Not very far from this monastery there was another monastery which was in ruins; only the foundation was visible. It was commonly known as 支那 Chih-na or Chinese monastery which, it was said, had been built by the great King Shih-li-chi-tuo Śrī-Gupta.[3] There were more than twenty monks from the land of the Great T'ang. This Chih-na was Kuang-chou (Canton). Mahāchīna 莫訶支那 Mo-ho-chih-na was the capital, it was also called 提婆弗呾羅 T'i-p'o-fu-tan-luo, Devaputra,[4]

---

name of Ādityasena, the son of Mādhava-Gupta and the grandson of Mahāsena-Gupta is mentioned. Ādityasena assumed the Imperial title of Mahārājādhirāja. The Chinese monk, here mentioned the name of a King Jiḥ-Chün. In Chinese the word Jih is Āditya (sun) and Chün means Sena (army) The monk probably mentioned the King Ādityasena belonging to the Later Guptas who ruled Magadha assuming Imperial title after the death of Harṣavardhana. Like other Hindu rulers he was also tolerant to other religion.

1. China.

2. This Mṛigasthāpana monastery described by I-ching in the seventh and eighth century, has been identified with Mṛigasthāpana Stūpa somewhere in *Varendrabhūmi* (Northern Bengal) by Foucher. An illustrated manuscript of A.D. 1015 containing a painting of the same *stūpa* has been kept in Cambridge University.

See Dr. N. R. Ray, *Bangalir Itihas*, p. 811; Dr. D. Mitra, *Buddhist Monuments*, p. 235.

3. According to Dr. N. R. Ray Śrī-Gupta and Mahārāja-Gupta the great grandfather of Samudra-Gupta of the Gupta Dynasty is the one and the same person. Śrī-Gupta was a great supporter of Buddhism though he himself was a Hindu.

4. The Emperors and rulers of the Great Roman Empire, Persia, India and China where the great civilisation prevailed used high sounding titles like Kaisara (Caesar), Shahan-shah, the King of Kings, Mahārājā and Devaputra respectively, which is suggestive of the Divine theory of Kingship.

which means in Chinese the son of Heaven. During his visit there were more than twenty monks from China. They followed the track known as Ko-yang, passed through 蜀川 Shu-ch'uan (modern Sze-ch'uan)[1] and reaching the Mahābodhi Saṅghārāma paid offerings to the sacred traces. The distance between Sze-ch'uan and this Saṅghārāma was more than five hundred yojanas.

They were received by the King with great respect for their piety. The king donated them a village of considerable extent and made an endowment of twenty-four villages for their maintenance.

Afterwards all the Chinese monks died. This village was partitioned and the land came into possession of aliens. When the pilgrim visited the place only three villages were in the possession of the Deer-Park (Mṛgasthāpana) monastery. Five hundred years had already elapsed since the Chih-na monastery had been built. At that time, measuring of land etc. was done with utmost care. This land then (during the time of the Pilgrim's visit) belonged to 提婆跋摩 T'i-p'o-po-mo, Devavarman[2], the king of Eastern India. The King returned the temple

1. Besides the Central Asian route, there were two more over-land routes from China to India. One, through Yün-nan Province, Upper Burma and Assam, was not commonly used. Another was through Tibet and Nepal to India.

2. In the accounts of Chinese monks I-ching and Seng-che, mention is made of a Buddhist Dynasty ruling at Samataṭa. This Dynasty is undoubtedly the Khaḍga Dynasty of Ashrafpur (30 miles north-east of Dacca, Bangladesh) inscriptions. There a bronze votive stūpa alongwith two copper plates were found. In those two plates, the names of Khaḍgodyama, Jātakhaḍga, Devakhaḍga and Rājarājabhaṭa have been mentioned. On the pedestal of stone image of goddess *Sarvāṇī* at Deolbāḍi in Tippera, the name of Prabhāvatī, the wife of Devakhaḍga and the mother of Rājarājabhaṭa has been engraved. I-ching here has mentioned of a King Devavarman of Eastern India and Seng-chi has mentioned the name of Rājabhaṭa a Buddhist King of Samataṭa. According to Dr. N. R. Ray Devavarman of I-ching may or may not be Devakhaḍga of the Khaḍga Dynasty but Rājabhaṭa of Seng-chi is undoubtedly Rājarājabhaṭa of the Ashrafpur copper plate inscriptions.

See Dr. N. R. Roy, *Bāngālir Itihās*, pp. 453-454; Nalini Nath Dasgupta, *Bānglāya Baudhhadharma*.

and its land to the villagers to avoid expenses as pilgrim monks in large numbers were coming from the land of the son of Heaven (China). He also said, "It is easy to make a nest like a magpie but to find a fortunate one to enjoy it, is really very rare".

"One must strive for world's salvation. Now someone should represent the Emperor requesting him to show his magnanimity for this sincere and worthy cause."

The Chin-kang-tso, Vajrāsana and the Mahābodhi temple had been erected by the King of Ceylon. In olden days the monks coming from Ceylon always remained in this temple.

The Nālandā monastery was about seven yojanas to the north-east of the Mahābhodhi which was built by an old king named Śakrādityā 室利鑠羯羅昳底 Shih-li-shuo-chieh-luo-tieh-ti for a Bhikṣu 曷羅社槃 Ho-luo-she-p'an from North India. The foundation of the building in the beginning was on a small scale but, later on, this King's son and successors successively continued this noble work on a very large scale.

This marvellous building surpassed all the buildings in grandeur and artistic workmanship. It was one of the most splendid ones in India. It is pretty difficult to describe the artistic skill and beauty of this temple. However, the description is given in brief: The shape of this Saṅghārāma was four square like a city with vertical eaves on the four sides; and with a lofty enclosing wall all around. There was a long corridor around the monastery. The three-storeyed building had brickpaved rooms. The building was more than one Chang[1] in height. The rooms had wooden cross-beams, ceilings had no tiles, the roofs were brickpaved. At the back of the temple, there was direct road by which one could conveniently walk round the temple. There was open space at the back of each room, with a high and stiff enclosing wall. This imposing monastery had a thirty or forty feet high enclosing wall with rows of well-modelled stucco figures.

As usual the monastery consisted of a number of monks' cells and they were nine in rows. The floor-space of each cell was more than hundred square feet. The windows were on the

1. A Chinese measure of ten feet.

back wall facing the cornice. The cells had a fixed, high single-leaf door without screens so that through one door all the cells could be seen. Going out of the room, one could clearly see the four sides. The monks would rather inspect each other than to allow any privacy among them.

At the end of the four corners, four big halls of brick-work were built. It is said that the Bhadanta Buddha 大德 Ta-te[1] once lived here. The main entrance was on the west wall through a large portico of which the roof rested on pillars. The wall was skilfully and marvellously carved out with curious figures and figurines. The entrance was connected with all the cells but originally there were separate gates. Going forward, there stood four pillars erected at a regular distance of two steps. Though the door was not very big, it was very strong. Everytime during meal hours, the doors were closed in order to protect the sacred place from any irregular and unpleasant happening.

The inner courtyard of the establishment was more than thirty Pu[2] 步 paces in area. This was laid with bricks; the smaller one was either of seven or five paces in length. The floor, back and front walls as well as the eaves were all mosaic, made of bricks large and small—some as small as dates and peaches. They were plastered thickly with a paste which was a mixture of finely powdered lime, earth, jute-fibres, oil and jute-fluff.

This paste was kept for days together to soak and mix, then it was used for plastering the bricks. The green grasses were put on the plastered bricks for three days. After the paste dried up, the polishing was done with soap stone and coloured with vermillion or red juice or something like that. Finally, it was rubbed and polished with oil, which gave to the brickwork the look of a mirror. The flights of stairs of the hall were also polished like this. After completion, people would walk over them—no crack would appear even after ten to twenty years. The colour would

1. Bhadanta, most honourable term for Buddha or for a monk used by the Hînayânists.

2. A land measure of 5 Chinese feet, 240 sq. 'pu' being equal to one mow or 733-½ sq. yards.

surely fade away if the limejuice was not applied. There were about eight such temples. The tops of the temples were evenly connected and similar plan, uniform designs were followed all-through. To the east of the temple, it had either one or three rooms. Right in the foreground were the Buddha images; at the back and front of this temple large and small images could be seen.

A separate structure was erected for the image of the Buddha at some distance outside the temple.

The big courtyard outside the south-west of the monastery was surrounded by innumerable big and small votive *stūpas* 窣堵波 Su-tu-po[1] and *Caityas* 制底 Chih-ti which were known in olden days as 塔者託略 T'a-che-o-lüeh, Dagoba and 支提者託 Chih-t'i-che-o respectively. These were about hundred in number. It was

1. Originally a funeral mound erected by the Buddhists to commemorate the sacred site or to enshrine the relics (*Dhātu*) of the Buddha or of his principal disciples. Much before the introduction of images of the Buddha, *stūpa* symbolised the Parinirvāṇa of the Buddha. Later on, stūpa became the symbol of the Master himself in the eyes of the devotees who satisfied their religious cravings by worshipping the *stūpa* as a representative of the Buddha. This practice of *stūpa* worship continued even when images of the Buddha were introduced.

The *Mahāparinirvāṇa Sūtanta* says that just before the death of the Master, his principal disciple, Ānanda, was instructed by the Lord to erect a *stūpa* over his ashes on the cross road like a *stūpa* of an universal monarch. So the practice of constructing *stūpa* was pre-Buddhistic. Many important *stūpas* were built on the relics of the Buddha and on the sites which were very closely and dearly associated with the life and the activities of the Lord.

Not only the King Aśoka as it is narrated by Hsüan-chuang, erected 84,000 *stūpas* (controversial) in India but also the common people, lay devotees built many stūpas and this was considered as an act of profound merit.

The shape of a *stūpa* is like a hemispheric dome with a *harmikā* (square box) crowned by an umbrella on the top. The passage round the *stūpa* is meant for circumambulation. The *stūpas* were built as an object of worship inside *Caitya* hall.

For details see Percy Brown—*Indian Architecture*. *H.C.I.P.* Bharatiya Vidya Bhawan, Vol. 2 (The Age of Imperial Unity) pp. 487-493; Grünwedel Gibson and Burgess—*Buddhist Art in India*, pp. 19-26. ; Dr. D. Mitra, *Buddhist Monuments*, pp. 21-30.

difficult for the author to recollect the vast number of sacred relics over there. These were erected over different sacred vestiges and adorned with gold and priceless lustrous stones.

The monks and their disciples had to observe the rules and ceremonies of the monastic life. The rules and precepts of the monastic life have been narrated in the 中方錄 *Chung-fang-lū*[1] and 寄歸傳 *Chi-kuei-chuan.*[2]

The oldest man, irrespective of his learning and attainments, was regarded only as director. Every night, the main gate was to be locked and the key was handed over to the head of the monastery. There was no sub-director known as Karmadāna or 維那 Wei-na[3]. But the founder of the establishment was, in fact, honoured as the master of the temple, Ssu-chu. In Sanskrit he was known as 毘訶羅莎弭 Pi-ho-luo-sha-mi[4], Vihārasvāmin. The person who was in charge of announcing time and circulating information regarding the affairs of the monastery to the resident monks, was known as 毘訶羅波羅 Pi-ho-luo-po-luo, Vihārapāla[5]; which means one who "protects the monastery". The person supervising the mess was known as 羯磨陀那 Chieh-mo-t'o-na, Karmadāna which means administrative staff, in general, it is Wei-na.

If the monks had some business, they would assemble to discuss the matter. Then they ordered the officer, Vihārapāla to cir-

1. *'Record of Madhyadeśa'*. The name of the book referred here presumably is the work of I-ching. Takakusu could not find this book in the India Office collection. But he thinks it may be found either in the Buddhist library of China or Japan or Korea.

2. I-ching while staying at Śri-bhoga in A.D. 692, sent the manuscript of *Nan-hai-chi-kuei-nei-fa-chuan*, a *'Record of the Inner law sent home from the southern sea'*, through another Chinese priest Tao-tsin who was returning to China. The work was translated into English by the most celebrated Japanese scholar J. Takakusu.

See J. Takakusu—*ARBRPIMA* pp. xviii-xxi.

3. A director of duties, who was the second in rank in the administration of a monastery.

4. The patron or the bestower of a monastery was known as the master of the monastery or Vihāraswāmin.

5. The guardian of a monastery was known as the protector of the monastery or Vihārapāla in Sanskrit.

culate and report the matter to the resident monks one by one with folded hands. With the objection of a single monk, it would not pass. There was no such use of beating or thumping to announce his case. In case a monk did something without the consent of all the residents, he would be forced to leave the monastery. If there was a difference of opinion on certain issue, they would give reason to convince (the other group). No force or coercion was used to convince. There were some monks who were in charge of the treasury of the monastery. Even if there were two or three resident monks, the officer (in charge of the monastery) would send monks of lower rank with folded hands to ask their permission for spending money. With their unanimous consent, they would be allowed to spend. Without the consent of all the resident monks, nobody could decide the affairs of the monastery. If anyone used the money without giving explanation, even if it were a quantity of rice in husks, that person would be expelled from the monastic life.

In case a monk bragged and used other's belongings, he was sarcastically and jokingly called Chü-lu-po-ti 俱攞鉢底 Kulapati.[1] The translation of the word is Chia-chu, the head of the family. He was disliked not only by the adherents of Buddhist faith but also by God. The decision taken by anyone without the consent of others was regarded as a sin against one's religion. This might be for the welfare of the monastery but it was finally considered as committing a grave sin. A wise monk would never do such things.[2]

Previously, there were ninety-six schools of heretics but during the time of I-ching's visit, only ten sects were left. At the time of any religious meeting, the monks holding their own faith would sit together. Generally the monks and nuns would not quarrel for front or back seats. The residents of the monastery, professing different faiths, would not move or sit together at the time

1. A head of a family. A householder who practises Buddhism without becoming a monk. The use of this term for a monk was considered to be an insult.

2. See D. D. Kosambi, *The Culture and Civilisation of Ancient India*, p. 176.

of study. The rules and regulations of this establishment were very strict and austere.

The officers known as 典事 Tien-shih and 佐史 Tso-shih, inspected the dormitories every fortnight and examined the rules and regulations observed by them. The names of the monks were not entered into the official register.[1] In case an inmate did anything wrong, his case and mode of punishment given to him were decided by all the fellow monks. Consequently, all the monks and the disciples were afraid of each other. Although the ordinary comforts of life were denied to them, it (this type of life) was extremely beneficial for the good of others.

I-ching recollected one incident while he was in the capital. He had seen a man drawing the picture of Jetavana vihāra without real knowledge. In order to acquaint a large number of people with the real fact, he just gave a short description of the monastery (Nālandā).

In the land of five Indies i.e., all over India, there were innumerable big monasteries. The King of the country ordered his subjects to use 漏水 Lou-shui, Clepsydra[2] or water-clock. It was not difficult to measure (the length of) hour of the day and night with this instrument. A night was divided into three parts[3]—the first and the third were occupied by meditation and chanting.[4] During the middle hour, the monks could

1. China had a unique custom of maintaining an official register of the clergy of the country The famous monk Chih Tao-lin protested against this system in a written letter to the Emperor in A.D. 399.

In T'ang China, the preparation of the monks' registration started in A.D. 799. The compilation was done once in three years and recorded in 4 copies—one to be kept in local prefecture , one with the Bureau of National Sacrifice and the third one with the Court of State Ceremonials. Such a registration helped the state to have an idea of the exact population of the clerics.

2. The "Clepsydra was a contraption consisting of a small perforated bowl floating in a large one filled with water, time being noted by each immersion of the small bowl and announced regularly" S. Dutt, (*Monks and Monasteries in India*, p. 335).

This instrument of water clock was not only used in the Nālandā monastery, but it was universally used in big monasteries of India. I-ching has given a detailed description of this water-clock in his famous work *Nan-hai-chi-kuei-nei-fa-chuan*.

See Takakusu, *ARBPRIMA*, pp. 144-145.

3. *Prathama Yāma, Madhyama Yāma, Paścima Yāma,* first half of the night, mid-night, and last half of the night.

4. Takakusu, *ARBRIMA*. (The Ceremony of Chanting) pp. 152-166.

take rest conveniently. Innumerable devices and methods (of regulating time) had been elaborately described in Chi-kuei-chuan.

Though he made a humble attempt to describe the plan of the monastery in short, he apprehends anyone coming here may not be able to understand properly the plan drawn by him. He hopes there will be no hurdle to visitors coming to this monastery. If he appeals to the Emperor, requesting him to construct a monastery according to this plan, then Rājagṛha would be in China without much difference. Hence it was necessary to draw a sketch of Nālandā.

The name of the monastery Shih-li-na-lan-t'o-mo-pi-ho-luo Śrī Nālandā Mahāvihāra was translated into Chinese as 吉祥神龍大住處 Chi-hsiang-shen-lung-ta-chu-ch'u[1] the lucky dragon spirit palace. The kings, high officials, their family members, big temples in India used the appellation 室利 Shih-li[2] before their names. The meaning of the word Shih-li is 吉祥 Chi-hsien, lucky omen—it means honourable. Nālandā was the name of a Nāga[3] (Dragon). In the vicinity of the

1. Nālandā (Lat. 25° 8'N; Long. 85° 27'E district Patna, Bihar) lies 7 miles to the north of Rajgir. Harṣavardhana of Kanauj (A.D. 606-647), a great patron of Buddhism donated revenue of a hundred villages for the maintenance of this great establishment. Nālandā Mahāvihāra by this time became the premier Buddhist institution not only in India but its prestige as an educational centre of supreme importance became known throughout the Buddhist world. Its fame and honour continued till the end of the twelfth century. The Chinese travellers like Hsüan-chuang, I-ching stayed and studied in this institution and they spoke of a high standard of learning and disciplined life of the inmates and brilliant attainments of the reputed teachers of the monastery. The students who 'stole the name of Nālandā were all treated with respect' wherever they went.

During the time of the Pāla rulers (eighth-twelfth century) Nālandā rose ever to greater prosperity and fame. One of the luminaries of the university, Padmasambhava went to Tibet and founded Lamaism there.

After Hsüan-chuang, I-ching, many more Chinese and Korean monks visited Nālandā.

2. This is a popular appellation used as a prefix to the names of various deities and men. *Śrī* in Sanskrit means beauty or prosperity or luck. The goddess *Lakṣmī* is also known as *Śrī*.

3. In Chinese mythology Nāga or Dragon is a fabulous serpent with

temple there was a dragon (Nāga) by the name 那迦爛陀 Na-chia-lan-t'o, Nāgananda. So was the name given to the monastery.

毘訶羅 Pi-ho-luo means 住處 Chu-ch'u (*āvāsa*) dwelling place. The name Nālandā was not correctly translated. All the seven monasteries were very similar in general appearance and lay-out; if you see one, you have seen all the seven. The road at the back of the monastery was a public thoroughfare—straight and even. One could have a clear picture of the entire establishment from south. The real view of the same was always available through western door. Hundred paces (20 pu) to the south was a ***stūpa*** (*Su-tu-po*) more than hundred feet high, where in olden days the Honourable Tathāgata remained for three summer months. The Sanskrit name of the ***stūpa*** was 莫攞健陀俱胝 Mu-luo-chian-t'o-chü-ti, Mūla-gandha-kuṭī[1]. It was known as 根本香殿 Kan-pen-hsiang-tien, *Mūlagandha* (monastery) temple in Chinese. More than fifty paces (pu) to the east of the door of the temple, there was still a much higher ***stūpa*** than the Mūla-gandha-kuṭī. This *stūpa* of brickwork was erected by the King 幼日王 Yu-jih-wang, Bālāditya.[2] The ornamentation of the stūpa was

---

supernatural power. *Nāga* or snake also plays an important part in Indian mythological stories. In the *Dictionary of Chinese Buddhist terms* (p. 247, A). Soothhill has described "as dragon it represents the chief of the scaly reptiles; it can disappear or can be manifest, increase or decrease, lengthen or shrink. In spring it mounts in the sky and in winter it enters the earth. Dragons are regarded beneficent bringing the rains and guarding the heavens, they control rivers and lakes and hybernate in the deep."

See Anthony Christie. *Chinese Mythology*. p. 111.

1. The root temple is 'the chief shrine of the Buddha', the root and fragrant residence of the Buddha. Mūla-gandha-kutī Vihāra was erected in these places like Sārnāth, Nālandā, Vaiśālī wherever the Buddha spent his time.

2. He belonged to the Later Gupta Dynasty when the Imperial power was completely disintegrated due to internal struggle and foregin invasion. Narasiṃha-gupta assumed the title of Bālāditya, who according to Hsüan-chuang defeated the Hūṇa Chief, Mihirakula. About the time and identity of Bālāditya, there are controversies. According to some scholars *Kumāra-gupta*, the son of Narasiṃha-gupta was known as *Bālāditya*. Dr. Roy Choudhuri identifies this *Bālāditya* with Bhānu-Gupta.

delicate and superb. The seat in the hall with mosaic floor was made of gold and was studded with jewels. Offerings were made generally of rare and precious things. The hall had an image of the Buddha Tathāgata in *Dharma-cakra-Pravartana-mudrā*[1] (turning the Wheel of Law).

Again, to the south-west, there was a very small *caitya* of more than ten feet high. It was here that a brahmin holding a bird in his hand was coming to ask the Buddha many questions. So it was known as 雀離浮圖 Ch'üeh-li-fou-t'u Sparrow *stūpa*.[2] To the west of the Mūla-gandha-kuṭi temple was the Buddha's tooth-stick tree 佛齒木樹 Fo-ch'ih-mu-shu and not willow branch. Again, to the west of this temple was an "altar of precept" 戒壇 Chieh-t'an[3], more than ten square feet in area.

Like the early Gupta rulers, Bālāditya was a great patron of Buddism though he was a follower of Brāhmaṇical faith. Under the active patronage of the Gupta rulers and in the atmosphere of toleration, Buddhism flourished in India. Bālāditya was a donor of the Nālandā monastery; he built a three storeyed monastery and temple. He marked the occasion by a religious convocation and invited some Chinese monks to attend the function.

See—A. Ghosh. *Nālandā*, 4th Ed. p.46, *H.C.I.P.*, Bharatiya Vidya-Bhavan, *Classical Age*, pp. 42-43; S. Chattopadhyaya, *Early History of Northern India*, pp. 222-224.

1. Before image-worship came into existence, symbol-worship was very popular in the history of Buddhism. In the beginning of the Christian era, Bhakti movement started in Buddhism. The Buddha was no longer a teacher or a superman. He was deified; the image-worship of the Buddha could somewhat satisfy the craving and devotional impulses of the masses. Before the introduction of image-worship, a symbol like Bodhi tree, Wheel of Law represented various aspects of the Buddha's life. The Buddha delivered his first sermon at Sārnāth and this event is known as *Dharma-cakra-pravartana* or moving the 'Wheel of Law'.

The pilgrim refers here an image of the Buddha in *Dharma-cakra-pravartana-mudrā*.

2. Hsüan-chuang while describing the Nālandā establishment has referred to a tope (*stūpa*) at the spot where a Tīrthika holding a bird in his hand asked the Buddha about life and death. I-ching also has mentioned the Sparrow *stūpa* more than 10 ft. high on the same spot referred by Hsüan-chuang. According to him, it was erected outside the west wall near the tank of Nālandā.

See Watters, Vol. II, pp.170-171 (Reprinted in Peking, 1941).

3. The altar where a novice receives the commandments from the preceptors.

The compound walls of brickwork were, however, plain and more than twenty feet high. The wall had a niche, five Chinese feet high, with a small *caitya*. The eastern corner of the altar contained brickwork base, inscribed with sacred Buddhist texts.[1] In breadth it was two chou[2] and in length either fourteen or fifteen chou and was more than two chou in height. On it blooming lotuses were carved with white lime. These lotuses were about two inches high and more than one foot in circumference. There were fourteen or fifteen flowers manifesting the traces of the lotus-like footprints (or steps) of the Buddha.

Going from this temple south to Rājagṛha was thirty li. The Ch'iu-feng and Chu-yüan Gṛdhrakūṭa or the Vulture Peak and Veṇuvana, Bamboogrove were all in the vicinity of the capital. Going south-west to the Mahābodhi Saṅghārāma seven *yojanas*[3] direct to the south was the 尊足山 Tsun-tsu-shan, Gurupādagiri[4] sage's foot mountain. The city of 薛舍離 Hsieh-she-li Vaiśālī was situated twenty-five yojanas to the north of the Nālandā Saṅghārāma and the Deer Park or Mṛgadāva[5]

1. Some fragmentary brick inscriptions have been found from the core of a votive *stūpa* of the main temple at Nalandā. These inscriptions contain the tenets epitomizing the teachings of the Buddha.—It follows:

Ye dharmā hetu-prabhavā hetuṁ teṣāṃ Tathāgatohyavadat.

teṣāṁ ca yo nirodha evaṁ vādī Mahā-śramaṇaḥ.

'Tathāgata has revealed the cause of those phenomena which spring from a cause, also (the means of) their cessation. So says the Great Monk'. These inscriptions contain the *Nidāna-Sūtra* or *Pratītyasamutpāda Sūtra* (the *Gāthā* of the Chain of causation).

2. Cubit.

3 Indian measure of length. It was described as one day's march of royal army in ancient India. Two English miles make one Indian *Krośa* and 4 *Krośas* make one *yojana* i.e. 8 English miles. *Yojana* is nearly 40 or 30 or 16 Chinese li; according to Hsüan-chuang 40 Chinese li was equivalent to one *Krośa*.

4. The mountain of the venerable preceptor Mahākāśyapa. Cunningham has identified this place with the three rugged and barren hills near Kurkihar (Lat. 24° 49'N; Long. 85°15'E District Gayā, Bihar) a small village, 16 miles to the north-east of Gaya. Dr. R. C. Mazumdar identifies the place with a small hill Gurpa on the south-east of Bodh-Gayā in Bihar. The present name of Gurpa is the same as Gurupādagiri.

See *J.R.A.B.*, Vol. II, 1906, pp. 77-83.

5. Sārnāth (Lat, 25° 22'N; Long. 83° 1'E. District Vārāṇasi, Uttar Pradesh) 4 miles to the north of Vārāṇasi is the site of ancient Mṛgadāva.

twenty yojans to the west. The city of 耽摩立底Tan-mo-li-ti Tāmralipti was sixty or seventy *yojanas* to the east. It was situated on the mouth of the sea from where one had to sail for China.

About three thousand five hundred monks were living in the Nālandā monastery. This establishment was in possession of 201 villages. The kings of successive generations had donated those villages permanently for the resident monks.

驛 I is translated into Sanskrit as 踰繕那 *Yü-shan-na, yojana.*

The infinite ocean, the home of dragon, and the river Lo[1], the home of the holy tortoise are divided by the Heavenly river. On the long distant track for horses across the desert, not a single traveller would be seen. Consequently, very few people could have any real picture of the situation through hearsay. The image made by the artist though corresponded to the original, still there was something lacking in it. The drawing of the ancient theme would always inspire the new generation. All the visitors would reverentially remember the Lord Buddha and thus their divine souls would be elevated.

The first chüan of Eminent monks who went to the West in search of Law during the Great T'ang rulers.

Sārnāth is one of the four sacred places for the Buddhists. The Buddha preached his first Sermon or moved the Wheel of Law at Sārnāth. This event is known as *Dharma-cakra-Pravartana.*

For details see Dr. D. Mitra, *Buddhist Monuments*, pp. 66-69.

1. The river 'Lo' delivered to Yü the Great, Emperor of the Hsia Dynasty (2205 B.C.—1818 B.C.) a transcendent tortoise. This divine tortoise had the numbers from one to nine at the back.

See the chapter 顧命 Ku-ming of the *Annals* 書經 and *Shu-ching*, 47.

CHAPTER II

15 MONKS

Written bv the Tripiṭaka Master I-ching

道琳法師 Tao-lin Fa-shih. The monk Tao-lin was a native of 江陵 Chiang-ling in 荊州 Ching-chou.[1] His Sanskrit name was 尸羅鉢頗 *Shih-luo-po-p'o*, Śilaprabha. He was known as 戒光 Chieh-kuang in Chinese (Śīlaprabha). When he was very young, he renounced the world and resolved to become a Buddhist monk. At the age of twenty, he fervently searched for an able teacher and the Truth. He collected the *Vinaya Piṭaka* 律藏 Lü-Ts'ang, controlled his passions and acquired profound knowledge.

He spent most of his time in meditation and thus quietened down the waters of the heart, to behold the Buddha as the moon reflected in still water. He was endowed with very good qualities of heart. He was of pure and humble nature, refined, modest and truthful. Taking oblations in the pure and crystal-clear water of the fountain, he calmed down his mind, washed his mouth with pure water and thus nurtured his inner soul. He seldom retired for rest; major part of the day and night he would sit and study. He took his meal only once in a day.

Many years had already passed, when the great religion (Buddhism) had flooded China in the East. But the Intuitional School[2] had just started, yet at the same time, the canonical texts

1. It comprised the modern states of Hu-nan, Hu-pei, Kuang-si, Kuei-chou and Sze-ch'uan. One of the 9 chous or divisions of the Empire made by the Emperor Yü.

2. Ting-men: The system of meditation of the Intuitional School. It was first founded in China by Bodhidharma, commonly known as Ta-mo in Chinese. Different dates have been recorded for his arrival in China. The earliest source material concerning Bodhidharma is the Lo-yang chia-lan-chi by Yang Hsüan-chih (C.T.T. Vol. 51, No. 2092, p. 999) completed in A.D. 547. A different date and time of his arrival is given in another source *Hsu-kao-seng-chuan* (*Further Biographies of Eminent monks*) (C.T.T. Vol. 50, No. 2060 p. 425).

emphasising the importance of the monastic discipline were also very rare. So he eagerly longed for visiting the far-off India to procure the sources and the history of the canonical rules of the *Vinaya Piṭaka.*

Then, he with a mendicant stick, reached the South Sea in a foreign ship and from there set sail for India. On his way he passed through copper pillar T'ung-chu and arrived at Lang-chia. He crossed 訶陵 Ho-ling and 裸國 Luo-kuo[1] to reach India. He received very warm and affectionate welcome from the kings of those countries he passed through. He spent a couple of years there and then he reached Tan-mo-li-ti, Tāmralipti in East India. He spent three years there in studying Sanskrit language.

In spite of the divergences of opinion, it may be presumed that Bodhidharma was in China in the second half of the sixth century A.D.

However, Bodhidharma was universally considered as the real founder of the contemplative form of Mahāyāna or esoteric school in China. It is known as Ch'an from Sanskrit *Dhyāna* which is said to be an Intuitive School. It does not depend on canon or texts. This school follows an immediate way instead of gradual meditation. Hui-neng the sixth patriarch of the seventh-eighth centuries popularised this school. Till the eleventh century this was the most prevalent school in China. Indian Dhyāna, Chinese Ch'an, Japanese Zen.

1. 'Luo' in Chinese means 'naked'. Luo-kuo or Luo-jen-kuo means the land of the naked people. I-ching, on his way to India, passed this island (in Bay of Bengal). He has given here a graphic description of the island (Nicobar) that agrees to some extent with the Venetian traveller Marco Polo's account of this place of the thirteenth century. But Takakusu thinks the description of the Arab navigators of the ninth century is very much like the description given by I-ching.

According to the Arabs, the island of Nicobar is Langabatus or Lankhabatus, very thickly populated, where men and women go out naked. They barter their commodities of cocoa-nuts for iron.

According to Marco Polo, the two islands of Nocueran (Nicobar) and Andaman are situated about 150 miles away from the Kingdom of Lambri. The inhabitants of these islands are almost savage; men and women go out naked without covering any part of the body. These places are rich in forest, and grow cocoa-nuts, a variety of drugs, and sandal woods—red and white. (Revised from Marsden's translation and edited by Mannel Komroff. *The Travels of Marco Polo*, New York, p. 281).

All these three accounts of the seventh, ninth and thirteenth centuries are more or less the same. A group of islands known as Andaman and Nicobar is spread in the Bay of Bengal. The extreme north point of the Andamans lies in

He rejected the old precepts, accepted the important ones and studied thoroughly the Vinayas of I-ch'ieh-yu-pu *Sarvāstivāda* school. Not only he studied the canonical rules of the Vinaya but also tried to make a synthesis of Knowledge with Dhyāna—meditation. The pilgrim spent much of his time in studying carefully 耽咒藏 Tan-chu-t'sang *Dhāraṇi Piṭaka.*[1]

He next witnessed the changing influences (of the Law) that took place in Mid-India, paid offerings to the sacred shrines of Chin-kang-yü-tso, Bodhimaṇḍa and performed sacred ceremonies to the image of Bodhisattva. Then he proceeded towards the Nālandā monastery where he learnt the real significance of the *Mahāyāna Sūtra* and *Śāstras*. He spent many years there, and completely mastered (saturated with) *Abhidharma Kośa*. Next he visited the Vulture's Peak mountain, 杖林山園 Chang-lin-shan-yüan *Yaṣṭivanagiri*[2] and 鵠樹 Ku-shu, Wild goose

---

13° 34' 3"N and extreme south point of the Nicobars is 6° 45' N. See *The Imperial Gazetteer of India*, New Edition (Reprint) Vol. V, pp. 350-4.

1. *Dhāraṇī* is synonymous with the word rakṣā, Pāli-Paritta.

Dhāranīs are protective magical charms, spells, mantras, exorcism against bad omened stars, poison, snake-bite, for recovery from diseases, longivity and spells for rebirth in the Western Paradise etc. There are numerous *Dhāraṇīs* and this collection of *Dhāraṇīs* may be called *Dhāraṇī Piṭaka*. The *Dhāraṇīs* constitute a large part of *Mahāyāna* literature. These are very peculiar kind of Buddhist literature which are diametrically opposed to the original teachings of the Buddha. If any one repeats the mantras or *Dhāraṇīs* for a long time, it will surely produce some mystic power.

The five *Dhāraṇīs* known as "Pañcarakṣā" are extremely popular in Nepal. These are (1) *Mahā-Pratisarā*, (2) *Mahā-Sahasrapramardinī*, (3) *Mahā-Māyūrī*, (4) *Mahā-Śītavatī*, (5) *Mahā-Mantrānusāriṇī*.

As early as third century, *Dhāraṇīs* constituted a portion of the Sūtra literature but were made popular chiefly in the eighth century when the Tantric teachings of Yogācāra system was introduced in China by Śubhākarasiṃha, Vajra-bodhi and Amoghavajra, which resulted in the growth of the *Tantra* school in China.

See Winternitz, *HIL* Vol. 2, pp. 380-386; Binoytosh Bhattacharya, *The Indian Buddhist Iconography*, p. 14; *CTT*. Vol. I, Nos. 1034-1036, 1070-1072A, 1073, 1074, 1092.

2. Yaṣṭivana (Jethian) lies six miles to the south-west of Rājagṛha. The Buddha visited this place and Aśoka is said to have built a *stūpa* there.

Hsüan-chuang narrates that more than 100 li to the east of the Buddhavana mountain there was a dense forest of bamboos. This was Yaṣutivana or stick-wood forest. I-ching, here, says it was stick-wood park or a hill park. Cun-

forest (*vana*)[1]. While he was living there, he with great respect and sincerity developed his honesty, loyalty and spirit. He travelled all over South India in search of 玄謨 Hsüan-mu (Monk).

Then he proceeded to West India where he spent hardly a year at Luo-ch'a, Lāṭa country. There he established an altar, got acquainted with 明咒 Ming-chu[2] *Vidyā*. Sometimes he tried to explain the teachings of that *Śāstra*.

Generally, the meaning of 明咒 Ming-chu in Sanskrit is 毘睇陀羅必棏家 *P'i-t'i-t'o-luo-pi-kan-chia* *Vidyādhara Piṭaka*. 毘睇 *P'i-t'i*, Vidyā has been translated as 明咒 Ming-chu. 陀羅 T'o-luo in Chinese means 持 *Ch'ih* '*dhara*'. 必棏家 Pi-kan-chia is 藏 Ts'ang, *Piṭaka*. Thus, it is called *Vidyādhara Piṭaka*.[3] The Sanskrit text, it is told, contained 100,000 *ślokas*. It might have been translated into Chinese three hundred chüans, (chapter, fasciculi). Now (at the time of I-ching) most of those translations were lost, only a few were extant.

After the *Mahāparinirvāna* of the Great Sacred One (Buddha), 阿離野那迦曷樹那 A-li-yeh-na-chia-ho-shu-na Ārya

---

ningham says that this place is modern Jakhtiban (*Indian Antiquary*, 1901, p. 621). According to B.C. Law it is about two miles from Tapavana in Gayā, Bihar (*Geography of Early Buddhism*, p. 45).

See Watters Vol. II, pp. 146-148; *Mahāvagga*, p. 35, R. 36.

Aurel-Stein: *Indian Antiqiary*, 1901, p. 621.

1. Hsüan-chuang saw a Hamsa tope or Wild goose tope on the eastern peak of the Indra śāla-guhā (identified with Giriyak) at Rājagṛha. The Wild goose tope was erected there to commemorate the incident when a wild goose fell down to satisfy the hunger of the Hinayānist monks living in the monastery on the eastern peak of the Indra sāla-guhā. I-ching presumably mentioned the wood on the eastern peak of the mountain where the incident took place and the wild goose tope was built.

2. Mantras of mystic knowledge.

3. *Vidyādhara piṭaka*, according to La Vallee Poussin (*JRAS* p. 433, f), is another name of *Dhāraṇī piṭaka* or *Mantra piṭaka*. The literal meaning of *Vidyādharapiṭaka* is a collection of mantras for the purpose of excorsism, some of which are included in the *Saṁmyukta piṭaka*. It consists of different *dhāraṇīs*, *vidyā mantras*, *tantras*, *yoga*, *tantras* etc.

Nāgārjuna[1] that is Nāgārjuna Bodhisattva preserved the true spirit if the *Piṭaka*.

One of his disciples, known as 難陀 Nan-t'o[2], Nanda, was a brilliant scholar, and was very much proud of his knowledge; he paid special attention to this text. He spent twelve years in Western India, wholeheartedly studied the *Vidyā* or Spell and acquired great knowledge of the my sticmantras. Every mealtime he chanted the mantras and food would fall from the sky.

1. We do not have any precise information about the life of *Ārya* Nāgārjuna. Scholars are of different opinion about the date of his birth, his native place etc. Dr. P. C. Bagchi thinks Nāgārjuna was a contemporary of Kaniṣka, (A.D. 78-101), the Kuṣāna King, who convened the fourth Great Buddhist Council. Tradition associated him with a galaxy of renowned teachers like Nāgārjuna, the great exponent of *Mādhyamika Philosophy*, Aśvaghoṣa etc. According to Tibetan tradition, Nāgārjuna, the famous Mahāyāna scholar of the second century A.D., was the high priest of Nālandā. Commonly accepted view is that he was a native of South India or Vidarbha (Nagpur).

The founder of the *Mādhyamika philosophy*, the composer of *Madhyamika-Kārikā* (Verses on the Middle Path), the Nāgārjuna Bodhisattva was a mystery and wonder in the Buddhist history. As a profound philosopher of the *Mādhyamika* system, he "created a revolution in Buddhism and through that in the whole range of Indian philosophy." (T.R.V. Murti, *The Central Philosophy of Buddhism*, Preface). Nāgārjuna's philosophy is known as 'Middle Way' between the *Sarvāstivāda* individual realism and the *Sautantric* universal idealism, between assertion and negation. His philosophy is also known as *Śūnyavāda* or the philosophy of voidness.

Kumārajīva translated the biography of Nāgārjuna in A.D. 405 into Chinese and also the three treatises known as Chung-lun (Treatise on the Middle), *Pai-lun* (Treatise in one hundred verses), and *Shiḥ-erh-men-lun* (Treatise on the Twelve Gates) and Kumārajīva has described Nāgārjuna as a great magician, an alchemist and a great sorcerer. Through his translation Kumārajiva established an important Mahāyāna school in China known as *San-lun* or the School of three Treatises.

The *Mahā-Prajñā-Pāramitā Sūtra* or *Śāstra* is the largest of the works of Nāgārjuna. The Sanskrit original is lost but preserved in Chinese in 100 fasciculi (Ñanjio's Cat. No. 1169). This is known in Chinese as *Ta-chih-ta-lun* translated again by Kumārajīva.

See Winternitz *HIL*. Vol. II, pp. 341-351; Watters Vol. II, pp. 202-206; Dr. P.C. Bagchi, *India and China*; T.R.V. Murti, *The Central Philosophy of Buddhism*; P. C. Roy—*History of Chemistry in Ancient and Mediaeval India*, (Indian Chemical Society, Calcutta 1956—pp. 116-119); "Life and Legends of Nāgārjuna," *JRAB*, 1882 Part I, pp. 115-120; CTT Vol. 50, pp 185; *Life of Nāgārjuna*) by tr. Kumārajiva.

2. I can neither find nor suggest any identification.

sky. No sooner did he recite the mantras and ask for food with magic bowl than he obtained it from the sky. He could get all the desired objects with this magic bowl in his hand. Supposing the mantras were not chanted the bowl would vanish in no time.

Therefore, the great monk Nanda was afraid that his knowledge of the *Vidyā* would be of no use if it was not practised regularly. He collected 12,000 *ślokas* which later on were compiled into a separate school of thought. Each and every word of the printed text was carefully compared. Although the language and the words of the book were same, the meaning and applications were completely different. Until it was expounded orally no one could understand and realise the significance of the mantras.

Later on, when the *Śāstrācārya* 陳那 Ch'en-na Diṅnāga[1] studied his works, he was astonished to find his lofty and noble ideas, profound knowledge and his extreme attachment to the subject.

1. Diṅnāga's life has been recorded by Tāranāth, the Tibetan historian Bu-ston and others. Bu-ston's history presents a whole series of life sketches, though mostly legendary, of Nāgārjuna, Vasubandhu, Diṅnāga and others. Their accounts say that Diṅnāga was an illustrious pupil of Vasubandhu. Diṅnāga belonged to the end of the fifth century A.D.

He was born in Kanchi (modern Conjevaram) in the south, in a Brāhmin family. He came to the north and became a disciple of Vasubandhu, the most brilliant teacher of this time. About the celebrity of the teacher, F. Th. Stcherbatsky records, "Among the great names of later Buddhism, the name of Vasubandhu occupies an exceptional position; he is the greatest among the great. He is the only master who was given the title of the second Buddha. His teaching was encyclopaedic embracing all the sciences cultivated in India at his time". (*The Buddhist Logic*, Vol. I, p. 32.)

Diṅnāga's early works consisted of a summary of *Abhidharma-Kośa-Marma-Pradīpa*, and of *Aṣṭa-Sāhasrikā-Prajñā Pāramitā-Sūtra*. But as a founder of Buddhist Logic (*Nyāya*) his name is remembered throughout the ages. His main work in *Buddhist Logic* preserved in Tibetan, is *Pramāṇa-Samuccaya*. Another work *Nyāyamukha* is extant only in Tibetan and Chinese, and *Nyāya-Praveśa* is extant only in original Sanskrit.

The work of Diṅnāga was translated into Chinese by Hsüan-chuang and I-ching in A.D. 649 and A.D. 711 respectively.

See F. Th. Stcherbatsky, *The Buddhist Logic*; S.C. Vidyabhushan, "*Medieval School of Indian Logic* (Calcutta University, 1909).

Touching the Sūtra affectionately, he said with a deep sigh—"If he (Nanda) attains perfection in *Hetu Vidyā*[1] could I be compared any longer with him in scholarship ? Not only a wise man could ocomprehend the range of his knowledge but also a stupid one could understand his profound scholarship." This *Dhāraṇī Piṭaka* was never very popular in China.

Consequently Tao-lin desired to protect his mysterious Sūtra. Because this *Dhāraṇī Piṭaka* says, "one may ascend to heaven sitting on the dragon-drawn vehicle, one may order hundreds of gods as one's slaves. One's desired object may be achieved only by reciting the mystic gestures and formulae"

While I-ching was at Nālandā, he regularly went to the altar and wholeheartedly tried to study this Sūtra; he worked quite hard but could not attain full success. His primary aim was to propagate this idea among a vast multitude of heterodox people. So he wrote down only a general outline.

Tao-lin proceeded towards North India from Western border. He visited and saw the transforming influence (of Doctrine) in K'e-hsi-mi-luo, Kashmir and then he arrived at Wu-ch'ang-na, Udyāna. There he searched for proper guidance for meditation and collected 般若 Pan-Jo[2], *Prajñā-Sūtra.*

1. *Hetu Vidyā* or Logic, one of the five *vidyās* (Wu-ming), was included in the syllabus for Indian children. The other four *vidyās* were *Śabda vidyā* (Grammar and Philology), *Cikitsā vidyā* (Science of Medicine), *Śilpasthāna vidyā* (Arts and Crafts), and *Adhyātma vidyā* (Metaphysics). The knowledge of Logic helped the students to sharpen their mental faculties, thus enabling them to debate and deliberate in accordance with logical rules.

I-ching states that after acquiring proficiency in *Śabda vidyā* a monk scholar could devote himself to Logic and *Abhidharma-Kośa.*

2. *Prajñā Sūtra* or *Prajñā-Pāramitā Sūtra* constitutes an important and voluminous section of the Mahāyāna literature. The growth and development of the Mahāyāna was very rapid in the first and second century A.D., due to the foreign influence says Keith, when a foreign Dynasty was ruling in India. The foundation of the Mahāyāna, in a sense, is *Prajñā-Pāramitā* or Perfection of Wisdom. Keith calls *Prajñā* the "twin-sister of Sophia or Gnosis of Asiatic Greece" (A.B. Keith: *Buddhist Philosophy*, p. 216).

The earliest group of Mahāyāna Sūtras is known as *Prajñā-Pāramitā Sūtra* in Sanskrit. It enables one to reach the other shore of the world. There are five large recensions in Sanskrit: *Śata Sāhasrikā Prajñā-Pāramitā* in 100,000 verses, *Pañcaviṃśatikā Sāhasrikā* in 25,000 verses, 18,000, 10,000 and 8,000

Next, he set on his journey for Chia-pi-shih where he offered great reverence to the sacred lotus skull[1] 烏率膩沙 Wu-shuo-ni-sha, *Uṣṇiśa* of the Lord, (it was the cranium of the Buddha).

After the expiration of Tao-lin and I-ching who would be deputed to carry on this mission?

I-ching next arrived at Kedah 羯荼 Chieh-ch'a[2] in the South Sea. It was narrated later on, by some foreigners from north, that he met two monks in Hu[3] country (either Tartar or Mongolia), agreeing in description with some of his friends, one of them was Tao-lin. He (Tao-lin), with another monk 智弘 Chih-hung, was returning to his own country. It was

---

verses respectively. The earliest of these *Sūtras* is *Aṣṭasāhasrikā Prajñā Pāramitā Sūtra*.

As early as the Han Dynasty, *Aṣṭa Sāhasrikā Prajñā-Pāramitā Sūtra* was translated into Chinese by Chih-ch'an. Towards the end of the third century, two translations of 25,000 Wisdom Sūtras were completed by Dharmarakṣa in A.D. 286 and by Mokṣala in A.D. 291. The Prajña school was dominant in China throughout the fourth century when the Sūtras were read, discussed and debated by the Buddhist monks and literati of China.

See Winternitz, *H.I.L.*, Vol. II, pp. 313-317; N.C. Dutt, *Mahāyāna Buddhism*, pp. 43-44; E. Zürcher, *B.C.C*, pp. 100-101, 124-126.

1. In Sanskrit the meaning of *Uṣṇīsa* is, either a turban or the hair done in a knob on the top of the head. But here it means differently. I-ching's monk paid reverence to the Ting-ku or Cranium of the Buddha at Kapisa. Watters considers that a new meaning has been given to the term. The term *Uṣṇīśa* here means 'Cranial Protuberance', Karoti which is one of the thirty-two signs of Great man, *Mahāpuruṣa*, Ta-ch'en-fu.

Fa-hsien also says that the city of Hilo possessed the *Uṣṇīśa* of the Buddha. Hilo, during his time, was a dependency of Kapisa.

Hsüan-chuang narrates that this relic was kept in a casket in the tope at Hilo. Hilo has been identified with Hidda. I-ching's pilgrim paid offering to this sacred relic of the Buddha in Kapisa that must be Hilo, Hadda or Hiḍḍa.

2. The Chola rulers of South India had direct relation with East Asian countries, specially with the Śailendra rulers of Śrī-vijaya (Sumatra). The names of the countries conquered by Rājendra Chola (A.D. 1014-1044) are mentioned in the inscriptions of A.D. 1024 and 1030. The most prosperous island that the Cholas conquered is Śrī-vijaya and the last is Kadara, the chief strong-hold of the Śailendra rulers at that time. Kadara or Kataha is identified with modern Kedah or Chieh-ch'a of the Chinese, in Malaya.

See Reginald Le May, *The Buddhist Art in Siam*, p. 37; R. C. Mazumdar, *Hindu Colonies*, pp. 37-40.

3. It is a general term applied to any foreigner by the Chinese. Originally 'Hu' was a Central Asian nomadic tribe, either Mongols or Tartars.

said that on his way back home, he was prevented to advance further by highway brigands. So he had to come back again to North India. He was fifty-six years old.

曇光律師者 T'an-kuang Lu-shih, Kṛṣṇamegharaśmi was a native of Chiang-ling in Ching-chou. He renounced the world, left his native place and reached the capital city.

He became the disciple of the Vinaya master 誠 Ch'eng. He (T'an-kuang) was a man of great literary taste and an eloquent speaker. He studied the classics of both of his own country and of outside countries too and with devotion and respect observed the canonical rules of discipline. He was always extremely courteous and polite.

He reached South from where he started his voyage, crossed the vast boundless ocean, with intense desire for worshipping the sacred relics of the Buddha. He first arrived in West India and therefrom he went to 訶利鷄羅 Ha-li-chi-luo Harikela[1] on the eastern limit of East India. No one had any information or knowledge of the whereabouts of this strong-built and middleaged monk. Probably he was trekking at that time, either over the mountain or on the river. There at Harikela, it was told, that he met a monk from the land of the T'ang rulers. He was fifty years old at that time.

He was very warmly received by the king of Harikela and was appointed as the head of the monastery there. He procured many sacred sūtras in original and Buddha images. He was fond of beating (the monks of the monastery).

He fell sick here and passed away in a foreign land.

慧命師者 Hui-ming-shih. Prajñājñapti. The monk Hui-ming also came from Chiang-ling in Ching-chou. He was a man of

1. Harikela was one of the renowned centres of learning in Eastern India in the seventh century. I-ching's Ha-li-chi-luo has been identified with Harikela. The Chinese monks who visited this place were greatly honoured by the rulers who were ardent Buddhists. Harikela has been identified with Candradvipa, Bakharganj Subdivision (Bangladesh) comprising major parts of eastern Bengal including the coastal region.

See Dr. N. R. Ray, *Bāngālir Itihās*, pp. 139-140.

honest and affectionate disposition, of high moral principle and of clear understanding. He not only studied the classics of China but also of outside countries. He had a soaring ambition. He reposed in the hope of seeing the sacred river[1] and directed his mind towards Veṇuvana, which always inspired his thought and imagination. He started his voyage for 占波 Chan-po, Champā.[2] In his voyage, he had to undergo much distress due to typhoon in the sea. He reached the copper pillar of Ma-Yüan, took rest in the capital and then went back to China.

玄逵律師者 Hsüan-k'uei Lü-shih. The Vinaya master Hsüan-k'uei Mahāmārga was a native of Chiang-ning 江寧 in 潤州 Jun-chou.[3] He belonged to a very noble and honourable clan Hu 胡. He was well versed both in history and literature. He himself was extremely courteous, righteous, devoted to *Dharma* and respectful towards fellow monks. A man of great reputation for his broad and extensive outlook,

1. The ancient Nairañjanā river, modern Lilajan. It is considered very sacred as Gautama Buddha attained Buddhahood on the bank of this river.

2. The ancient Hindu Kingdom of Champā comprised the modern states of North and South Vietnams or southern portion of old Annam. It also comprised the modern provinces of Quang-nam in the north and Bin-Thuan in the south. It extends from 18° to 10° of N. latitude. The elegant name of Champā was derived from the name of the people of the land, Chams. The position of Champā served as a connecting link between India and China. The northern boundary of Champā reached the Chinese Empire. The extent of Champā changed from time to time. In the second century A.D. the Hindu colonisers had already started reaching the coast of Annam either by sea or through Cambodia. Champā was the first Hindu kingdom founded in this area.

The Chinese pilgrim I-ching in the last year of the seventh century had mentioned the names of those countries, who greatly revered the 'Three Jewels'. In the list he included the name of Champā too. That Buddhism got royal patronage and had good hold on the people of Chams, is proved by the fact (*Chinese Annals*, Maspero, *T'ong Pao*, 1910, p. 514) that in A.D. 605 a Chinese General carried off 1350 Buddhist manuscripts all "written in a script of Indian origin", after a military conquest of Champā. See Sir Charles Eliot, *Hinduism and Buddhism*, Vol. III, Chapter XXXIX, pp. 137-150; R. C. Mazumdar, *Hindu Colonies*, Chap. IV, pp. 149-174; Dr. P. C. Bagchi, *India and China*, pp. 21-22; C. P. Fitz Gerald, *The Southern Expansion of Chinese People*, pp. 1-4, 28-30.

3. During the time of the Sui rulers it was known as Jun-chou and in the T'ang period Tan-yang in Chiang-su, (Kianzg-su) Lat. 32° 10'N, Long. 119° 29'E, one of the ports open to foreign traders.

the Vinaya master left home when he was very young. As he grew up, he commanded respect and honour. His progress and achievements in the field of religion were unprecedented and unparallelled. Not only extensively he studied the Vinaya texts (Book of Discipline), but also he had specialised in meditation. He observed strict discipline which was rare among his friends; he always attended discussions and deliberations of the Buddhist Sūtras and did make special study in 玄義 Hsüan-I.[1] A man of great literary merit, he acquired mastery over ancient Chinese calligraphy. The Vinaya-master Hsüan-k'uei used only three garments[2] (like Buddhist śramaṇa). He took the right corner of the robe and put it over the left shoulder without letting it stay on the arm.

He had the habit of taking off shoes as he entered the temple; but on his tour, he always used them. He cared very little even if people laughed at him. He never relaxed in bed; he spent his time in sitting and meditating. What did he care for a comfortable bed? He refused to have food in large quantity. He lived on by begging only. He would always avoid the big eating house.

Everyone is fond of straw-shoes and knows the art of making them but these tear out in no time. During his long wandering life, his feet would be exposed. Alas, what a suffering!

He had common ideals with his companions but he had great power of reasoning. He could bring a storm in calm water. He was not dogmatic and conventional as the common people were. He was the only one who was so much conscious and alert about the Truth. How could he associate himself with common people who were in darkness (of ignorance) and intoxication (of attachment)?

1. The teachings of the Buddha were systematically organised and developed on the basis of Indian Buddhist scriptures and commentaries by venerable monk Chih-i (A.D. 538-597) and on this basis he estabiished the famous T'ien-t'ai school in China. Hsüan-i is the method of teaching of this school. See Soothhill—Dictionary, pp. 194-195.

2. Three types of garments collectively called *Tricīvara* which every monk must use—The *Kāśāya,* i.e. *Saṅghāti* or the 'double cloak'; The *Uttarāsaṅga* or the 'upper garment'; the *Antarvāsa* or the 'inner garment'.

He travelled from place to place and then reached 丹陽 Tan-yang[1]; there he made an agreement with a man to go to India on a pilgrimage. Immediately, he bade good-bye to his elder brother and friends in south. How sad was the separation from his brother and friends ! But he cherished the lofty ideal of propagating the religion which dominated his life and thought. With this aim in view, he reached Kuang-chou[2] where he was down with pneumonia. Once he felt that he had been tied up with the disease and he possibly could never go to the far-off land. He was very much disgusted and disappointed and went back to his native place of 吳 Wu[3] and 楚 Ch'u[4]. He was only twenty-five or twenty-six years old.

Later on, a monk named 哲 Che reached India and told people that Hsüan-K'uei, a famous Chinese monk, had fallen sick and passed away ! Alas, how unfortunate he was ! His life had proved—how difficult it is to achieve one's own objectives ! He had a sincere desire and hope of acquiring the doctrine of reality, beyond limitation of positive and negative, the substance of Dharma; but all his hopes were in vain.

Again he had the hope of bringing back the gift (the Law of the Buddha) from India. He finally had to abandon the desire for 龐樹 Lung-shu,[5] Nāgārjuna's doctrine.

So, I (I-ching) comment with profound emotion—"The sage had passed away ! Who would come to succeed him ? What a bad luck that he had such a short life ! Alas ! his towering ideas were shattered into pieces. Like budding flowers he withered

1. In other three editions it is 楊 instead of 陽 yang.

2. Modern Canton.

3. The province of Chiang (Kiang)-su. Wu was one of the three kingdoms from A.D. 229 to 280. The state of Wu comprised Che-kiang (Chiang) province Su-chou being the capital.

4. Ch'u was the name of a feudal state which existed from B.C. 740 to B.C. 330. It comprised the Provinces of Hu-nan, Hu-pei, part of Kuei-chou and extended upto An-hui, Chiang-si and Ho-nan.

See Chou Yun-hsi, *The first Map*: *Ancient China in Transition*.

5. In other two editions it is 龍 Lung.

away. To understand a higher ideal is easy, but how difficult it is to put the same into practice in life !

"He had all the blessedness of Karma and virtue at the young age. He had passed on the lamp of Truth to the posterity. He had strong determination and aspiration. I, I-ching like to keep his illuminating and brilliant life immortal by writing his biography so that he would be remembered by the generations to come, for many long autumns."

Once the monk Hsüan-k'uei said "I will leave Kuang-chou (Canton) for 桂林 Kuei-lin.[1] As a token of remembrance I compose this poem for the monk."

The verse consists of five characters, —"My heart goes to the sacred land of Buddhist temples. I dream to move in the land of the Buddha. I suffer from illness from young age. I, however, could not accompany my friends to India. All my high aspirations and hopes are dashed to the ground. Once the leaves fall from trees they can never go back to their original places. My heart's desire of the past had never been fulfilled. Will that auspicious day ever come, when with the help of a cup or bowl[2] only, I shall be able to cross and reach India ? Shall I be able to witness the magnificient flow of Dharma in India ?"

I-ching spent the first year of the Hsien-heng period[3] in the Western capital[4] in hearing and studying religious discourses. At that time he had in his company Ch'ü-i, a teacher of the Law of Ping-pu,[5] Hung-wei, a teacher of the Śāstra of Lai-chou[6] and

1. Kuei-lin mountain in Canton. It also means monastery.

2. There was a monk in China, in the fifth century, who could cross a river with the help of a cup or bowl. Our author must have referred to the monk 杯度 Pei-tu.

3. This era was started in A.D. 670 by the T'ang Emperor Kao-Tsung.

4. In ancient Chinese works Hsi-ching (Western capital) was known as Cochin-China. This name was also given to various capital cities under different Dynasties. Ch'ang-an, Lo-yang, T'ai-yuan and even Kyoto in Japan were sometimes known as Western capital.

5. Ping-pu in Shan-si.

6. Lai-chou (Lat. 37° 10'N, Long, 120° 10'E), in Shan-tung province.

two or three other Bhadantas also. They made an agreement together to pay a visit to the Vultures Peak mountain (Gṛdhrakûṭa) and set their heart on the Tree of Knowledge (Bodhidruma).

The old age of the mother of the venerable monk Yi and his love for home in Ping-chuan[1] forced him to return home. Hung-wei, on the other hand, on meeting Hsüan-chang at Chiang-ning,[2] set his mind on An-yang[3], Sukhâvatī (The Pure Land). Hsüan-k'uei accompanied (I-ching) upto Kuang-fu but like others he also changed his mind. Only I-ching started his journey with a young monk Shen-hsing from 晉州 Chin-chou.[4]

Unfortunately, he parted with his own friends in the Divine Land, who followed their own way, while he did not have a single new acquaintance in India. If at that moment he hesitated (to take a journey) his desire would not have been fulfilled. Being very much grieved at heart in his lonely life of solitary wanderings, he composed two verses imitating the one on the fourfold sorrow.[5] "I had passed through thousands of different stages during my long solitary journey. The threads of sorrow had disturbed my thought hundred-folds. Why did the shadow

1. See No. 3.

2. In Chiang (Kiang) -su province. Formerly it was an Imperial residence and was called Nan-ching.

3. One has to recite or chant the name of Amitābha daily to be born in the Western Paradise or the Sukhâvatī.

4. The province of Shan-si. It was a feudal state under the great Chou Dynasty (B.C. 1122-256 B.C.)

5. I-ching composed the poem imitating the poem written by Chang-heng (A.D. 78-139). During the rule of the Han Emperor Shun-ti (A.D. 126-145), 張衡 Chang-heng's fame as a great historiographer spread far and wide. He was also a celebrated mathematician and astronomer. He constructed an Uronosphere which was considered as celestial globe. He incurred displeasure of the Emperor who denounced him as a magician.

A pair of odes on the eastern and western capitals (Ch'ang-an, Lo-yang) was written about A.D. 87 and the third ode followed in A.D. 110 during the time of his temporary retirement.

See Needham, Joseph Vol. IV, 3, p. 86.

of my body walk alone on the borders of Five Indies? Then again I console myself......An excellent general can resist an aggressive army but the resolution of a gentleman will never change.[1] If I am sad for short span of life and always complain of that, how can I fill up the 長祇 Ch'ang-chih, long Asaṅkheya age" ?[2]

In the third year of the Hsien-heng period, I-ching kept the summer-retreat (Varṣā or Vassa)[3] in devotional exercises in Yang-fu. In the early autumn he unexpectedly met an Imperial. envoy 馮孝詮 Feng Hsiao-ch'üan of 龔州 Kung-chou[4] With his help I-ching reached the city of Kuang-tung, and fixed the date with the owner of a Persian[5] ship to sail for the South.

1. *Confucius Analects*. Chapter IX, 25. James Legge's translation, *The Four Books*. Arthur Waley's translation "You may rob the three armies of their commander-in-chief but you can not deprive the humblest peasant's opinion". See Arthur Waley, *The Analects of Confucius* (Third Impression), p. 144.

2. I-ching here has given the reference of Bodhisattva who has to pass through Asaṅkhya ages on charity.

3. The third chapter of the Mahāvagga deals with the age old custom of retiring of the monks during the three months of the rainy season. According to this rule, the wandering recluses had to remain in a fixed place and they were strictly forbidden to travel without any fixed local habitation. This practice is known as 'Vassavāsa'. The monks spending the rainy-retreat had to observe certain rules and regulation and to devote their time in devotional prayer and meditation.

In China, the Buddhist monks also followed this tradition. This retirement was known in China as summer-retreat and the first retreat according to their calendar starts on the "first day of the dark half of the fifth moon and the second summer-retreat is on the first day of the dark half of the sixth moon. The first summer-retreat ends in the middle of the eighth moon while the second ends in the middle of the ninth moon." (Takakusu, *ARBRIMA*, p. 85, 219).

4. During the period of the Sung Dynasty, 平南 P'ing-nan was known as Kung-chou. It was in Kuang-si (Lat. 23° 32'N, Long. 1 10° 03'E).

5. In ancient time, foreign trade had been conducted mainly by camel caravan with the Roman Empire through the Central Asian silk route. But the T'ang period (A.D. 618-907) ushered a new era in the history of China's maritime trade with foreign countries like India, Malayan countries and Persia. In fact, overseas trade of China was at first in the hands of Persians and Arabs. Oceanic trade between China and other countries resulted in an unprecedented

In the meantime, he accepted an invitation from the envoy Feng Hsiao-ch'üan and went to 廣州 Kuang-chou.[1] The envoy again became I-ching's Dānapati, a patron. The envoy's younger brothers 孝誕 Hsiao-tan and 孝軫 Hsiao-chen—both Imperial envoys and ladies Ning and P'eng and other members of the family gave him parting gifts. Before his departure, they gave him excellent food and other necessaries (for the journey). Everyone of them tried their best to help him so that I-ching would not be in difficulties during his voyage. But they were still worried and apprehensive of difficulties he might face in a foreign land. He could feel the parental affection in them, giving whatever the orphan desired to have. They all became his great shelter and refuge and gave all possible assistance to visit the wonderful regions.

The power of the Feng family enabled I-ching to make the pilgrimage (to the Holy Land). Irrespective of the monks and laity, all in Lin-nan[2] were extremely grieved at the time of his departure. Even the learned scholars of north felt sad at their departure, thinking they would not be able to see them again.

In the eleventh month they started their voyage looking towards the constellations 翼 I[3] and 軫 Chen[4] and leaving 番禺 P'an-yü[5] behind them. Sometimes (on his journey) I-ching directed his thought towards far off Mṛgadāva,

---

prosperity of China under the T'ang rulers. During the last part of the seventh century I-ching mentioned the Persian ships coming in and going out from the port of Canton.

1. Kuang-chou, Canton, Kuang-tung; comprised two district cities of Nan-hai and P'an-yü, the capital of the province; Lat. 23° 08' N.,111°17' E. During the time of the Wu Kingdom it was known as 番州 P'anchou and at the time of the T'ang Ch'ing-hai.

2. South of Plume Range i.e. Kuang-tung and Kuang-si.

3. One of the 28 Chinese Zodiacal constellations. Its corresponding element is fire and the animal is snake. According to Indian astronomy there are 27 Zodiacal constellations.

4. Another of the 28 Chinese Zodiacal constellations. Its corresponding element is water and the animal is earth-worm.

5. Kuang-tung, Canton.

the Deer Park and sometimes he was engrossed in thought of paying a visit to the Cock-foot mountain (Kukkuṭapādagiri).

That was the time when blowing of the first monsoon just began. The ship, with a pair of ropes suspended from a hundred cubit long mast, proceeded towards the Shu-fang, Red South[1]. Leaving behind the constellation 箕 Chi[2] (as the ship proceeded) her two sails, five lengths (canvas) each were blown away. While they were ploughing through the vast ocean, breakers looked like huge mountains on the sea. Joining sideways with a gulf of stream, the huge waves seemed to be dashing against the sky like clouds.

It was less than twenty days journey to reach Bhoga where he disembarked and stayed for six months, gradually learning Śabdavidyā Śāstra (Grammar). He received help from the King who sent him to Malayu (which has now been corrected as Śrībhoga) where he spent two months and then he left for Chieh-ch'a, Kedah.

In the twelfth month, he embarked on a royal ship from there and set sail for Eastern India. From Kedah it was a little more than ten days sail towards north to reach the land of the Naked People (Insulas Nudorum). Looking towards the east, the shore —one or two li in extent—contained nothing but 椰子 Yeh-tzu (Nārikela—cocoa-nut) trees, dense forest of betel-nuts[3] and betel-palms. It was pleasant to look at.

As soon as the ship advanced towards the shore, the natives, seeing the vessel, came rushing in hundred small boats. They reached the ship with cocoa-nuts, bananas, articles made of canes and bamboos and wanted to barter their commodities.

The most important thing they needed was iron; in exchange for five or ten cocoa-nuts they wished to get a piece of iron as large

1. See Takakusu, *ARBRPIMA*, pp. 8, 9, fn.8.

2. A Zodiacal constellation—Sagittarius, Dhanu. In Chinese it is said, Sagittarius loves wind and Taurus (Bull or Vṛṣa) loves rain. "Chi-hao-feng, Pi--hao-yü."

3. Areca nuts generally are used by the Indians with betel leaves for chewing.

as two fingers. The men of that place were all naked, the women covered their bodies with leaves. The merchants in joke offered them clothes but they showed their unwillingness to wear any clothes by waving their hands.

It was said that this country was in the direction of south-west of Sze-ch'uan. This land never produced iron; gold and silver were not common. But the main products were cocoa-nuts and tubers, on which the natives lived. Paddy was rare. Therefore, iron was regarded by them as most precious and valuable. Iron was known as 盧呵 Lu-ho,[1] Lohā in that island.

Generally, the natives of this place were not dark. They were of medium height. They were skilled in making cane-baskets. No other country could beat them in this skill.

If anyone refused to barter articles with them, they would immediately attack him with poisonous arrows; even a single one would prove fatal.

They sailed on for about half a month in north-west direction and then they reached Tāmralipti which was the southern limit of Eastern India. It was more than sixty yojanas from the Mahābodhi Saṅghārāma and Nālandā. Here I-ching met for the first time, the teacher Ta-Ch'eng-teng, Mahāyāna Pradīpa and stayed with him for one year, studied Sanskrit (the language of the Brahmā) and practised Vyākaraṇa (Grammar—a treatise on words and the structure of Sanskrit).[2]

Next, I-ching with the teacher Teng took the road straight to the West, and hundred merchants accompanied them to Mid-India. From the Mahābodhi Vihāra at a distance of ten days

1. Lauha in Sanskrit.

2. The reading of the text (Taisho Ed.) is 學梵語習聲聞論 Hsüeh-fan-yü, hsi-sheng-wen-lun. But in the three editions of the Sung, Yüan and Ming Dynasties, the syllable 聞 Wen is omitted. According to the Taisho's reading the translation will be, he "learnt Sanskrit (The language of the Brahmā) and practised the Śāstras of the Śrāvakas or the Hīnayāna." But I think the reading of the three editions is better. Takakusu also translated as 'practised the science of words instead of Hīnayāna Śastras.' (Takakusu *ARBRPIMA*, p. xxxi).

journey, they crossed a big mountain and bogs. This dangerous and perilous road was difficult to cross. It was better and safer to travel in a company of men rather than alone.

All through, I-ching was very weak and tired due to various seasonal diseases. He wanted to avail the company of the merchants but as he was very much exhausted and tired he could not go with them. He still continued to move on, after walking for about five li, he found that he required long rest and liked to stop for hundred times. There were more than twenty fellow priests of Nālandā with them. In the company of those priests, the venerable Mahāyāna Pradīpa proceeded in advance. I-ching was left alone to walk in the dangerous pass. When the sun was about to set in, immediately bandits and robbers came down from the mountain and surrounded him. Placing arrows on their bows, they shouted loudly, and one by one they glared at him and insulted him. They first snatched away his upper garments. Then they stripped him off his lower garments. Even the girdle which was with him, was also taken away from his naked body. At once he felt that he was on the point of death and he would not see the world again. If he was pierced by their arrows and lances, all his hopes to visit and pay offerings to the sacred land would be dashed to the ground. 'A man of fair complexion', according to the sayings of the land, should never be spared and he should be sacrificed before the altar. The story of this dreadful custom made him more terrified. Then he entered into a bog, besmeared his body with mud and covered it with leaves. He resumed his journey slowly with the support of a stick.

The sun had already gone down. It was quite dark and the inn was quite far off from this place. At the second watch of the night, he met the company of his fellow travellers. He could hear the venerable Teng calling out for him from outside the village. When they met, Teng offered him clothes to wear. First he took him to a tank and then after a wash they entered into a village. From there they moved on towards north and after a couple of days travel, they first reached Nālandā where they worshipped the Mūlagandhakuṭī, the Root Temple.

Next he went to the Vultures' Peak mountain and visited the place where heaps of clothes were kept folded. Later on, he paid a visit to the monastery of Great Enlightenment, Mahābodhi[1], where he worshipped the real image of the Buddha.[2]

The priests and the laity of 山東 Shan-tung[3] (at the time of his departure from China) had presented him pieces of fine and thick silk. He made 袈裟 Chia-sha, Kāṣāya[4] using those silk pieces of the exact size of Tathāgata and offered it with great veneration to the image. The Vinaya-master Hsüan of 濮州 Pu-chou[5] had given him hundreds and thousands of canopies to be offered on his behalf, at the altar of the Lord. The Dhyāna-master 安道 An-tao of 曹州 Ts'ao-chou[6] had requested him to worship the image of the Buddha which he did. I-ching with utmost reverence and undivided mind

1. The Mahābodhi Saṅghārāma was originally built by a Ceylonese monk. According to the report of Wang Hsüan-t'se, the King Meghavarma sent an envoy to the court of the famous Samudra-Gupta (A.D. 335-376) of the Gupta Dynasty. Samudra-Gupta immediately gave permission to build a monastery for the accommodation of the Ceylonese monks and pilgrims.

The Chinese travellers Fa-hsien and Hsüan-chuang visited this Saṅghārāma during the fifth and the seventh century respectively. Both of them stated that this Mahābodhi Saṅghārāma was constructed outside of the north gate of the Bodhi Tree.

See S. Beal, *Fo-kuo-chi*, C.T.T. ed. Vol. 51, No. 2085, p. 857.

Beni Madhav Barua, *Gayā and the Buddha-Gayā*, (Calcutta 1934), pp. 180-181; Dr. Debala Mitra, *Buddhist Monuments* (Calcutta 1971) pp. 60-63.

2. Hsuan-chuang heard the story of carving of an image of the Buddha in 'true likeness' by Maitreya. Once in this temple of Mahābodhi, Maitreya, in the guise of a Brahmin, started to carve an image with scented clay and a lamp inside the closed door of the temple and completed the 'beautiful image of the Buddha in true likeness' in little less than six months. I-ching and other two pilgrims Hsuan-chao and Chih-hung saw this beautiful image of the monastery. I-ching alludes to this event.

3. A province of modern China, situated in the lower Yellow river region.

4. One of the three Civaras or robes.

5. Shan-tung, Lat. 35° 48'N. Long. 115° 33'E.

6. District in Ts'ao-chou Fu (Shan-tung), Lat. 34° 56' 38'. Formerly it was a kingdom in Shan-tung.

prostrated himself (the knees, the elbows and the head touching the ground) before the image. He first prayed for China that the four kinds of benefits[1] may prevail in the Dharmadhātu (in the realm of the Law) among all the living beings there.

He wished to meet the honoured Maitreya under the Nāga-tree[2] and to determine the true teaching (of various schools, the teaching which explains the truth of Bhūtatathatā) and to attain unexcelled and perfect wisdom 無生智 Wu-sheng-chih,[3] which is not subject to births.[4]

Next he visited all the sacred places, passed through 方丈 Fang-chang[5] (in Vaiśālī) and then reached Kuśīnagara. Wherever he went, he was sincere and devout. He entered into the Mṛgadāva, Deer Park, climbed the Kukkuṭapādagiri, Cockfoot mountain. He spent ten years in the Nālandā monastery and collected the *Sūtras*.

After some time he retraced his steps to go back and reached Tāmralipti. Before he reached there again he met a band of

1. Four kinds of benefits conferred by Parents, teachers, elders and the monks, or "by 1. the Buddha, 2. King, 3. Parents and 4. benefactors". (*ARBRPIMA* p. 196, fn. 3).

2. The tree of Nāgapuṣpa will be the Bodhi Tree of Maitreya, the 'Buddhist Messiah' when he will come to the earth. Mesua roxburghii, Rottleria tintocorca piper belet. Apte's Sanskrit English Dictionary.

3. The knowledge of immortality, the knowledge which helps an Arhat to be free from the chain of transmigration.

4. The four forms of births (1) 'T'ai-sheng. Jarāyuja, birth from womb, (2) Tan-sheng, Aṇḍaja, birth from eggs, (3) Hsi-sheng, Saṁśvetaja, birth from moisture, (4) Hua-sheng, Anupapādhika, birth by transformation.

See *Vajracchedikā Prajñā-Pāramitā Sūtra*. (Translation by Kumārajiva). *CTT* Vol. VIII, p. 749.

English translation by the Rev. S. Beal, Chaplain R.N., *J.R.A.S.* 1863.

5. Fang-chang means ten cubits in Chinese. Originally Vimala-kīrti, a wealthy merchant, a great devotee and contemporary of the Buddha had a room in Vaiśālī, which was measured after many centuries by the Chinese envoy Wang Hsüan-t'se in A.D. 643. The measurement of the room was ten cubits in length and breadth. So the room of Vimalakīrti came to be known as Fang-chang. Later on, the abode of a head priest and even monasteries were known as Fang-chang.

robbers. He narrowly escaped the fate of being killed by their marauding swords. Thus he managed to exist from morning to night. (This only expanded the span of his life.)

He sailed from this port to reach Kedah carrying more than 500,000 Ślokas[1] of the Sanskrit Tripiṭakas. Out of these, about some thousand Chüan had been translated into Chinese.

On his way back he stayed in the crowded city of Śrī-vijaya.

善行師 Shan-hsing. The priest Shan-hsing, Sugati was a native of Chin-chou.[2] At an early age he left his own native place[3] for Tung-shan[4] (or monastery) to inquire into the Way (Buddhism).

As he grew, he studied the rites on Discipline and expressed his feelings to learn Vidyāmantra, spells. Mild and humble, frugal and simple by nature, he became the disciple of I-ching and followed him to Śrī-vijaya but always remembered his own country.

When he got ulcer, he took a small boat and returned to China at the age of a little over forty.

靈運法師者 Ling-yün. The monk Ling-yün came from Hsiang-yang.[5] His Sanskrit name was Prajñādeva. A man of strong will and determination, of uncommon qualities, he renounced the world at an early age. He was impatient to pay homage to the "sacred relics" of the Buddha. So he accompanied the monk Che in his voyage. They reached India after crossing the South Sea.

He studied thoroughly the Sanskrit language. He was exemplary to others. He commanded great respect and honour from the king and the people wherever he went.

1. Sung, hymn of praise. A stanza of thirty two syllables either in four lines of eight each or two of sixteen.

2. It comprises most of Shan-si province.

3. Sang-tzu. Native place. Mulberry and Lindera 'King of trees'. These two names indicate the native place. These are generally planted by parents around home.

4. Eastern hills. Near the district of Ho-hsi in Yün-nan Province. Tung-shan also means monastery.

5. Prefectural city in Hu-pei. Lat. 32° 06'N, Long. 113° 05'E.

He sketched the image of Maitreya which was an exact replica of the image under the Wisdom Tree. The size was in conformity with the original one. His superior artistic designs excelled even the skilful workers. Later on, he devoted his life to the cause of Buddhism in China. He possessed a rare ability to translate the Buddhist texts.

僧哲禪師者 Seng-che Ch'an-shih. Bhikṣu Darśana Dhyānācārya. The Dhyāna-master Seng-che was a native of 澧州 Li-chou. From childhood he was honest, dignified, pure and was inclined to Buddhism. His power of understanding was very great He was sharp in debate, clever in arguments and an eloquent speaker; it seems he was always in the banquet. He was serious and quiet by nature.

He deeply and enthusiastically studied the different collections of the Vinaya and mastered the entire system of Dhyāna. He finally raised that general outline of both the *Mādhyamika* and *Śata Śāstra*, which were in his opinion indispensably and entirely connected with Chuang and Liu.[1] He had an absorbing passion for making pilgrimage to the sacred places. So he set sail for India. After reaching the Western land, he crossed through (many places) begging alms as a Buddhist priest.

Visiting many sacred places of surrounding countries he advanced towards Eastern India. He reached Samataṭa, 三摩呾吒 San-mo-tan-t'e.[2] The king of the country was

1. One of the most celebrated philosophers and historians of ancient China (B.C. 80-9 A.D.). He was the author of the Han-shu or the *Historical Record of the Han Dynasty* (B.C. 206-220 A.D.). He started the modern style of historical composition. He served the Imperial rulers from young age and held various offices under the Han Emperor Hsüan-ti and two of his successors. He was inclined toward Taoism and supernaturalism.

See William Frederick Mayers, *The Chinese Readers' Manual* (Reprinted in China, 1939), p. 140, No. 404.

2. Hsüan-chuang says, "This country (Samataṭa) which was on the seaside and was low and moist, was more than 3000 li in circuit. It had more than 30 Buddhist monasteries and above 3000 Brethren, all adherents of the Sthavira school. There were about 100 Deva-temples, the various sects lived pell-mell; and the Digambara Nirgranthas were very numerous" (Watters, II, p. 187).

曷羅社跋乇 Ho-luo-she-po-t'o.[1] The king was a great admirer of "Three gems" 三寶 San-pao[2] and was a zealous 烏波索迦 Wu-po-so-chia, Upāsaka.[3]

The Dhyāna-master was a zealous, enthusiastic and sincere adherent of Buddhist Faith. His love and perfect devotion for the Faith was rare in the past and so would be in future. Everyday he made one hundred thousands of Buddha images according to the model of the Lord with clay and recited one hundred thousand ślokas from the *Mahā-Prajñā-Pāramitā sūtra.* Same amount of fresh flowers were also offered to those images daily by himself. The heaps of flowers gathered there would sometimes reach human height.

At the time of royal outing, the royal carriage would be ready, the image of Avalokiteśvara would be carried in front of the procession. The flags, festoons and banners would flutter and sound of drums and music would fill the air. The image of the Lord was carried by the monks and the lay devotees at the head of the procession, followed by the king. More than four thousand monks and nuns dwelling in various cities received offerings for their maintenance from the king. Every morning an officer was

---

Samataṭa of this passage has been identified with the site of modern Jessore in Bangladesh. (Cunningham *AGI.*, p. 501); and Watters identified it with the modern district of Faridpur in Bangladesh. According to Dr. N. R. Ray modern Tippera was a part of Samataṭa from the sixth century to the twelfth century A.D. and the entire land extending from the eastern bank of the Ganges and the Bhāgirathī to the mouth of the river Meghna was known as Samataṭa.

See Dr. N.R. Ray, *Bāngālir Itihās,* pp. 141-142.

1. Chavannes has rendered the name of the King Ho-luo-she-pat'o as Harṣabhaṭa. But this King has been identified by some scholars with Rājarājabhaṭa, the son of Devakhaḍga of the Buddhist Kaḍga Dynasty who extended his power over Samataṭa.

Dr. N. R. Ray thinks that the king mentioned by our author is definitely the same as king Rājarāja (bhaṭa) of the two Ashrafpur copper plate inscriptions.

2. The Buddha, the Law and the Order.
3. The term for a Buddhist laity who followed the five commandments.

sent to the monastery who would go from room to room with folded hands to ask about the welfare of the resident monks. The officer, on behalf of the king, would inquire whether venerable monk Che passed the night peacefully. The monk in turn would bless the king by saying "May the honourable king be free from all diseases, may he live long to raise the prestige and honour of the country and may he rule the country peacefully".

The royal officer before returning from the monastery would discuss the affairs of the State.

The intelligent, virtuous and wise men of India had extensively studied the *Sūtras* of the eighteen schools[1] Shih-pa-pu (as existed in India) and they could explain clearly the Five Learnings, Pañca Vidyā and great *Śastras.* These men of letters and eminent scholars from every corner assembled there in the capital. It was the popularity and kindness of the king which spread far and wide that drew a large number of people there. He was a jewel among all the kings.

The monk Che was living in this Rāja-vihāra[2] receiving special honour and respect from the king. He studied Sanskrit and gradually improved a great deal.

1. The first schism in the Buddhist Saṅgha resulted in the development of two sects,—the Theravāda and the Mahāsāṅghika. Later on, there appeared eighteen schools, even before the time of Aśoka. Ten schools among them gradually established their own positions and developed their own literatures. These principal sects are known as *Sthaviravāda* (*Theravāda*), *Haimabata, Dharmagupta, Mahīśāsaka, Kāśyapīya, Sarvāstivāda, Mūla-sarvāstivāda, Sammatīya, Mahāsāṅghika* and *Lokottaravāda.* An account of eighteen schools of Buddhism from the original treatise of Vasumitra was translated into Chinese by three different authors. The Tibetan and Chinese translations of Vasumitra's work give different accounts of the Great schism.

See 2500 *Years of Buddhism* (Ministry of Communication and Broadcasting, Govt. of India, 1956.). pp.97-122;

Rhys Davids, The Sects of the Buddhists, *J.R.A.S.* 1891, pp. 409-22;
Rhys Davids Note on 18 schools *J.R.A.S.* 1892, pp. 1-7.
Indian Antiquary 1880, December, pp. 299-300; A.C. Bannerjee, *Principal Schools and Sects of Buddhism.*

2. The Gunaighar (18 miles to the north-west of Comilla, Bangladesh) copper-plate inscription of Vinayagupta, the Gupta ruler dated A.D. 507 refers to a monastery called Rāja-vihāra, evidently built by a king.

I-ching could not meet the monk Che. On his arrival in the monastery he heard that the monk, who was over forty, once lived there.

玄遊 Hsüan-yu, the disciple of the monk Che came from 高麗 Kao-li. He accompanied his teacher to Simhala where he was ordained as a monk. There he lived for the rest of his life.

THE ABOVE-MENTIONED FIFTY MONKS

智弘律師者 Chih-hung Lu-shih, Mahāprajñā. The Vinaya-master Chih-hung belonged to Lo-yang.

He was the nephew of 王玄策 Wang Hsüan-t'se[1] who had been sent by the Emperor as an envoy to the Western world. From childhood Chih-hung realised the unreality of this world. He abhored the company of the rich, frivolous and the worthless people. He preferred to give up this life of enjoyment and settle down somewhere far from the crowd.

He left home, went to Shao-lin 少林 monastery[2] and lived mainly on roots and fruits. He derived great pleasure from classics (Chinese). He himself was a good writer. He did not

1. Ma Tuan-lin, a scholar of unrivalled erudition, belonging to the declining period of the Sung Dynasty (A.D. 960-1278 A.D.) and the rising of the Yüan Dynasty (A.D. 1280-1341 A.D.) recorded an important event, when the T'ang Emperor T'ai-Tsung sent Wang Hsüan-t'se as a head of a new mission to the court of Harsha, the king of Kanauj, India, in A.D. 641. He was again sent as envoy in A.D. 643. In the next mission in A.D. 646, Wang Hsüan-t'se arrived in India, when King Harshavardhana had already died. The envoy received a check at the hands of Arjuna or Aruṇāśva who usurped the throne in A.D. 648. Wang Hsüan-t'se went back to Tibet and with the help of the famous King Srong-btsan-Gampo, defeated Aruṇāśva and took him to China as a prisoner-of-war. This story of the Chinese envoy has little historical value. A very cordial and intimate relation was established between India and China just after Hsüan-chuang's return to China from India.

2. Shao-lin monastery is situated on the Sung mountain in Hu-nan Province. This monastery is specially famous for its nine years association with Bodhidharma (Lo-yang-chia-lan-chi) who first started the Intuitional school (Dhyāna or Ch'an) in China.

like the noise and hubbub of the world. He liked the quiet and peaceful life of the monks and sages.

He left 巴水 Pa-shui[1] for San-Wu[2] 三吳 where he relinquished everything, put on monk's robe and became a mendicant under the guidance of the preceptor 瑳禪 Ts'o-ch'an, Dhyānaraśmi. He wanted to imbibe the wisdom of his venerable teacher, but could not succeed. After trying for many years, he learned the Doctrine of the Lord. Hereafter, he went to 蘄州 Ch'i-chou[3] where the Dhyānamaster 忍 Jen was living. Under his guidance, Dhyānaraśmi practised purifying his body and mind but could not awaken his soul.

Next, he crossed the 湘 Hsiang[4] river, passed over the 衡嶺 Heng-ling[5] mountain, entered the Kuei-lin monastery and hid himself in a solitary place for many years studying the religion. There he became the disciple of the Dhyānamaster Chi. He stayed there enjoying the beauty of the mountain and river. The solitude and natural beauty of the vast forest enamoured him. So he wrote (directed his pen) poems describing his inner feelings aroused by the surrounding gloomy fountains and hills. These poems expressed his extreme soft feelings for his far-off home.

Then he acquired excellent knowledge from the teacher of San-wu and learned many things from the talented scholars of Chin-chiang. He was of very pleasant character and was never affected by anyone's flattery.

1. A part of Ho-nan and Shen-si. Eight rivers— 霸 Pa, 滻 Ch'en 涇 Ching, 渭 Wei, Feng, 鎬 Kao, 潦 Liao, 潏 Chü also called Pa-ch'üan. Tse Yüan Vol. I, p. 162, folio 2.

2. Tan-yang. During the time of the T'ang, it comprised parts of Chiang-su (Kiang-su) and Anhui.

3. Ch'i-chou in Huang-chou Fu. Hu-pei (Lat. 30° 03'N, Long. 115°, 25'E).

4. A large tributory of the Yang-tze. It flows through Hu-nan.

5. One of the five sacred mountains in central Hu-nan.

He left China with a fervent desire to visit and pay homage to the Western lands. Fortune favoured him; he happened to meet the Dhyānamaster 無行 Wu-hsing and came to an agreement with him (to sail for Western countries).

He reached 合浦 He-p'u[1] and sailed for the boundless sea. Due to unfavourable wind he could not proceed farther and remained at 上景 Sheng-ching.[2]

He resumed his journey again and reached Chiao-chou where he passed the summer retreat. Next, at the end of winter, he embarked a ship from the port, reached Śrī-bhoga in South Sea. The experience they gathered in their travel was recorded in the narrative of the Dhyāna-master Wu-hsing. They passed two years in the monastery of Great Enlightenment. With pious mind and sincere devotion, he worshipped the Lord. There he practised and recited the Sanskrit Śāstras. Thus he improved his language gradually. After learning the Śabda Śāstra (a Treatise on words and their meanings), he acquired the ability to understand Sanskrit scriptures. He also studied the rules and ceremonies of the Vinaya texts and *Abhidharma*. He already could expound *Kośa* and achieved great proficiency in *Hetuvidyā* (Logic).

In the Nālandā monastery he specially learned the Mahāyāna and sitting on the Bodhimaṇḍa of the monastery of Faith, he learned the Hīnayāna. As a famous monk, he was very strict and rigorous in following the rules of the Orders. Being a very diligent and mindful student, he never wasted a single minute. He also studied the Vinaya Sūtras composed by the monk 德光 Te-kuang, Puṇyaprabha. He was talented enough to translate (into Chinese) immediately whatever he heard. As a traveller, he possessed nothing but note-books. Very seldom he reposed; always he kept sitting. He had no desire. Pure, simple and honest, he was not only respectful to his superiors and elders but also polite to subordinates and young monks.

1. A district forming the prefectural city of Lien-chou, Kuang-tung; Lat. 21° 39'N; Long. 108° 59'E.

2. See *ARBRPIMA*. p. 12, fn. 4.

He visited the Vulture's Peak mountain near Rājagṛha, Mṛgadāva or Deer Park, Jetavana Vihāra, 天階 T'ien-chieh[1] Deva Sopāna, Āmravana[2] or Mangogrove and the caves for meditation.

The long cherished dreams of visiting these places were realised. He expressed his deep gratitude and reverence for these places. He always offered his own garments and food to others. In the Nālandā monastery best food was served and Rājagṛha supplied all the necessities of life.

After living in Mid-India nearly for eight years he advanced towards Kashmir in the North. Kashmir was as if his own home. The monk 琳公 Lin-kung, it was told, was the companion of Chih-hung. The whereabouts of the monk was not known to the writer. However, he contributed in translating sacred texts into Chinese.

無行禪師者 Wu-hsing Ch'an-shih. The Dhyāna-master Wu-hsing belonged to Chiang-ling in Ching-chou. In Sanskrit he was known as 般若提波 Pan-jo-t'i-po Prajñādeva. It means 慧天 Hui-ti'en (Prajñādeva) in Chinese. He was a man of gentle, humble and pure disposition. He possessed the culture and refinements which he inherited from his birth. Extremely virtuous and kind, he had great ambition. His love for learning was great, from childhood he frequently

1. Hsüan-chuang describing his visit to Sāṅkāśya narrates, "..Within the enclosing wall of the Monastery were Triple stairs of precious substances in a row south to north, and sloping down to east, where Ju-lai descended from the Trayastriṁśa, heaven". Watters suggests that the district Sāṅkāśya took the name of Devāvatāra or Devāvataraṇaṁ, which means in Chinese "Place of Deva's Descent". I-ching has used the word T'ien-chieh, instead of T'ien-hsia-chü'. T'ien-chieh in Sanskrit is Devasopāna or Devāvatarṅaṁ. Śāṅkāśya or Sankissa is in Farrukkabad district, Uttarpradesh. Here at Sāṅkāśya the Buddha descended in the company of Śakra and Brahmā by means of a staircase from the Trayastriṁsa heaven. This event is known as the miracle of Sāṅkāśya.

2. Not much before the Parinirvāṇa of the Buddha, Āmrapāli, the famous courtesan of Vaiśāli made a formal performance of offering a mango-grove for the Buddha and the brethren. The Buddha accepted the gift from her. She changed her life and became a great divotee of the Lord.

visited the library. At twenty, the prime of his life, he was honoured with an Imperial officer's post[1] 金馬門 Chin-ma-men.

He studied thoroughly the classics of hundred schools of philosophers[2] and three Chinese Classics.[3] This genius and talented monk was reputed as the most learned man in his province. The glow and radiance of his pure knowledge illuminated

1. Chin-ma-men or the Golden Horse Gate means the Han-lin-yüan or the Imperial Academy or the Board of Academicians.

In ancient Chinese bureaucratic system of education, the Han-lin Academy was the highest educational institution, which prepared scholars to get an entry into the Imperial services.

The Emperor Wu-ti of the former Han Dynasty (B.C. 206-A.D. 23) placed a bronze horse in front of the Imperial Academy. So it was known as Cnin-ma-men.

2. During the Warring states period, specially from B.C. 500, 'Hundred Schools of Thought' over-flooded China by hundreds of philosophers with different ideas and thoughts. The most important schools were the Confucian, the Taoist (Lao-tze) and the Mohist. The school of Mo-tze propounded the philosophy of 'Universal love', utilitarianism and pacificism. During the middle and the later part of the Warring states period, another group of philosophers also known as the 'School of Names' (Ming-chia) included the Dialecticians, whose thinking was much like that of the sophists of Greece. In B.C. 280-233 another group of philosophers came into existence; their school was known as the 'Legalist school'. The Legalists have been called totalitarians by modern thinkers. Late in the same period, we find another school known as the Diplomatists or T'sung-heng-chia. The emergence of the Hundred schools with different views did not create any conflict among themselves. They were tolerant towards one another. "Pai-hua Ch'i-fang, Pai-chia Cheng-ming". See Fung Yu-lan, *History of Chinese Philosophy*, (trans. by Derk Bodde), Vol. 2 Princeton 1953.

3. A new theory of "Mysterious learning" or Metaphysical school was introduced by the scholar-officials of the feudal rulers during the last part of the Han Dynasty and during the period of Three Kingdoms. "This was one of the scholastic philosophies combining idealism and sophistry and, in form, it followed the traditions of Taoism and the school of Names, interpreting Confucian classics in terms of the philosophy of Lao-tze and Chuang-tze".

Hou Wai-lu, *A Short History of Chinese Philosophy*, p. 31. The Three Classics included the three works of Lao-tze, Chuang-tze and Book of Changes (I-ching).

the entire San-chiang[1] and seven lakes.[2] He was a fountain-head of knowledge that watered the different rivers. He enjoyed the fruits of his previous Karma.

He had great admiration for the Buddhist doctrines, the door to enlightenment.

Fortunately, he met five eminent men who guided him in his pursuit of knowledge. He lived in the Teng-chieh monastery and for the first time started studying Buddhism with other disciples sitting on the altar of the monastery. The monk Hui-ying (Prajñāvīra) of the 大福田 Ta-fu-tien monastery became his Upādhyāya (teacher) which in Chinese is known as 親教師 Ch'in-chiao-shih, one's own teacher or He-sheng.

Prajñādeva became the best disciple of the preceptor 吉藏 Chi-ts'ang (Śrigarbha).

Each and every generation is marked by great men. He concentrated on the study of the Law and thus he devoted his time in dwelling in Dhyāna. He left domestic life and lived outside the society. He had the capacity to discuss and expound subtle metaphysics. Though he was young, his fame even surpassed that of his elders.

Along with more than twenty people he, as a fully ordained monk, received the entire Commandments at the altar. Among all the disciples receiving instructions, he was indisputably the best. There was nothing left to add to his range of extensive knowledge. Residing in the dark cave of a mountain, he recited 法華妙典 Fa-hua-ch'ao-tien *Saddharma-Puṇḍarika* and other Mahāyāna Sūtras. He did not require even one month to complete the seven rolls[3] (chūans) of the Sūtras.

1. There are various explanations of the term San-chiang (Three Rivers); but generally it indicates the ancient mouths of the river Yang-tze. The three rivers of Yang-chou—(i) Wu-sung, (ii) Chi'en-t'ang river in Chiang (iii) P'u-yang.

2. In ancient time, it was said that there were seven lakes in the state of Ch'i. At present it comprises the entire boundary of Hu-pei province.

See Tz'u-hai *Dictionary*, p. 8

3. Chūan in Chinese means a roll of paper. But it also means a book or a volume.

It has been rightly said: A bamboo fishing trap is a means to catch fish; similarly searching for reasons is a means to reach the Truth. He must search for a real preceptor with great spiritual understanding, who would be able to direct him to practise Dhyāna and thus would help him to be free from all the worries of the world and to achieve salvation.

Therefore, he with a mendicant-staff went to Chiu-chiang[1] and from there reached 三越 San-yeh[2]. He travelled over the mountain 衡 Heng[3] and settled down in 金陵 Chin-ling.[4] In the peaceful surroundings of the monastery on the Sung[5] 嵩 and the 華 Hua[6] mountain he retired and recited the Sūtras for long.

He travelled all over the big mountains in North. His sole aim was to acquire perfect knowledge and wisdom. He wanted to carry with him the principle and system of intent contemplation

1. Chiang-si; it is also the district city of Te-hua; Lat 29° 42'N; Long 116° 08'; one of the ports of the Yang-tze. This region was known as Chiu-chiang (Nine Rivers) during the time of Chin Dynasty. According to W.F. Myer, it means the entire region through which the nine branches of the river Yang-tze flow (*CRM*, *B.* 362).

2. The three principalities of Yüeh in the second and first century B.C. (i) Wu, the modern Chinang-su (Kiang-su) and part of Che-chiang, (Kiang) (ii) modern Fu-chien (Kien) and part of Che-chiang (Kiang), (iii) modern Kuang-tung and part of Tonkih.

3. Heng-shan in central Hu-nan, one of the beautiful mountain spots, was considered as one of the five sacred mountains of China. It is also a district in Heng-chou Fu, Hu-nan, Lat. 27° 14'N, Long. 112° 38'E.

4. Modern Chiang-ning province. Formerly an Imperial residence and therefore called Nan-ching or Southern capital. Lat. 32° 05'N, Long. 118° 47'E. Originally it was Chin-ling but it changed its name during the T'ang period; it was called Chiang-ning. At present Chin-ling Buddhist Text Society at Nanking preserves more than 120,000 printing blocks of Buddhist scriptures (Chao Pu-chu, *Buddhism in China*, p.2, Peking 1960).

5. Loftiest of the five peaks of the mountain in Ho-nan.

6. The mountain Hua in Shen-si province on the west. One of the sacred mountains of the Chinese Buddhists. The Hua mountain is the abode of Kṣiti-garbha Bodhisattva.

to North. His craze was to imbibe the knowledge and perfection in minute details of the great Dhyānamaster.

He crossed the dangerous mountains of the West and reached the East where he studied the pure and genuine knwoledge of the eminent Vinayamaster 道宣 Tao-hsüan.[1]

He listened to the (discussion of) the old and new Śāstras and Sūtras, discussed all the ancient and modern ceremonies and rules.

His knowledge was like boundless, fathomless ocean and high precipitous mountain.

Later on, Wu-hsing with the fellow-monk Chih-hung started on voyage. It took only a month to reach Śrī-vijaya in favourable east wind. The king of the country welcomed him with utmost cordiality, scattering golden flowers and grains (in front of him) as he was a very honourable special guest. The four necessaries[2], 四事 Szu-shih of a monk were offered to him.

Knowing the monk had come from the land of the great T'ang rulers, the king showed him extra respect and honour.

The monk Wu-hsing reached Mo-luo-yu in fifteen days on royal ship. They took another fifteen days to reach Kedah.

1. Tao-hsüan (A.D. 596-667) a contemporary of Hsüan-chuang, eminent monk and celebrated Buddhist historian of the T'ang Dynasty, was the author of eight works (NC App. iii, 21). His important works are *Hsu-kao-seng-chuan* (*Further Biographies of Eminent monks*. CTT. 50. No. 2060, 425-707), *Kuang-hung-ming-chi* (Further collections of Essays on Buddhism, CTT 52, N. 2103, p 97), and *Fo-tao lun-heng* (Essays on the controversy between Buddhism and Taoism, CTT, 52, 372a).

Tao-hsüan was an important person in founding a new Vinaya school, Lü-tsung or the Disciplinary school on the basis of the Caturvarga Vinaya of the *Dharmagupta* school. This sect is sometimes called Nan-shan or Southern mountain, because Tao-hsüan lived in a monastery on Chung-nan mountain near Ch'ang-an.

2. The four necessaries are, (1) piṇḍiyulopa-bhojanam (taking food by begging only), (ii) pamsukulacivaram (using rag clothings collected from dust heaps), (iii) rukkha mūlasenāsanam (sitting or lying under a tree), (iv) putimuttopheṣajjam (using only excrements and urine as medicine).

See N. Dutt, *Early Monastic Buddhism*, Ed. 2, Calcutta, 1971, p. 154; *JRAS* 1891, pp. 476-77.

At the end of winter, he sailed again for the West. It took another thirty days to reach 那伽鉢亶那 Na-chia-po-t'an-na[1]. From there it was two days sail for Ceylon,where he saw and paid offerings to the Tooth of the Buddha. He sailed from Ceylon for the north-east by ship and after about a month's sail reached Harikela which was situated on the east of Eastern India. It was a part of 贍部州 Shan-pu-chou, Jambu-dvīpa[2]. There he stayed for one year and then moved towards Eastern India gradually with his constant companion Chih-hung. Nālāndā was more than a hundred yojanas from there. After resting for some time, he advanced towards the monastery of Great Enlightenment.

The king not only made all arrangements for his stay in the monastery but also honoured him by appointing him as the abbot of the monastery which was highly esteemed in the West. The abbot only had the right of discussion whereas the resident monks could only get boarding and lodging—that was all.

Next the Dhyāna-master turned towards Nālandā. There he heard discourse on Yoga and learned 中觀 Chung-kuan.[3]

He made a special study of *Kośa* and the canonical rules of the Vinaya with great interest.

Again he advanced towards 羝羅荼寺 Ti-luo-ch'a Tila-dhaka monastery,[4] two yojanas west of Nālandā monastery.

1. Nagapattinam was an important centre of Buddhism. Dhyānācārya Wu-hsing, during his travel in India, visited Nagapattinam (Lat. 10° 45'N, Long. 79° 50'E, District Thanjavur, Tamil Nadu). It was a port opened to foreign trade.

A Buddhist temple was constructed at the request of a Chinese ruler for the Chinese Buddhists during the time of the Pallava ruler Narasiṃhavarman II (A.D. 695-722). It is said that a Chinese architect and designer was employed for the construction of the temple.

2. India.

3. Chung-kuan is one of the San kuans (三觀). It is the via media between the ideas of voidness and unreality of everything.

4. I-ching, here, places the monastery of Ti-luo-ch'a or Ti-lo-t'u in Magadha about two yojanas west of Nālandā. According to Cunningham,

The great monk of the monastery could excellently expound the *Hetuvidyā* (Logic). Sitting on the fragrant bamboo mat, he often studied the works of Diṅnāga and Dharmakīrti[1]. He was perhaps able to open the sombre door of Buddhism and unveil the mystery of it.

He lived on begging alms only once a day. His wants were very few. He always lived as if he was beyond the realm of this world of mortal beings. In his free time he translated 阿笈摩經 *A-chi-mo-ching*, *Āgama Sūtra* and narrated the events of the Mahāparinirvāṇa 如來涅槃 Ju-lai-ni-fan of Tathāgata. This was the summary consisting of three chüans. Before his return to China, he completed the translation of the Vinayas of the *Sarvāstivāda school*. Though he could not make much progress in translating other Śāstras, his translation (Vinaya) agreed with the translation done by the monk Hui-ning. The splendour of India could not shake Wu-hsing's love for the Divine Land (China). He always desired to go back to China taking the route through North India.

A day after, I-ching came from Nālandā to see him off. Both of them travelled about six yojanas towards east. Then with a very heavy heart they bade farewell to each other. They wished

---

Ti-luo-ch'a of I-ching is the same monastery of Ti-luo-shih-ka narrated by Hsüan-chuang. Cunningham states that Ti-luo-shih-ka is the Tiladaka i.e. modern Tittara. Fergusson is of opinion that it was in the Barabar hills in district Gayā.

See Cunningham *AGI*, pp. 521-523; Watters II, pp. 105, 106, 107.

1. Dharmakīrti was born in a Brahmin family of South India in A.D. 635. Intelligent and skilful, he attained great proficiency in five arts, in the Vedas, Vedāṅgas as well as in grammar. From childhood, he attended the discourses on Buddhism. Later on, he became an ardent, devout Buddhist of brilliant intellect. He was ordained by Dharmapāla of Nālandā. In logical discourses and debates and understanding he even surpassed Diṅnāga. Dharmakīrti is the author of many monumental works. His *Nyāyabindu*, the *Pramāṇa-vārtika-kārikā, Pramāṇaviniścaya* are some of his works on logic. *Nyāyabindu* is extant in original Sanskrit. He may be placed on the seventh century since I-ching during his travel in India A.D. 671-695, has praised Dharmakirti as a great logician after Diṅnāga.

to see each other again. They parted with tears. It was really a very moving scene. They wiped off their tears with sleeves of their robes. The monk Wu-hsing was fifty-six years old at that time.

His perfect faith in and great devotion for the Buddha was remarkable. It was a great pleasure for the Dhyāna-master to watch the Wisdom Tree in foliage at the advent of spring every year, and to enjoy bath in the Dragon lake, Lung-ch'ih during that season. The Bamboo grove would be fresh yellow. He loved to collect flowers and offer them to the Vulture's Peak mountain.

During the spring time, generally all assembled together to celebrate the festive occasion.[1] The Buddhist brethren, laity in myriads from far and wide poured spontaneously into this place and sprinkled water on the Wisdom Tree.

In spring, the Vulture's Peak mountain would be flooded with palm sized yellow flowers that looked like pure gold. Everyone would rush to the mountain to pluck flowers. The wild forest was aflame with abundance of yellow flowers known as 春女華 Ch'un-nü-hua, Vasanta Mallikā.[2]

Once, I-ching with the Dhyāna-master Wu-hsing climbed the Vulture's Peak mountain and made devotional offerings there. They felt extremely grieved at heart when they looked towards their own land from the top of the mountain.

I-ching composed this poem expressing his feelings in mixed metres.

"We witness the transformation of the sacred mountain peak and glance at the ancient city of Rājagṛha. Thousands of years

1. During the reign of the King Bimbisāra, various festivals and fairs were arranged in the capital. One such type of fair was known as Giragga-Samājja. The word Giragga means, as the commentator says, the festival on the top of a mountain. It also means that which are seen from the top of a mountain. Even now, on every full moon day in the month of Kārtika i.e. October-November, a fair is held at the village Giryak.

See Dr. Amulya Chandra Sen, *Rājagṛha O Nālandā*.

2. "Having blossoms in Spring": Cordia Latifolia—Monier Williams, *Sanskrit English Dictionary*, p. 930.

had already passed but the water of the lake remains pure and clear as it was before, and the Bamboo grove remains evergreen. The vague reminiscence of the past had thrown back its reflexion on the hard roads (of the city), but everything is in ruins.

七寶仙臺 Ch'i-pao-shan-t'ai Saptaratna ṛṣi sopāna is the thing of past now. Previously when the Lord preached the Law, the heavenly flowers of variegated colours were scattered below. Now there is no dripping music of the flowery rain. These are the past events now ! What a pity I was not born then ![1] What great pain I feel (when I think) that this world is a burning house which deceives the worldly people. How sad that the island of pearls and gems is always obscure like the high peak of the mountain ![2]

I have travelled beyond the boundary and in imagination I have crossed the Seven Seas and also the whole universe. The three disturbed realms are sinking into heterodoxy and falsity. Things are all in disorder and confusion. There is no real Truth. Its complete comprehension can only be achieved by compassion and generosity. By removing the 塵 . Ch'an[3] (six guṇas) and calming down one's desire, one can discover the profound Doctrine. When one sacrifices one's own body and seeks complete annihilation of one's own being to initiate the mind,[4] this pāramitā is known as Shih 施 Dāna,

1. The same feelings overwhelmed the great poet Rabindra Nath Tagore when he visited the temple at Bodha-Gayā. 'Why was I not born when he, at the touch of whose feet the whole universe was sanctified, personally walked through Gayā; why did I not directly feel the sacred impact of his presence, with my body and soul ?'

Rabindra Nath Tagore, *Buddha-deva, Rabindra Rachanāvalī Vol. II*, p. 469 (Centenary Edition, Govt. of West Bengal Publication, Calcutta, 1368 B.S.)

2. According to Indian mythology, India is encircled by seven seas viz. Lavaṇa, Ikṣu, Surā, Sarpiḥ, Dadhi, Dugdha, Payaḥ. Jambuplakṣāhvayau-dvipau Śālmaliścāparo mahān ! Kuśaḥ Krauñcastathā Śākaḥ Puṣkaraścaiva Saptamaḥ // Ete dvīpāḥ Samudraistu Sapta Saptabhirāvṛtāḥ Lavaṇekṣu-surāsarpirdadhi dugdhajalaiḥsamam // *Agnipurāṇa* 108, 1-3.

3. In Sanskrit it means "Secondary element" an attribute of the "five elements". These six guṇas are those of sight—cakṣu, sound—karṇa, smell—nāsikā, taste—jihvā, touch—tvak, thought—manas.

4. Thought, Manas. It is explained as material, worldly things.

Charity.[1] Putting all the different passions under restraint and devoting to the Commandments like pure white pearls, is known as Chieh, Śīla,[2] moral conduct. Patience as armour protecting firmly against all evils, known as 忍 ren, kṣānti,[3] Endurance. Only by observing untiringly these three (pāramitās) one can traverse the two vehicles.

By forgetting one's toil, and overcoming innumerable obstacles, ceaselessly labouring in the interest of one's pursuits—is known as 勤 Ch'in, Vīrya,[4] fortitude. When one is deeply absorbed in meditation and lost in transcendental thought it is known as 定 Ting, Samādhi,[5] Abstract meditation. The sword of wisdom that cuts away the illusion of thick fogs and frost (ignorance) is known as 慧 Hui, Prajñā[6], Wisdom. 大劫 Ta-chieh, Mahākalpa time is eternal. One may cultivate (these pāramitās). One may change one's heart by observing daily these six cardinal virtues or pāramitās, (六時 Liu-shih). Thus one will attain complete annihilation (of desire) and will repose on the bank of the river Hiraṇyavatī 金河 Chin-he,[7] eternally."

They chanted and expounded Sūtras temporarily in the Kukkuṭa grove for achieving all-round merits. The sound of preaching the Tiuth by the holy disciples still revibrated (could be heard). They had entered into the dragon palace in the deep sea in search of abstruse and mystical books[8]; they had stayed in the hermitage

1, 2-3. First three of the six Pāramitās.

4. The fourth of the six Pāramitās.

5. The fifth Pāramitā. Abstract meditation which ultimately leads to Nirvāṇa.

6. The sixh Pāramitā-Prajñā or Wisdom. It is the only way which helps men to reach the shore of Nirvāṇa.

7. The Parinirvāṇa of the Buddha took place in the suburb of Kuśinagara or Kusināra (District Deoria, Uttar Pradesh) on the bank of ancient Hiraṇyavatī (modern Gandak).

8. Nāgārjuna, the founder of the *Mādhyamika* philosophy and one of the mystics of later Buddhism, is said to have gone deep into the sea to collect literatures. I-ching is perhaps referring to this story.

in the hills for the Truth. Due to propagation of the Law, generation after generation, Buddhism is still in existence.

The pathway of desert, river and snowy mountains is indistinct even in the early morning. The vast beach of limitless ocean is greatly disturbed even at night. To save one life, one has to sacrifice thousands of lives.

The great knowledge or the lamp of Truth had been transmitted from the teacher to the disciples from generation to generation. Though the long journey was perilous and hazardous but great panorama would enchant the travellers who encountered such great difficulties.

The two vintages of the Nü-luan mountain were still visible in the east. The three turns of the Wheel of Law 三輪 San-lun[1] (which the Buddha turned) in the Deer Park in the west, still flashed (in his eyes). The lake[2] of the city of Śrāvastī[3] was still there and could be seen in the north. He greeted the sacred mountains with caves and five elegant peaks[4] and hundred

1. The three wheels supposed to be the deeds of the Buddha or his body, mouth or discussions, mind or ideas. The first rolling onwards of the Wheel of the Law.

2. A tope was built on the spot where five hundred Śākya maidens were insulted and mutilated by the King Virudhaka, the son of Prasenjit of Kośala. Later on, those maidens were purified and enlightened by the Buddha. Very close to the tope at Śrāvastī, there was a large dried pond where Virudhaka caught fire and died while he was enjoying the boat riding with the ladies of the harem. I-ching is probably referring to this event of Śrāvastī.

3. Śrāvastī, situated on the bank of the Acirāvatī (modern Rāpti) the capital of the kingdom of Kośala (Oudh) was one of the most favourite resorts of the Buddha. The Aṅguttara Nikāya gives the names of the places at which the Buddha with his followers put up or took his retreat diuring the three months of Vassa. The great establishment of Jetavana-vihāra was gifted to the Buddha by the well known merchant Sudatta-Anāthapiṇḍika of Śrāvastī. The Buddha passed maximum numbers of Vassa at Jetavana and delivered most of his sermons here.

Śrāvastī has been identified with the modern villages of Saheth-Maheth (Lat 27° 30'N, Long. 82° 2'E), in Districts of Gonda and Bahraich, Uttar Pradesh.

See T. W. Rhys Davids. *JRAS* 1891, p. 339.

4. The five sacred mountains associated with the life of the Buddha: (1) Vaibhāra, (2) Saptaparṇi, (3) Indraśaila, (4) Gṛdhrakūṭa, (5) Sarpa-Saundika-Prāgbhāra.

tanks around the city. The brilliant fresh flowers brightened every corner. The Bodhi Tree looked glorious with the advent of spring.

With a mendicant-stick, he proceeded towards the mountain and walked slowly in the Jetavana. He visited the place where the Buddha discarded his robes and also the mountain delivered by heaven.

I-ching offered big golden flowers to the shrines of the Buddha. While he was circumambulating the Buddha's altar and was watching these old shrines he felt as if he was very near to the Buddha.

The city of Rājagṛha in India still carried in its bosom the reminiscences of the past activities.

"I am far away from my motherland; pang of separation makes me very much grieved. I always remember my home when the cold wind blows on the Vulture's Peak and the Nairañjanā river flows by. I listen to the discussion of the Law happily. I never feel that I am growing older day by day. My aims and objectives in India have been fulfilled. Now I must return to the Divine Land (China) carrying the stick and the Sūtras."

法振禪師者 Dhyāna-master Fa-chen Dharmavikampana came from Ching-chou. In personal appearance he was a tall, handsome man with elegant manners and was kind in expression. He washed his feet in the waves of meditation, remained unperturbed and purified himself in the water of ocean (Dhyāna). To be respectful and dignified was his guiding principle. He was a constant follower of Dharma. He recited the rules and precepts of the Vinaya and the Sūtras. Sometimes he lived on the hills or at the bank of rivers.

He had insatiable desire to visit the Western regions without delay and to pay devotional homage to the sacred shrines. He, therefore, with the Dhyāna-master Ch'en-wu and Dhyānajāgratāyana, another monk of his own native place, Ch'en-ju, the Vinayamaster of Liang-chou studied throughly the sacred books, of his own country and of outside countries too.

He was not the only one who possessed merits but in his travel, he was accompanied by friends with common ideas and objectives and merits like him. The monk, therefore, left San-chiang with two friends, embarked on a ship and arrived at Sheng-ching and from there they resumed their voyage to reach the north of K'e-ling. After travelling over many places and crossing many islands they reached Kedah.

After a short while, the monk Ch'en fell sick and passed away at the age of thirty-five or thirty-six. Some days after, a man met those two monks; they set sail together and returned to the east. They hoped to go to Chiao-chih. They reached 瞻波 Chan-p'o, Champā This country is known as Lin-yi (Chinese name of Champā), where the monk Ch'en-wu died.

It was told by the people of Champā then that the monk Ch'en-ju alone went back to his own country. He was greatly esteemed and admired by everyone though he failed to fulfil his objectives.

These three monks went out of their country, but why none of them succeeded (in reaching India)?

大律法師者 [1]The Great Vinaya and Law master belonged to Li-chou, entered into an ecclesiastical life at an early age and grew simple, austere, honest and frugal. He had very few wants; therefore he lived on begging alms and performing the duties (of a monk). He hoped to pay offerings to the sacred shrines of the Lord and a visit to the sacred city of Rājagṛha.

Everytime he said in despair "I would not be able to see Śākyamuni, the father of Mercy (Karuṇāmaya). The idea of Maitreya, of 天宫 T'ien-kung, Devaloka (Tuṣita heaven)[2] inspires my heart. I could neither see the Bodhi Tree nor could I watch the glorious flow of the 祥河 Hsien-he, Lucky river. How

1. In the Sung edition and in the Imperial Record, it is 律 Lü and not 津 and in the Sung, Ming and the Yüan Dynasties editions it is 法師 Fa-shih and not shih only.

2. Maitreya's Paradise, the fourth Devaloka where all the Bodhisattvas were to be born before they finally appeared on the earth as Buddha.

can I gather together all the emotions arising from the six organs of senses and practise to attain (six pāramitās) in three Asaṅkhyeya,[1] San-chih 三祇者 without visiting those places".

Thereupon, in the second year of 永淳 Yung-shun (Ch'un)[2] period, taking a monk's staff, he voyaged in the South Sea with many companions in the beginning, but later on, they decided not to proceed further. He was, therefore, left alone. He followed the Chinese envoy with the Buddhist Sūtras and images. They embarked on a ship and reached Śrī-vijaya Island after more than a month's voyage, and remained there for a couple of years. He could not understand the language spoken by the people of K'un-lun. He studied Sanskrit books there.

He led a very pure and simple life and with one heart and mind received the whole of the Commandments, Yüanchu. I-ching met the monk here only. The monk wanted to return to China with the hope of requesting the Emperor to build a monastery in the West that would serve the great purpose of human welfare. So he udertook the perilous sea-voyage.

Thereupon, on the fifteenth day of the second month of the third year of 天授 T'ien-shou era[3], he set sail for Ch'ang-an. He took with him ten chüan of miscellaneous Buddhist Sūtras and Śāstras newly translated, four chüan of 南海寄歸内法傳 Nan-hai-chi-kuei-nei-fa-chüan (*Record of the inner law or religion sent from the South Sea country through one who returns*) and two chüan of *Hsi-yü-chiu-fa-kao-sheng-chuan* (Memoirs of eminent monks who visited Western region or India and its neighbouring countries in search of Law).

1. In every Mahā Kalpa there are three Kalpas: (1) Period of destruction (Pralaya), (2) Period of formation (Sthiti), (3) Period of reproduction (Sṛṣṭi). In order to become Buddha, every Bodhisattva attains six Pāramitās in three Asaṅkheya and 100 Kalpas to attain 32 signs.

2. This era was started by the third Emperor Kao-Tsung of T'ang Dynasty in A.D. 682.

3. The Dowager Empress Wu of the T'ang Dynasty usurped the throne for twenty years. She changed the Dynastic title and adopted the title Chou in A.D. 690. In order to commemorate this event, she began a new era in the same year.

Eulogising, it is said "since childhood you have insatiable longing for Dharma and very firm determination. You had already travelled all over China in search of the Truth and went to Western Land (India) as well to collect more information (about Buddhism). Later on, you went back to the Divine Land to propagate the vastness and extensiveness of 十法 Shih-fa, Daśadharma[1] for the welfare of the living souls. Thousands of autumns had passed away but you have not grown old."

The four more monks qualified to be included in the Record of the South Sea (Record of the Buddhist religion as practised in that region).

Pi-ch'u-chen-ku Lü-shih. The Vinaya-master Bhikṣu Chen-ku was known as 娑羅笈多 Sa-luo-chi-tuo, Śālacitta in Sanskrit. The translation of it in Chinese is Chen-ku, firm and erect. He belonged to 滎川 Jung-ch'uan in Cheng.[2] His family name was 孟 Meng. From his childhood he grew kind and compassionate and directed his attention towards Hui-yuan.[3] At the age of fourteen he lost his father.

He realised the unreality of life and that the Law of the Buddha alone is real.

Thereupon, self-possessed and mindful, he desired to pay a visit to the sacred places. With this aim in view he went to the monastery of 等慈寺 Teng-t'ze-Ssu[4]—the monastery of

1. The powers of the Buddha bestowing correct knowledge. The Power of (1) understanding between right and wrong, (2) of knowing what is the Karma of every being, (3) different stages of Dhyāna liberation, (4) the power of giving moral direction to living beings, (5) of knowing actual conditions of all beings, (6) of giving direction and resultant consequences of all laws, (7) of knowing all causes of mortality, (8) powers and faculties of all beings, (9) end of all beings, and (10) destruction of all illusions.

See—W. E. Soothhill—*A Dictionary of Chinese Buddhist Terms.*, p. 46 (b). 51a.

2. A feudal state under the Chou Dynasty. Modern K'aifeng in Honan (Lat. 34° 46'N, Long. 113° 56'E).

3. A celebrated monk of the T'ang period (A.D. 618-907), lexicographer, compiled a dictionary of sounds and meanings of the Buddhavataṁsaka Sūtra *NC* No. 1606.

4. This temple was constructed during the Chen-Kuan period (A.D. 627-650) of the T'ang Emperor T'ai-Tsung in Cha'ng-an.

Universal Compassion where the monk Yüan was living at Fan-shui[1] 汜水 He extended his services to the abbot of the monastery. The religious fervour in him was greatly heightened and thus he achieved the ability to recite the great Buddhist Sūtras. Unfortunately, his preceptor passed away after three years.

Later on, he visited the 林慮 Lin-lü and other monasteries in 相州 Hsiang-chou[2] to seek a teacher for religious guidance. He wished to unveil the mystery of meditation. He could realise that his comprehension of the Law was not enough. His power of discrimination between real and unreal was very much limited.

He again proceeded towards the Kingdom of 東魏 (the Eastern Wei rulers) Tung Wei[3] to hear (the discourses) and study the text 唯識 *Wei-shih, Vijñaptimātratā*.[4] Next going to 安州

1. According to Han Dynasty record Fan-shui was the name of a river in Ho-nan . During the Sui Dynasty this was the name of a place in Ho-nan. Modern name of the place is K'ai-feng in Ho-nan.

2. Hsiang-chou is modern Chang-te (Lat 36° 07'N, Long. 114° 30'E) in Ho-pei province. During the Wei Dynasty, it was known as Hsiang-chou.

3. The Eastern Wei Dynasty ruled only for sixteen years from A.D. 534 to 550. Their capital was at Yeh in Ho-nan province.

4. Asaṅga, the elder brother of Vasubandhu, was responsible for converting Vasubandhu from Hīnayāna to Mahāyāna. These two brothers initiated and formulated the doctrines of the Idealistic school in India. The scholars differ about their dates; some assign them to the fourth century, others to the fifth. After his conversion to the new faith, Vasubandhu made a supreme contribution to the Vijñānavāda by writing the monumental work *Vijñapti-mātratā-Siddhi*. He propounded his philosophy of Vijñānavāda in two classical treatises *Viṁśatikā* and *Triṁśatikā* in twenty and thirty verses respectively. His philosophy repudiates all belief in the reality of the material objective world supporting that the Citta (Vijñāna) of Cittamātra (Vijñānamātra) is the only reality.

Paramārtha or Chen-ti, a native of India, first introduced the idealistic teachings of the Indian masters Asaṅga and Vasubandhu to the Chinese Buddhist world by translating the Sūtras belonging to the *Vijñāñavādin* school. During the T'ang period, the *Salakṣaṇa*, Fa-hsiang or the Idealistic school was developed by Hsüan-chuang and K'uei-chi. Hsüan-chuang translated the *Vijñāpti-mātratā-Siddhi* with all the Indian commentaries into Chinese. Later on, he summarised all these into one work, with Dharmapāla's commentary, *Vijñapti-mātratā-Siddhi-Śāstra*.

See Winternitz, *HIL* Vol. 2, p. 360, f.n.4.

An-chou[1] he studied 方等 Fang-teng[2] under the Great Dhyāna-master Yu.

Some days had passed by, a wonderful form suddenly appeared before him. Again he left for Ching-chou, passed through many mountains and rivers still seeking for perfect knowledge. He wanted to know what was not known before.

Next, reaching Hsiang-chou, he met the Dhyāna-master Shen-tao and received from him the knowledge of victorious deeds of Amitābha. Then he left this impure and corrupt world and desired to take shelter in heaven, the abode of eternal tranquillity and virtue. He always thought of receiving the same pain and agony as was felt by the 大士 Ta-shih, Mahāsattvas. Why does not Vijñaptimātratā change into Pure Land, Ching-fang ?

Next he proceeded towards the monastery of Great Enlightenment, the place of Dhyāna-master Pradipa, where he received instructions from his superior. Even at the teacher's utterance of half a word, he could grasp the whole meaning. He made an exclusive study of canonical rules with the Dhyāna-master. He carried on the important responsibility of (preaching) 五德 Wu-te[3] of 世尊 Shih-tsun, the Five Virtues of Lokeśvararāja,[4] the World-honoured One. He deeply studied various Sūtras and Śāstras. At that time he was a strong upholder of 四依 Szu-i Caturśaraṇa.[5] He was anointed with

1. An-chou Fu in P'ing-an.

2. The Vaipulya Sūtras or the Sūtras of 'infinite meaning' are the Mahājāna Sūtras, supposed to be preached by the Buddha before he first moved the Wheel of Law. Among the Mahāyāna Sūtras, the nine Sūtras are of great merit and regarded as the most important of all texts. These are the *Aṣṭasāhasrikā-prajñāpāramitā*, the *Saddharma-puṇḍarīka Sutra*, the *Lalitavistara*; the *Laṅkāvatāra*, the *Suvarṇaprabhāsa*, the *Gaṇḍvyūha*, the *Tathāgata-guhyaka*, the *Samādhirāja* and the *Daśabhūmiśvara*. These are called the 'Vaipulya Sūtra'.

3. At the end of three month's rainy retreat, every monk had to confess or had to acquire five virtues at the Pravāraṇā ceremony. These are : "Freedom from predilection, from anger, from fear, not to be easily deceived, discernment of shirkers of confession".

See N. Dutt. *Early Monastic Buddhism*, Vol. I, p. 293.

4. 'The Lord of the World', 'World-honoured One', which has been the epithet of every Buddha.

5 The four requisites (Catupaccayā) of Bhikṣu. They are usually given

the principle of 八解 Pa-chieh, eight stages of mental concentration, aṣṭa vimokṣa[1] that greatly influenced the different sects. His prodigious wisdom and profound knowledge of 六度 Liu-tu, six Pāramitās, was high like the crest of a mountain. He was not confused with five earthly dirts (that taint the true nature) 五塵 Wu-ch'en.[2] He was undisturbed by nine distresses 九惱 Chiu-nao[3] and excelled outwardly in the four currents 四流 Szu-liu[4] and inside he lit the knowledge of 三定 Santing.[5]

He was greatly respected by monks and laity both equally and was regarded as the Chief of the Sect. He was specially invited and permitted to enter the divine capital. He spent many years in the Pūrvārāma 東寺 Tung-Ssu[6] under the Dynastic rule of the Wei. The monk Ku was a little more than twenty years old. There sitting at the feet of Dhyāna-master, he acquired brilliant scholarship in complete Commandments 圓具 Yüan-chü.

---

in the Pāli texts as Civara, Piṇḍapāta, Senāsana, and gilan-paccaya-bheṣajja (*Majjhim-Nikāya*. I. 33). But in the *Dīgha Nikāya* 11, 35, ghasacchadana for the first two.

1. Liberation or Release in eight forms. "The term vimokṣa is explained in the *Abhidharma-Kośa-Vyākhyā* as that which removes the veil covering the higher meditation. Its another meaning is that it makes the adepts turn their face from the phenomenal world."

N. Dutt. *The Early Monastic Buddhism*, pp. 268-69. For the eight stages of mental concentration see *Abhidharma-Kośa Vyākhyā* (Japanese Edition), pp. 666-669.

2. The objects of five senses are rūpa, rasa, gandha, śabda and sparśa which being worldly or dirty things, can taint the true nature.

3. The nine distresses vide 智度論Chih-tu-lun. Commentary on the *Prajñā-Paramita-Sūtrā*.

4. (i) Illusion due to imperfect perception, (ii) desire, (iii) existence, (iv) ignorance.

5. Three forms of Samādhi; (i) K'ung 空 mind made empty of 'me', (ii) Complete removal of the idea of form 無色 Wu-se, (iii) free dom from all desire 無願 Wū-yüan.

6. The monastery of Eastern grove was built by the authorities at the request of a Buddhist monk Hui-yung at Lu mountain. The name was Pūrva-vihāra. There was a similar notable monastery, Pūrvārāma to the north-east of Jetavana-Vihāra in India. It was so called because of its situation on the east of the city of Śrāvastī.

Then he took only one year in learning the general outlines concerning the laws of the Vinayas.

Again he advanced towards 安州 An-chou, spent three-years with the Vinaya-master 秀 Hsiu studying mindfully written explanations by the Vinaya-master 宣 Hsüan. Not a single question remained unanswered by him; he excelled even 鄔波離 U-po-li, Upāli.[1] He had gone through the five Pi'en.[2] He also received lessons from a Bhikṣuṇī, nun 毘舍女 Pi-su-ni. He had perfect comprehension of all that is abstruse in 聚 Ch'i-chü.[3]

According to the rules of Vinaya, he became a Parivrājaka, recluse, at the age of five; he was ordained before he attained maturity. Ten years had already passed when he left his own hearth and home. He achieved his goal, before he was twenty years old.

The Vinaya-master Hsiu was the best disciple of the Vinaya-master 興 Hsing (Abhyudaya) of 蜀郡 Shu-chün.[4] At the age of twenty he was fully ordained and continued his stay at Sze-ch'uan. There the monk Hsiu studied the Vinaya for four years from a monk teacher. Next he went to Ch'ang-an where he became a guest of the monk Hsüan and settled there.

The monk like a domestic goose drinking only the essence

1. Upāli, one of the most eminent disciples of the Buddha, belonged to a barber's family. Being ordained by the Buddha, he became a monk and desired to meditate in the forest. But at the advice of the Lord, he stayed among men and got his lessons on Vinaya directly from the Buddha. He regarded Upāli as one of the most renowned Vinayādharas. In the first council of Rājagṛha, he recited the whole Vinaya and decided all the questions regarding the Vinaya. It was a great privilege to learn Vinaya from Upāli, even when the Buddha himself was living.

See Upāli Vagga, *Aṅguttara-Nikāya.*

2. (i) Pārājika, (ii) Saṅghavaśeṣa, (iii) Prāyaścitta, (iv) Pratidoṣaniya, (v) Duṣkṛta.

3. The five above and two more (i) Sthūlātvaya, (ii) action and speech, Karma and Vāc.

4. The modern province of Sze-ch'uan, the capital Ch'an-tu was known as Shū-chün in ancient time.

from a vessel of milk mixed with water,[1] collected the essence of Perfect Knowledge for the happiness of the Paradise (Sukhāvatī), the isles of Blessedness. In sixteen years, he never left the teacher.

He studied thoroughly the discipline of numerous schools of thoughts. The Commentary of the Dhyāna-master was carefully preserved as a fundamental text of the sect. Then he went to San-yang in Pa-shui, and from there again proceeded to Kuang-chou, his birthplace, to report the achievement he had made. Then he moved to An-chou where he propagated the great and magnificent teachings of the Vinaya. The princes with all the grandeur welcomed him with honour and respect. The ancient Vinaya says that though there are different schools, yet the rules of Vinaya are followed uniformly by each one of them; there is no difference.

He lived in the Daśabala monastery 十力寺 Shih-li Ssu. He went to the abode of peace at the age of little more than seventy.

He was very simple and pure by nature. His eyes and ears were always alert to bring every matter to the notice of a superior. Oh ! what a gigantic pillar he was in the realm of the Buddha during that period ! He would be regarded as the greatest man by the posterity.

It is truly said that the pearls from the river[2] 漢 Han and jade of 荆 [3]Ching are from different places but both are attractive and fascinating. The twigs of cassia and the leaves of orchid have the same fragrance though they grow in different seasons.

1. This idea might have been taken from the famous Sanskrit Śloka of *Pancatantra Kathāmukhm*'.

Anantapāraṃ kila Śabdaśāstraṃ /
Svalpaṃ tathāyurbahavaśca vighnāḥ //
Sāraṃ tato grāhyamapāsya phalgu /
Haṃsairyathā kṣiramivāmbumadhyāt //

2. The south-eastern sea board between Yang-tze and Pearl rivers has many shorter rivers; the river Han is one of them flowing directly to the sea.

3. It comprised the province of Hu-nan, most of Hu-pei and part of Kuei-chou.

The monk Ku obtained the Vinaya texts and thoroughly studied them. With more efforts he studied the Sūtras and Śāstras. Moreover, he recited thousand times the *Saddharma-puṇḍarika Sūtra* (Lotus Sūtra), *Fa-hua-ching* and *Vimalakīrtinirdeśa-Sūtra, Wei-mo-ching.*[1] He regularly attended the prayer with sincere devotion and always remembered (the canonical rules). Though the monk Ku believed in 三業 San-yeh, Trividha-dvāra (karma) still he had equal interest in observing the four ceremonies Szu-i.[2]

Next, he went to Hsiang-chou and stayed there with a monk. Here he seriously listened to the discourses on 蘇呾羅 Su-tan-luo, the Sūtras (sermons of the Buddha) and searched for the mystery Tui-fa-ts'ang, *Abhidharmapiṭaka.* He understood fully the deepest thought of *Abhidharma* and followed a very temperate and frugal life.

Resting in the magic city[3] 化城 Hua-ch'ang (illusion) finally one reaches Ratnadvīpa[4] 寶渚 Pao-chu i.e. after

1. *Vimala Kīrti-Nirdeśa-Sūtra* is one of the outstanding work of Buddhist literature. It was extremely popular Mahāyāna Sūtra among the Chinese gentry. During the epoch of the Three Kingdoms, Chih-chien translated this Sūtra. Later on, during the period of the Chin (A.D. 265-317) Dharmarakṣa and the Indian Upāsaka Chu-shu-lan undertook the translation of the same Sūtra before Kumārajīva went to Ch'ang-an. The original name of this Upāsaka is not known. Dr. P. C. Bagchi has rendered this name as Śuklaratna and Matsumoto, Saṅgharakṣa (Zürcher, *BCC.* IIA, pp. p. 346.)

Vimalakīrti was a great devotee of the Buddha, a man of profound wisdom and of enormous wealth. Vimalakīrti, a famous householder of Vaiśāli, discussed the 'Gate of Unique Law' sitting side by side with Manjuśri. This scene has been depicted on the Lung-men caves many a time. The best translation of the Sūtra was done by Kumārajīva and its commentary was written by Seng-chao. 魏書釋老志 Wei-shu-shih-lao-chih).

Saddharma puṇḍarīka Sūtra was a favourite scripture of the large masses of the Buddhist society during the period of the six Dynasties but *Vimalakīrti-Nirdeśa-Sūtra* was much more popular with the Chinese intellectuals and gentry classes.

2. The four rituals or ceremonies taught by the Master Confucius: (i) Literature, (ii) Personal Conduct, (iii) Being one's true self, (iv) Honesty in social relationship.

3. Magic city in the *Saddharmapuṇḍarīka Sūtra.*

4. Illusory island in the same Sūtra.

resting in imperfect Nirvāṇa finally one achieves the goal of perfect Nirvāṇa.

Crossing the river Hsiang-shui[1], the monk Ku advanced towards Lu-shan[2] 盧山 He admired the noble principle of the Lord that relieved the world.

He lived in the Tung-lin monastery where he propagated his ideas.

He had a passionate desire to pay a visit to Ceylon to have a glimpse of the Buddha's Tooth and other sacred places. In the 垂拱 Ch'ui-kung period,[3] he went to Kei-lin with mendicant-stick and followed the principles of the Buddha wherever he travelled. He gradually arrived at a distant mountain valley where he was graced with the blessings of the Lord to continue his journey. Next he reached and stayed at P'an-yü in Canton. The Buddhist disciples living there requested him to teach the Vinaya treatises. That was the glorious age when three Upādhyāyas (Buddhist officers)[4] were appointed by the great pious

1. The Upper reaches of the stream are known as T'ai-pai river. The river Hsiang-shui is to the south-east of Pao-chi in Shen-Si.

2. The mount Lu is situated to the south-west of the district Hsing-tze in Chiang-si (Kiang-si) and to the south of Chiu-chiang, a port on the Yangtze. The mount Lu is famous for its natural beauty, and it was a very popular centre for tne Buddhist learning. A monastery was built on the eastern slopes of the mountain called the Tung-lin-Ssu (Monastery of Eastern grove). It was finished in A.D. 386. Saṅghadeva, a Kashmirian mor k who translated the *Sarvāstivādin literature* into Chinese, lived in Lu-shan.

See *TCTI. Lu-shan-chi*, Vol. 51, p. 1024, No. 2095.

3. This era was started in A.D. 685 by the Empress Wu of the T'ang Dynasty.

4. These officers seem to be like the Dharmamahāmātras, a class of officials, created by the King Aśoka. The mention of Dharmamahāmātras is found in the Rock Edict V. The activities of these officials were manyfold. The main idea of Aśoka was to promote the moral welfare of his subjects. So he appointed Dharmamahāmātras to spread Dharma, to bestow grants, and to look after the welfare of the different contemporary sects like Buddhists, Jains, Ājivikas and others. The activities of the Buddhist officials appointed by the Ta'ng ruler were mainly to promote Buddhism, to propagate moral law and justice in the country.

T'ang ruler, with the hope to kindle again the Buddha-Sun that removes the darkness of ignorance. The Buddha-truth, like a barque, ferries men out from the sea of mortality to Nirvāṇa. In the end, this imposing and dignified monk became a symbol of Vinaya. So Ku commanded respect and was very much sought after.

He discussed and expounded the teachings of 毘柰耶 P'i-nai-yeh, Vinaya, at Tripiṭaka Bodhimaṇḍa 三藏道場 San-ts'ang-tao-ch'ang for nine years and completed seven P'ien, chapters (Pārājika, Saṅghavaśeṣa, Prāyaṣcitta, Pratidoṣaṇīya, duṣkṛta—Karma and Vāk—action and speech). He not only excellently taught the Buddhist disciples but also properly guided the laity.

The Ācārya (Preceptor) 闍梨 Tu-li of the 制旨 Chih-chih monastery was greatly respected by everyone of that period. Sitting on the platform, every time he encouraged his diseiples with his excellent method of teaching and with untiring zeal and sincerity.

The Ācārya with a lofty and high moral character, left home at an early age. Even at the age of seventy, he observed respectfully the rules of Wu-p'ien. Only the blessed one can attain the highest wisdom.

The able guidance of the Ācārya helped him in crossing the waves of Dhyāna pond and led him to reach the deep ocean of the Law to attain Nirvāṇa. After surmounting the rocky height of "thought range" one can reach the lofty peak of the highest prajñā. He perfectly realised the illusory nature of the world and was aware of the fact that mind is the fundamental source of all things. Though everything in the universe is unreal, the deeds of beings produce results. He played the supreme role of a bridge across the stream (of life). His continuous writing on the Sūtras piṭaka served the purpose of providing mental nourishment to all. In fact, his exposition on enlightening knowledge, had great influence on mankind. He advised conscientious people to combine the highly esteemed Vinaya with Teachings.

Taking leave of his disciples, the monk Ku retired to mountain valley. He desired to dwell as a recluse under the pine trees and to cultivate meditation, the object of his heart's desire. The abbot of the 蒙謙 Meng-ch'ien temple specially went to meet the head of the 賓迎 P'in-yang monastery and told him that the young monk Ku was an embodiment of the highest truth, knowledge, compassion and forgiveness. Day and night he selflessly served the people and respected their view-points.

The monk Ku wished to enter into a life of rest and meditation in a monastery. He cherished the desire to build a barrack (for the monks) with a long corridor having direct connections with roads and steps and to reconstruct the foundation (of the building) and to dig a pond round the monastery. His sole aim was to propagate the purity and richness of Aṣṭavimokṣa, eightfold path of liberation. At that time, he constructed a platform where he hoped to explain to the people the essence of Ch'i-chu, Seven precepts. He also wanted to erect a mausoleum for the ashes of Buddhist priests[1] and behind it a Mahāyāna Bodhimaṇḍa at the back of the altar 戒壇 Chieh-t'an to cultivate and practise the purity and richness of Samādhi 法華三昧 Fa-hua-san-wei.[2] Though he had firm determination to carry out his plan, yet at the end he never succeeded in his pursuit. He continued to observe the reles and ceremonies of 布薩 Pu-sa, Upavasatha[3] and had already made the general sketch (of the

1. A cemetery where a generation of monks had left their ashes can be seen down below the Kṛṣṇagiri or Kanheri caves in Western India, about twenty five miles from Bombay.

2. *Saddharmapuṇḍarīka Sūtra* has mentioned the names of sixteen Samādhis such as Dhvajāgra Keyūra, Saddharma puṇḍarīka, Nakṣatrarāja vikṛdita etc. See H. Kern. *The Lotus of the True Law* (Translation), Ch. 23, p. 393.

3. The Buddhist rite of Upavasatha or Uposatha is marked with the citation of the Pātimokkha on every full-moon and new-moon day. In observing these sacred days the Buddhist monks should make self-examination and confessions. They keep fasting on these days. Hence these days are called Upavasatha. It is not an innovation started by the Buddhists. Fasting on the full-

building). Though he stayed with many preceptors, he was not sure whether to advance or retire.

I-ching went to the ship at the mouth of the river Bhoga to send letters as a credential to Kuang-chou through people requesting them to meet his friends and ask them who embarked on a ship and to keep ready the papers, ink cakes etc. for copying Sanskrit Sūtras and at the same time to find some means to hire scribes. The merchants at that time sailed in favourable wind and raised their sail to the utmost height. Thus he (I-Ching) was carried back; even if he asked to stop, there would have been no way. He realised from this that influence of Karma which determines the fate is beyond human planning.

Next, on the twentieth day of the seventh month of the Yung-ch'ang period (A.D. 689) they arrived at Kuang-fu. The monks and laity as well, met and received him with respect. He sighed and said to the resident monks of the 制旨 Chih-chih (The Edict)monastery that he (I-ching) went to the Western country with a primary hope of transmitting and spreading (the Law). On his way back he remained in the island of the South Sea. He took along with him (from India) texts containing more than 500,000 ślokas of the Tripiṭaka. It was absolutely nescessary that he must go there onee again But he was more than fifty years old; while crossing the running waves once more, the horses that pass through cracks[1] may not stay and to protect the life would be difficult.

If the time for the morning dew comes suddenly, to whom should these books be entrusted ? The sacred canon is considered to be the important doctrine; who would accompany him to collect these ? The right type of person who could easily translate the Sūtras must be found out. The assembly unani-

---

moon and new-moon days was observed in India even in earliest time. (*Śatapatha Brāhmaṇa* 111. The Darśapūrṇamāsa, Sacred Books of the East, Vol. XII, Part I.).

The Upavasatha-day ceremony in China differs from what it is in India,

1. 光陰如箭馬如过隙 See Takakusu *ARBPSHSS* p. xxxv f.n.

mously told him that a monk named Chen-ku, living not very far from that place, had studied the Vinaya from early age with absolute sincerity and perfection. If he was available he would be the best for him (I-ching). After hearing this, he said that Chen-ku would be the right type of man whom he was looking or since long.

Then, he sent a letter requesting Chen-ku to accompany him on his voyage roughly informing him about their preparation. Chen-ku also opened the letter and agreed to his proposal. He took leave of the quiet forest of Pines and stream (the solitary abode of the monk) with joy. In front of the hill of the Stone gate (north-west of Kuang-tung) he tucked up his sleeves, raised his skirt and entered the Chih-chih (The Edict) temple. They began to like each other and shared their feeling to remove the worldly dust. They sacrificed their five limbs (for the cause of religion). They concluded in friendship as if from ages they were friends. Though they did not meet each other before, still they were cherishing common aspiration and common desire. In the pleasant night they discussed various matters relevant to their future plan.

The monk Chen-ku said, "when virtue wishes men to meet they unite without any introduction. We are naturally united. Time has come when no one can stop it even if they want. May I then earnestly propose to propagate and spread the teachings of the Tripiṭaka together and thus help you to lit thousand lamps."

When they proceeded towards the mountain Hsia (near Kuang-tung) to bid farewell to the abbot Ch'ien and other residents of the temple, Ch'ien, the head of the temple, decided to perform every rite and acted accordingly. He never intended to keep them any longer with him; on the contrary, after knowing their aims and objectives, he extended his help and shared their happiness and joy. He was never worried for what he might be wanting for himself. He was sincerely giving assistance to others. Moreover, he lavishly provided them with money and other necessaries so that they would not be short of anything in their journey.

The priests and the lay followers of Kuang-fu gave them enough money and food. Then on the first day of the eleventh month of the same year (A.D. 689) they sailed by a merchant ship for Fan-yü.[1] From there they advanced towards Champā aiming to reach Śrī-vijaya after a long voyage so that they would become the ladders for every sentient being, or like a boat they would help them to cross the vast ocean of passion. It was a real joy for them that their long cherished resolution was going to be fulfilled. They hoped not to fall in the course of their long journey. The monk Chen-ku was then forty years old.

It is said that a wise man performs deeds due to his Karma of previous birth. At young age, he purified his thoughts and strived only for blessedness. To receive knowledge and kindness he was passionately searching for a renowned, superior and real preceptor. He was unconcerned about his own affairs and material gain. The monk Ku had only thirst for virtuous men and priceless things like Truth. He received and grasped the knowledge of the classics of the wonderful Dharma 妙典 Ch'ao-tien[2] and understood unchangeable reality and its true meanings hidden behind all phenomena. He was extremely virtuous and honest at heart, unblemished in character, prsosperous and fearless. Being indifferent to worldly glory and position, he longed to discard (this body) like old shoe. If he had to live in great difficulties he would not grudge for it. And he travelled all over like a busy bee in search of 色 Se[3] and 香 Hsiang[4], Rūpa and Gandha.

Giving up the comforts of life, he proceeded alone in search of Chinese cultural heritage. The philosopher Ku devoted his

1. It was a prefecture (district) on the South-Sea in Kuang-Chou (Canton).

2. Sūtras of the Mahāyāna School.

3. One of the five skandhas and one of the six Bāhya-āyatanas.

4. One of the Sadāyatana, six senses.

attention to voluminous literature to seek the knowledge of the Vinaya and thus he could succeed in discovering the principles of the network (of the Vinaya). Further, he made much progress in deep mysticism.

His long cherished desire was to extend his felicitations to the distant Wisdom Tree. Thereupon, with a staff of chenopodium he reached the Kuei-lin monastery. He was delighted in climbing the valley and it was a great joy for him to know the things of the world. Finally he followed the traditions of China. The monk Ku was again pleased to know the new religion that spread speedily in the South. He hoped to preach and spread the religion which was not done before. Congratulation for such strong determination. He could sacrifice his own self for the cause of others.

The monk became a good companion of I-ching and both of them reached 金州 Chin-chou.[1] They had the determination for noble action 梵行 Fan-hsing (which ensures a place in Brahmaloka). On this basis, they became very good friends. Like a brother he helped I-ching throughout their journey, either by sea or by l and.

When the aim and hope of lighting the lamp of preaching (Buddha's teaching) would be fulfilled in his long life, then alone he would be free from mortification. After reaching Śrī-vijaya he could feel that he had achieved the object of his long cherished desire. He listened to the discourses on religion which he had never heard before and watched those practices and customs which he had never seen before.

He translated many texts, at the same time he acquired much knowledge. He examined the customs and practices with great care and overcame the stalemate.

He saw new things, gathered new experiences and a new vista of law and culture opened before him. He had extensive knowledge and vast wisdom. Every time he encouraged himself to carry out the noble cause. Being respectful, frugal, laborious

1. Suvarnadvīpa.

and affectionate, he was never overshadowed with horror of death.[1] He was afraid that "Too many cooks spoil the broth". Moreover, a solitary man can relieve the suffering and distress peacefully. A flame of fire in favourable wind may cover thousands of lamps and put them into obscurity ![2]

The monk Chen-ku had one disciple whose family name was 孟 Meng and first name 懷業 Hsüan-yeh. He was known as 僧伽提婆 Seng-chia-t'i-p'o, Saṅghadeva. Though his grandfather originally belonged to the north, he had to live in the south as an Imperial officer; so his family also temporarily shifted to Kuang-fu. As a great patron of the Faith, he received religious instructions from the preceptor. Though he was tender in age, his determination was very strong. The officer (Saṅghadeva) met the head preceptor with an earnest desire of acquiring extensive knowledge. Hsüan-yeh wished to accompany his teacher. He was predestined to study Buddhism leaving his own home and family. He sailed for Śrī-vijaya. He quite understood the local language of K'un-lun, studied thoroughly Sanskrit books and chanted beautifully *Abhidharmakośa verses* and other Buddhist hymns. He became an attendant, and later on he became an interpreter. He was seventeen years old. (In three editions it is 七十 70 years old).

苾芻道宏者 Bhikṣu Tao-hung. His Sanskrit name was Buddhadeva. In Chinese it is 佛陀提婆 Chüeh-ti'en which means divine wisdom. He belonged to 雍丘 Yung-ch'iu in 汴州 Pien-chou.[4] His family name was 靳 Chin.

1. 朝聞道夕死可矣 Morning you hear, evening you die (Lun-yü, *Confucius Analects*, tr. by James Legge Book IV, Chap. VIII, Clarendon Press, 1893).

2. It is interesting to note the same idea in the Subhāṣita. 'Ekaścandrastamo hanti, na ca tārāgaṇo' pi ca'. Only one moon can remove the darkness which countless stars cannot do.

3. During Ch'un Ch'iu period Yung-ch'iu was the capital of a feudal state of Ch'i. The ancient city of Ch'iu was in present Ho-nan.

4. Modern K'ai-feng in north Ho-nan, forming also the district city of Hsiang-fu (Lat 34° 52'N, Long 114° 33'E). In ancient time this place was known as Pien-liang, T'ang period Pien-chou.

His father was a companion of a merchant. Therefore, he travelled all over the south. He crossed the rivers of the north, south and central China and climbed five mountains[1], scattered all over the country. In the course of his wandering life, he passed through 韶部 Shao-pu[2] and next he went to Hsia-shan.[3] He saw the lonely desolated cliffs and valleys, witnessed the solitude and serenity of the fountain-heads of streams, gathered new experiences and knowledge, and put on black robes[4] discarding ordinary clothes.

At his young age, Tao-hung was carried away from place to place like duck-weed by Karma without any hindrance. He travelled many places with his father and teacher, visited Kuei-lin that aroused his imaginations. He retired to a quiet place.

His father was known by the name Dhyāna-master Ta-kan. He went to the Dhyāna-master Chi to study esoteric or mystery of soul, spent a couple of years there and acquired knowledge about essential meaning of the doctrine, in general. Next he went to Hsia-shan. Then Tao-hung along with his father left home and became a monk. He acquired some knowledge in all the branches at the age of twenty. He left for Kuang-fu and entered the Buddhist monastery. Though he was young and his expectations were not much, still his ideal of life was very high. Hearing of I-ching's arrival, he wanted to pay a visit to this wonderful monk. On his inquiry, he was told that I-ching had been living in the 制旨 Chih-chih monastery. Immediately he reported to I-ching with a feeling of reverence and conventional courtesy. He discovered that both of them had the com-

1. In India there were five sacred mountains associated with the life of the Buddha. In China they had also five mountains considered very sacred by the Buddhists. These are Ching-shan, Pei-shan, Nan-shan, at Han chou and A-yü-wang-shan, King Aśoka mountain and T'ai-pai-shan at Ningpo.

2. I have not been able to find out the word Shao-pu but if it is Shao-chou, then it is 曲江 Ch'ü-chiang in Kuang-tung.

3. Hsia-shan, modern Ch'iung-lai is on the north-west of the huge mountain fringing the Sze-ch'uan Basin. Ch'iung-lai is the most majestic and magnificent scenic spot.

4. The Buddhist monks sometimes used to wear black robes.

mon ideals. He again and again felt very much tempted to meet him. Whatever may be in fate, one must make sacrifices (for acquiring greater knowledge). He heard that acquiring knowledge is like crossing the towering waves but to him it was nothing but waves of a small pond. Gazing at a huge whale of limitless sea, it appeared to him as if it was a small fish. After some time, he went to a far off place and bade farewell to the mountain-abode. He went back to Kuang-fu with the monk Chen-ku. Thereupon, he took voyage to the South Sea and reached Suvarṇabhūmi where he determined to copy the Tripiṭaka so that he would be remembered for thousands of years (thousand autumns).

He was intelligent, modest, and gentle with profound knowledge. He worked hard on different styles of Chinese calligraphy, studied again the philosophy of Chuang-chou. The Chapter 齊物 Ch'i-wu[1] was vain and meaningless to him, equally the teachings of 指馬 Chih-ma[2] appeared to be very far-reaching. He crossed many rivers, travelled on foot in the desert. Though the merit he acquired would not illumine but finally he must be praised for his heroic plan. How to carry out this? In search of Law, he cared very little for his own life; he never cared for his own happiness but was very much eager to work for others' happiness. He did not care for his own relations but the entire world became his own kith and kin. It was a joy for him to regard everyone as his own self. How could it be possible for him not to treat a man as a man but as a dog? This was his generosity and benevolence.

Arriving at Śrī-vijaya, he devotedly studied the Vinaya Piṭaka. He not only translated the Buddhist texts but also took notes on

1. Allusion to the famous metaphor in Chuang-tze, Chapter xxiv. The name of the Chapter is Ch'i-wu-lun. 齐物論) often used in Chinese Buddhist literature to elucidate the expedient nature of the doctrine.

2. It is probably an allusion from Shih-chi (The Historical Record). Chao-kao tried to put the second son of Ch'in Shih-Huang on the throne. He made a gift of stag to the prince, invited all the courtiers and said that it was a horse. They were to prove that it was a horse and not a stag. (指鹿為馬 ' Chih-lü-wei-ma).

scriptures with the aim of propagating (Buddhism). He wished that the lusture of 'Precept' like pearl would be again brightened up and would illuminate (the name of the Buddha). He aspired to attain perfect Nirvāṇa removing the thick screen of mortality. To complete a great task one has to start with a small beginning. He would be rewarded for the unlimited good he performed for the welfare of the world. He attained an esteemed position. He was twenty years old then.

苾芻法朗 Pi-ch'iu Fa-lang. His Sanskrit name was 達摩提婆 Ta-mo-t'i-p'o, Dharmadeva. In Chinese it means God of religion 法天 Fa-t'ien. A native of 襄陽 Hsing-yang[1] in Hsiang-chou,[2] he lived in the temple of 靈集寺 Ling-chi (Spirit temple). His surname was An-shih.

In fact, he belonged to a great enlightened aristocratic family. The members of the family were traditionally holding high offices in the Imperial services. At young age he left home with the hope of entering into an ecclesiastical life. He afterwards left his home and travelled all over, deserts and mountains, to the South. Reaching Fan-yü, I-ching informed to the traveller Fa-lang of his arrival. Though his knowledge was not very comprehensive, yet in fact, he hoped to be greatly attached to him. Lang desired to have the pleasure of the company of I-ching during his sea-voyage. It was not yet a month when they arrived at Bhoga. Since he reached there, he started practising (for the cause). The monk Lang, then concentrated in the profound classics of Hetuvidyā and studied it day and night. From sunrise to sunset, he pondered over and listened to the mystical and abstruse doctrine of Abhidharma. He then added the final basket to complete his knowledge. A mountain can be made with each basket of earth but it is incomplete even without one.

He devotedly studied the Tripiṭaka. He was determined to succeed in Wu-pi'en. He never shirked manual labour. He possessed profound knowledge and wisdom. The purpose of his life

1. It is a river port on the Han-shui in Hu-pei.
2. Hu-pei Province.

was to do good to others liberally and extensively; with this aim in view he untiringly copied down (the Buddhist scriptures).

He lived on alms. Keeping his shoulder bare and dirty bare foot, he observed all the important ceremonies and rituals reverentially. Though he never succeeded in his endeavour he had been striving hard to fulfil his desire. All his companions and followers desired to be self-contented. The monk was greatly respected because he had the unique habit of doing good to others. Respectfully and sincerely he always strove for the Truth.

His great desire was to save all beings. For the sake of future generations he would bear the great light of the Compassionate Maitreya. He was only twentyfour years old.

The monk Chen-ku and four others set sail for Śrī-vijaya and landed there. He spent three years at Śrī-vijaya, gradually studied and acquired proficiency in Sanskrit and Han (Chinese) literature. Then after a while, the monk Lang left for K'o-ling. He passed the summer over there; fell sick and died.

Chen-ku and Tao-hung preferred to stay at Śrī-vijaya for the cause, they did not return to Fan-yü. Both of them stayed together; rest of the monks went back to Kuang-fu. Not only they tarried long but also they waited for their (other two monks') return. The monk Chen-ku went to the Tripiṭaka Dharmamaṇḍa and widely diffused the teachings of the Vinaya. At the end of the third year, he got ill and passed away. Tao-hung went back alone and passed the rest of his life in the South. No news was available about Tao-hung after that. Though Iching occasionally wrote to him, there was no reply from the other side.

Alas ! all the four disciples sailed together and made sincere efforts to light the torch of Dharma. Who can predict the destiny of life? One may live long, one may be left behind. I-ching was extremely sorrowful at the recollection of this. The parable of a lin[1]

1. One of the four fictitious, supernatural animals of China, a fabulous creature of good omen whose appearance at the Imperial Court was a sign of heavenly favour. Its appearance would be followed either by good government or by a birth of a pious ruler. The male counterpart is Ch'i.

(a female unicorn) is difficult to describe. It is difficult to achieve great fortune because life is too short.

All the followers of the Buddhist Trinity (the field of blessedness) 福田 Fu-tien[1] should share the wealth (of wisdom) and cross (this sorrowful world).

All would be free from the torments of the world on attending the first meeting of Maitreya under the Dragon flower-tree[2] where he would preach the Buddha-truth.

1. The field of blessedness i.e. any sphere of kindness, charity or virtue.
2. Champaka tree, the Bodhi tree of Maitreya.

Biography of Eminent Monks
Who Went to the Western Region
in Search of the Law
During the Great Ta'ng Dynasty

CHINESE TEXT

No. 2066

①大唐西域求法高僧傳卷上

②幷序

③沙門義淨從西國還在南海室利佛逝撰寄歸幷那爛陀寺圖

觀夫自古神州之地。輕生④殉法之賓。顯法師則創闢荒途。奘法師乃中開⑤王路。其間或西越紫塞而孤征。或南渡滄溟以單逝。莫不咸思聖跡罄五體而歸禮。俱懷旋踵報四恩以流望。然而勝途多難寶處彌長。苗秀盈十而蓋多。結實罕一而全少。寔由茫茫象磧長川吐赫日之光。浩浩鯨波巨壑起滔天之浪。獨步鐵門之外。亘萬嶺而投身。孤⑥漂銅柱之前。跨千江而遺命(⑦䟦南國有千江口⑧也)或亡飡幾日輟飲數晨。可謂思慮銷精神。憂勞排正色。致使去者數盈半百。留者僅有幾人。設令得到西國者。以大唐無寺。飄寄棲然爲客遑遑。停託無所。遂使流離⑨蓬轉牢居一處。身既不安道寧隆矣。嗚呼實可嘉其美誠。冀傳芳於來葉。粗據聞見撰題行狀云爾。其中次第多以去時年代近遠存亡而比先後

太州玄照法師　齊州道希法師
齊州師鞭法師　新羅阿離耶跋摩法師
新羅慧業法師　⑩新羅求本法師
新羅玄太法師　新羅玄恪法師
新羅復有⑪法師二人
覩貨羅佛陀跋摩師
幷州道方法師　幷州道生法師、
幷州常⑫慜禪師　⑬常慜⑭弟子一人
京師末底僧訶師　京師玄會法師
質多跋摩師　⑮吐蕃公主嬭母息二人
隆法師　益州明遠法師
益州義朗⑯律⑰師　⑱朗律師弟子一人
⑲益州智岸法師　益州會寧律師
交州運期法師　交州木叉提婆師
交州窺沖法師　交州慧琰法師
信胄法師　⑳愛州智行法師
愛州大乘燈禪師　㉑唐國僧伽跋摩師
高昌彼岸智岸二人　洛陽曇㉒潤法師
洛陽義輝論師　又大唐三人
新羅慧輪法師　荊州道琳法師
荊州曇光㉓法師㉔又㉕大唐一人　潤州玄㉖逵律師
荊州慧命禪師
晉州善行法師　襄㉗陽靈運法師
澧州僧哲禪師(㉘哲禪師弟子㉙二人)　荊州無行禪師
洛陽智弘律師
荊州法振禪師　㉚荊州㉛乘悟㉜禪師
㉝梁州㉞乘如㉟律師　澧州大㊱津法師

右總五十六人。先多零落。淨來日有無行師道琳師慧㊲輪師僧哲師智弘師五人見在計。當垂拱元年。與無行㊳禪師執別西國。不委今者何處存亡耳

沙門玄照法師者。太州仙掌人也。梵名般迦舍末底(㊴唐㊵言㊶照慧)乃祖乃父冠冕相承。而㊷總髫之秋抽簪出俗。成人之歲思禮聖蹤。遂適京師尋聽經論。以貞觀年中乃於大興㊸善寺玄證師處。初學梵語。於是㊹仗錫西邁掛想祇園。背金府而出流沙。踐鐵門而登雪嶺。漱香池以結念。畢契四弘。陟葱阜而翹心誓度。三有途經速利過覩貨羅。遠跨胡疆到*吐蕃國。蒙文成公主送往北天。漸向闍闌陀國。未至之間。長途險㊺隘爲賊見拘。既而商旅計窮控告無所。遂乃援神寫契㊻仗聖明衷。夢而感徵。覺見群賊皆睡私引出圍。遂便免難。住闍闌陀國經于四載。蒙國王欽重留之供養。學經律習梵文。既得少通。漸次南上到莫訶菩提復經四夏。自恨生不遇聖幸覩遺蹤。仰慈氏所制㊼之眞容。著精誠而無替。爰以翹敬之餘。沈情俱舍既解對法。淸想律儀兩教斯明。後之那爛陀寺。留住三年。就勝光法師㊽中百學等論。復就寶師子大德受瑜伽十七地。禪門定瀲。㊾亟覩關涯。既盡宏綱。遂往弶(㊿巨亮反)伽河(51)北。受國王苫部供養。住信者等寺復歷三年。後因唐使王玄策歸鄉。(52)表奏言其實德。遂蒙降(53)勅。重(54)詣西天追玄照入京。路次泥波羅國。(55)蒙王發遣送至*吐蕃。重見文成公主。深致禮遇。資給歸唐。於是巡涉西蕃而至東夏。以九月而辭苦部。正月便到洛陽。五月之間途經萬里。于時麟德年中。駕幸東洛

① (原)麗本　② 〔幷序〕－(元)(明)　③ 〔沙門…圖〕二十四字＝〔三藏法師義淨奉詔譯〕九字(宋)(元)(宮)，〔唐三藏法師義淨奉詔撰〕十字(明)　④ 殉＝徇(三)(甲)*　⑤ 王＝正(明)　⑥ 漂＝標(宋)(宮)　⑦ 䟦＝跋(三)(宮)　⑧ 〔也〕－(三)(宮)　⑨ 蓬＝萍(三)(宮)　⑩ 〔新羅求本法師〕－(三)(宮)　⑪ 〔法師〕－(三)(宮)　⑫ 慜＝愍(明)　⑬ 〔常慜〕－(明)　⑭ (師)＋弟(宋)(元)(宮)，弟子一人明本作細註　⑮ 吐＝土(三)(甲)*　⑯ 律＝法(宋)(元)(宮)　⑰ 師＋(幷弟一人)夾註(宋)(元)(宮)，(智岸幷弟)夾註(明)　⑱ 〔朗律師弟子一人〕－(三)(甲)　⑲ 〔益州智岸法師〕－(明)　⑳ 愛＝受(宋)(宮)　㉑ 唐＝襄(三)(宮)　㉒ 潤＝閏(三)(宮)　㉓ 法＝律(明)　㉔ 〔又〕－(明)　㉕ 大唐一人四字明本作夾註　㉖ 逵＝達(元)　㉗ 陽＝州(宮)　㉘ 〔哲禪師〕－(三)(宮)　㉙ 二＝一(三)　㉚ 〔荊州〕－(明)　㉛ 乘悟明本作夾註　㉜ 〔禪師〕－(明)　㉝ 〔梁州〕－(明)　㉞ 乘如明本作夾註　㉟ 〔律師〕－(三)　㊱ 津＝律(宋)(元)　㊲ 輪＝倫(宋)(元)(宮)　㊳ 〔禪〕－(三)(宮)　㊴ 唐＝此(明)*　㊵ 言＝云(三)(甲)　㊶ 照＝昭(三)、　㊷ 總＝緫(三)　㊸ 善＝苹(三)(甲)　㊹ 仗＝杖(三)(宮)　㊺ 隘＝阨(宮)　㊻ 仗＝伏(三)(宮)　㊼ 〔之〕－(三)(宮)　㊽ 中百學＝學中百(三)(宮)　㊾ 亟＝函(元)　㊿ 〔巨亮反〕－(明)　(51) 北＝比(宮)　(52) 表＝奏(宮)　(53) 勅＋(旨)(三)　(54) 詣＝指(宮)　(55) 蒙＋(國)(三)(宮)

奉詔闕庭。①還蒙勅旨令往羯濕彌囉國。取長
年婆羅門盧迦溢多。既與洛陽諸德相見。略
論佛法綱紀。敬愛寺導律師觀法師等。請譯
薩婆多部律攝。既而勅令促去不遂本懷。所
將梵本悉留京下。於是重涉流沙還經磧石。
崎嶇棧道之側。曳半影而斜通。搖泊繩橋之
下。沒全軀以傍渡。遭*吐蕃賊脫首得全。遇
凶奴寇僅存餘命。行至北印度界。見唐使人
引盧迦溢多於路相過。盧迦溢多復令玄照
及使②傔數人向西印度羅③荼國取長年藥。
路過縛渴羅到納婆毘訶羅(*唐云新寺)覩如來澡
④盥及諸聖跡。漸至迦畢試國禮如來頂骨。香
華具設取其印文。觀來生善惡。復過信度國
方達羅*荼矣。蒙王禮敬安居四載。轉歷南
天。將諸雜藥望歸東夏。到金剛座旋之。那爛
陀寺淨與相見。盡平生之志願。契總會於龍
華。但以泥波羅道*吐蕃擁塞不通迦畢試途
多氏⑤捉而難度。遂且棲志鷲峯沈情竹苑。雖
每有傳燈之望。而未諧落葉之心。嗟乎苦行
標誠利生不遂。思攀雲駕墜翼中天。在中印
度菴摩羅⑥跛國遘疾而卒。春秋六十餘矣(多氏者即大食國也)
傷曰。卓矣壯志。穎秀生田。頻經細柳。幾步祁
連。祥河濯流。竹苑搖⑦芊。翹心念念。渴想玄
玄。專希演法。志託提生。嗚呼不遂。愴矣無
成。兩河沈骨。八水揚名。善乎守死。哲人利貞(兩⑧河即在西河八。水乃屬⑨京都)
道希法師者。齊州歷⑩城人也。梵名室利提婆
(唐云吉祥天⑪也)乃門傳禮義家襲搢紳。幼漸玄門少懷
貞操。涉流沙之廣蕩。觀化中天。陟雲嶺之峩
峩。輕生殉法。行至*吐蕃中途危厄。恐戒檢
難護遂便暫捨。行至西方更復重受。周遊諸
國遂達莫訶菩提。翹仰聖蹤經于數載。既住
那爛陀。亦在俱尸國。蒙菴摩羅*跛國王甚相
敬待。在那爛陀寺頻學大乘。住輸婆伴娜(在涅槃處寺名也)
專功律藏。復習聲明頗盡綱目。有文
情善草隸。在大覺寺造唐碑一首。所將唐國
新舊經論四百餘卷。並在那爛陀矣。淨在西
國未及相見。住菴摩羅跛國遘疾而終。春秋
五十餘矣。後因巡禮見希公住房。傷其不⑫幸
聊題一絕。⑬七言 百苦亡勞獨進。影四恩
⑭存念契流通如何未盡傳。燈志溘然於此過
途窮
師鞭法師者。齊州人也。善⑮呪禁閑梵語。與
玄照師從北天向西印度。到菴摩羅割⑯跛城
爲國王所敬。居王寺與道希法師相見。中鄉
國之好。同居一夏遇疾而終。年三十五矣
阿難耶跋摩者。新羅人也。以貞觀年中出⑰長
安之廣脇(王城⑱小名)追求正教親禮聖蹤。住那爛
陀寺。多閑律論抄寫衆經。痛矣歸心所期不
契。出雞貴之東境。沒龍泉之西裔。即於此寺
無常。年七十餘矣(雞貴者。梵云⑲矩矩吒⑳暋說羅。矩矩吒是雞。*暋說羅是貴。即高麗國也。相傳云。彼國敬雞神而取尊。故戴翎羽而表飾矣。那爛陀有池。名曰龍泉。西方喚高麗㉑爲矩㉒矩吒*暋說羅也)
慧業法師者。新羅人也。在貞觀年中往遊西
域。住菩提寺觀禮聖蹤。於那爛陀久而聽讀。
淨因檢唐本。忽見梁論。下記云。在佛齒木樹
下新羅僧慧業寫記。訪問寺僧。云終於此。年
將六十餘矣。所寫梵本並在那爛陀寺
玄太法師者。新羅人也。梵名薩婆愼若提
婆(*唐云一切智天)永徽年內取*吐蕃道。經泥波羅到
中印度。禮菩提樹詳檢經論。旋踵東土行至
土㉓谷渾。逢道㉔希師覆相引致。還向大覺寺
後歸唐國。莫知所終矣
玄恪法師者。新羅人也。與玄照法師貞觀年
中相隨而至大㉕覺。既伸禮敬遇疾而亡。年過
不惑之期耳
復有新羅僧二人。莫知其諱發自長安遠之
南海。汎舶至室利佛逝國西婆魯師國。遇疾
俱亡
佛陀達摩者。即覩貨速利國人也。大形模足
氣力習小教。㉖常乞食少因興易。遂届神州
云。於益府出家。性好遊涉。九州之地無不履
焉。後遂西遊周觀聖迹。淨於那爛陀見矣。後
乃轉向北天。年五十許
㉗右㉘一十人
道方㉙法師者。并州人也。出沙磧到泥波羅。
至大覺寺住。得爲主人經數年。後還㉚向泥
波羅于今現在。既虧戒檢不習經書。年將老
矣
道生法師者。并州人也。梵名栴達羅提婆(唐云
月天)以貞觀末年從*吐蕃路。往遊中國。到菩提
寺禮制底訖。在那爛陀學爲童子。王深所禮
㉛遇。復向此寺東行十二驛有王寺。全是小
乘。於其寺內停住多載。學小乘三藏精順正
理。多齋經像言歸本國。行至泥波羅遘疾而
卒。㉜可在知命之年矣

①還=遂(三)(宮) ②傔=傔(宋)(宮) ③荼=茶(三)(宮)* ④盥=盆(三),罐(宮) ⑤捉=投(宮) ⑥跛=跋(三)(宮) ⑦芊=竿(宋) ⑧河=國(三)(宮) ⑨京都=東都(三)(宮) ⑩城=成(三)(宮) ⑪〔也〕－(三)(宮) ⑫幸=達(三) ⑬七言宋元二本俱作夾註,〔七言〕－(明) ⑭存=在(三)(宮) ⑮呪禁=禁呪(三)(宮) ⑯跛=波(三)(宮) ⑰長=是(宋) ⑱小=山(三)(宮) ⑲矩=雞(三) ⑳暋=醫(三)(宮)* ㉑〔爲〕－(三)(宮) ㉒矩=吒(三)(宮) ㉓谷=山谷(三)(宮) ㉔希+(法)(三) ㉕覺+(寺)(三)(宮) ㉖常=嘗(明) ㉗〔右一十人〕－(明) ㉘〔一〕－(宋)(元)(宮) ㉙〔法〕－(宋)(元)(宮) ㉚向=同(宮) ㉛遇=敬(三)(宮) ㉜可在=在可(三)(宮)

常慜禪師者。并州人也。自落髮投簪披緇釋素。精勤匪懈念誦無歇。常發大誓願生極樂。所作淨業稱念佛名。福基既廣數難詳悉。後遊京洛專崇斯業。幽誠冥兆有所感徵。遂願寫般若經滿於萬卷。冀得遠詣西方禮如來所行聖迹。以此勝福迴向願生。遂詣闕上書請於諸州教化抄寫般若。且心所①至也天必從之。乃蒙授墨勅。南遊江表。敬寫般若。以報天澤。要心既滿。遂至海濱附舶南征往訶陵國。從此附舶往末羅瑜國。復從此國欲詣中天。然②所附商舶載物既重。解纜未③遠④起忽滄波。不經半日遂便沈沒。當沒之時商人爭上小舶互相戰鬪。其舶主既有信心。高聲唱言師來上舶。常慜曰。可載餘人我不去也。所以然者。若輕生爲物順菩提心。亡己濟人斯大士行。於是合掌西方稱彌陀佛。念念之頃舶沈身沒。聲盡而終。春秋五十餘矣。有弟子一人。不知何許人也。號咷悲泣。亦念西方與之俱沒。其得濟之人具陳斯事耳

傷曰。悼矣偉人。爲物流身。明同水鏡。貴等和珍。涅而不黑。磨而不磷。投軀慧巘。養智芳津。在自國而弘自業。適他土而作他因。覩將⑤沈之險難。決於己而亡親在物。常慜子其寡隣。穢體散鯨波以取滅。淨願詣安養而流神。道乎不昧。德也寧⑥堙。布慈光之赫赫。竟塵劫而新新

末底僧訶者(*唐云師子⑦慧) 京⑧兆人也。俗姓皇甫。莫知本諱。與師鞭同遊。俱到中土住信者寺。少閑梵語未詳經論。思還故里路過泥波羅國。遇患身死年四十餘

玄會法師者。京師人⑨也。云是安將軍之息也。從北印度入羯濕彌羅國。爲國王賞⑩職乘王象奏王樂。日日向龍池山寺供養。寺是五百羅漢受供之處。 即尊者阿難陀室灑末田地所化龍王之地也(室灑譯爲所教。舊云弟子⑪者非也)⑫復化羯濕彌羅王大放恩赦國內。 有死四千餘人勸王釋放。出入王宅既漸年載。後因失意遂乃南遊至。大覺寺禮菩提樹。覩木眞池。登鷲峯山。陟尊足嶺。稟識聰叡多繕工伎。雖復經過未幾而梵韻淸徹。少⑬攜經教思⑭反故居。到泥波羅⑮國不幸而卒。春秋僅過而立矣(泥波羅既有毒藥。所以到彼多亡⑯也)

復有一人。與北道使人相逐至縛渴羅國。於新寺小乘師處出家名質多跋摩。後將受具而不食三淨。其師曰。如來大師親開五正。既其無罪。爾何不食。對曰。諸大乘經具有⑰全制。是所舊習性不能改。師曰。我依三藏律有成科。汝之引文非吾所學。若懷別見我非汝師。遂强令進。乃掩泣而食。方爲受具。少閑梵語覆取北路而歸。莫知所至。傳聞於⑱北天之僧矣

復有二人。在泥波羅國。是*吐蕃公主嬭母之息也。初並出家。後一歸俗住⑲大王寺。善梵語并梵書。年三十五⑳二十五矣

隆法師者。不知何所人也。以貞觀年內從北道而出。取北印度欲觀化中天。誦得梵本法華經。到健陀羅國遇疾而亡。北方僧來傳說如此

㉑右二十人

明遠法師者。益州清城人也。梵名振多提婆(*唐云思天) 幼㉒履法訓長而彌修。容儀雅麗㉓庠序清遒。善中百議莊周。早遊七澤之間。後歷三吳之表。重學經論更習定門。於是棲隱廬峯經于夏日。既慨聖教陵遲。遂乃振錫南㉔遊。屆㉕於交阯。鼓舶鯨波到訶陵國。次至師子洲。爲君王禮敬乃潛形閣內密取佛牙。望歸本國以興供養。既得入手翻被奪㉖將。不遂所懷頗見陵辱。向南印度傳聞師子洲人云。往大覺中方寂無消息。應是在路而終。莫委年幾。其師子洲防守佛牙異常牢固。置高樓上幾閉重關。鎖鑰泥封五官共印。若開一戶則響徹城郭。每日供養香華遍覆。至心祈請則牙出華上。或㉗現異光。衆皆共覩。傳云。此洲若失佛牙並被羅刹之所吞食。爲防此患非常守護。亦有傳云。當向支那矣。斯乃聖力遐被有感便通。豈由人事强申非分耳

義朗律師者。益州成都人也。善閑律典兼解瑜伽。發自長安彌歷江㉘漢。與同州僧智岸并弟一人名義玄。年始弱冠知欽正理。頗閑內典尤善文筆。思瞻聖迹遂與弟俱遊。秀季良昆遞相攜帶。鵜鶘存念魚水敦懷。既至烏雷同附商舶。掛百丈陵萬波。越舸扶南綴纜郎迦㉙戍。蒙郎迦戍國王待以上賓之禮。智岸遇疾於此而亡。朗公既懷死別之恨。與弟附舶向師子洲。披求異㉚典頂禮佛牙。漸之西國。傳聞如此。而今不知的在何所。師子洲既不見。中印度復不聞。多是㉛魄歸異代矣。年四

三

①至＝志【三】【宮】 ②〔所〕－【宮】 ③遠＝達【宮】 ④起忽＝超忽【宋】【元】【宮】，忽起【明】 ⑤沈＝況【宮】 ⑥堙＝湮【三】【宮】 ⑦慧＝惠【三】【宮】 ⑧兆＝師【三】【宮】 ⑨〔也〕－【三】【宮】* ⑩職＝識【三】【宮】 ⑪〔者〕－【三】【宮】 ⑫復＋（勸）【三】【宮】 ⑬攜＝擕【三】【宮】 ⑭反＝返【三】【宮】 ⑮〔國〕－【三】【宮】 ⑯〔也〕－【三】 ⑰全＝令【三】【宮】 ⑱北天＝天竺【三】【宮】 ⑲大＝天【三】【宮】 ⑳〔二十五〕－【明】 ㉑〔右二十人〕－【明】 ㉒履＝順【三】【宮】 ㉓庠＝詳【三】【宮】 ㉔遊＝極【宮】 ㉕於＝于【三】【宮】 ㉖將＋（事）【三】【宮】 ㉗現＝見【三】【宮】 ㉘漢＝漠【宮】 ㉙〔戍〕－【三】 ㉚典＝與【元】 ㉛魄＝魂【三】【宮】

十餘耳

會寧律師益州成都人也。禀志操行意存弘益。少而聰慧投跡法場敬勝理若髻珠。棄榮華如脫①屣。薄善經論尤精律典。②志存演法結念西方。爰以麟德年中③仗錫南海。④汎舶至訶陵洲。停住三載。遂共訶陵國多聞僧若那跋陀羅。於阿笈摩經內譯出如來涅槃焚身之事。斯與大乘涅槃頗不相涉。然大乘涅槃西國淨⑤觀見目云。其大數有二十五千頌。翻譯可成六十餘卷。檢其全部竟而不獲。但得初大衆問品一夾有四千餘頌。會寧既譯得阿笈摩本。遂令小僧運期奉⑥表齎經還至交府。馳驛京兆奏上闕庭。冀使未聞流布東夏。運⑦期從京還達交阯。告諸道俗蒙贈小絹數百疋。重⑧詣訶陵報德智賢（若那跋陀羅也）與會寧相見。於是會寧方適西國。比於所在每察風聞。尋聽五天絕無蹤緒。准斯理也即其人已亡。傷⑨曰嗟矣。會寧為法孤征纔翻二軸啓望天庭。終⑩期寶渚⑪權居化城。身雖沒而道著。時縱遠而遺名。將菩薩之先志。共後念以揚聲。春秋可三十四五矣

運期師者。交州人也。與曇⑫潤同遊。仗智賢受具。旋迴南海十有餘年。善崑崙音頗知梵語。後便歸俗住室利佛⑬逝國。于今現在。既而往復宏波傳經帝里。布未曾教斯人之力。年可⑭四十矣

木叉提婆者（*唐云解脫天*也）。交州人也。不閑本諱。汎舶南溟經遊諸國。到大覺寺遍禮聖蹤。於此而殞。年可二十四五⑮耳

窺冲法師者。交州人。即明遠室灑也。梵名質咀囉提婆。與明遠同舶而汎南海。到師子洲。向西印度見玄照師。共詣中土。其人稟性聰叡善誦梵經。所在至處恒編演唱之。首禮菩提樹。到王舍⑯城遘疾竹園。淹留而卒。年三十許

慧琰⑰師者。交州人也。即行公之室灑。隨師到僧訶羅國。遂停彼國。莫⑱辯存亡

信胄法師。不知何⑲許人也。梵名設⑳喇陀跋摩（*唐云信胄）。取北道而到西國。禮謁既周住信者寺。於寺上層造一塼閣。施上臥具永貽供養。遇疾數日餘命輟。然忽於夜中云。有菩薩授手迎。接端居合掌太息而。終年三十㉑五

㉒右三十人

智行法師者。愛州人也。梵名般若提婆㉓（*唐云慧天）。汎南海詣西天。遍禮尊儀。至弶伽河北。居信者寺而卒。年五十餘矣

大乘燈禪師者。愛州人也。梵名莫訶夜那鉢地已波（*唐云大乘燈*也）。幼隨父母汎舶往㉔社和羅鉢底國。方始出家。後隨唐使㉕鄭緒相逐。入京。於慈恩寺三藏法師玄奘處進受具戒居京數載頗覽經書。而思禮聖蹤。情契西極。體蘊忠恕性合廉隅。戒纛存懷禪枝叶慮。以為溺有者假緣。緣非則墜有。離生者㉖託助。助是則乖生。乃畢志王城敦心竹苑。冀摧八難終求四輪。遂持佛像攜經論。既越南溟到師子國。觀禮佛牙備盡靈異。過南印度㉗復屆東天。往耽摩立底國。既入江口遭賊破舶唯身得存。淹停斯國十有二歲頗閑梵語。誦緣生等經㉘兼修福業。因遇商侶。與淨相隨詣中印度。先到那爛陀。次向金剛座。旋過薜舍離。後到俱尸國。與無行禪師同遊此地。燈師每歎曰。本意弘法重之東夏。寧㉙知志不㉚成遂奄爾衰年。今日雖不契懷。來生願畢斯志。然當為覩史多天業冀會慈氏。日晝龍華一兩枝用標心至。燈公因道行之次。過道希師所住舊房。當于時也其人已亡。漢本尚存梵夾猶列。覩之潸然流涕而歎。昔在長安同遊法席。今於他國但遇㉛空筵

傷曰。嗟矣死王。其力彌强。傳燈之士。奄爾云亡。神州望斷。聖境魂揚。脊餘恨而流涕。慨布素而情傷。禪師在俱尸城般涅槃寺而歸寂滅。于時年餘耳順矣

僧伽跋摩者。康國人也。少出流沙遊步京輦。禀素崇信戒行清嚴。檀捨是修慈悲在念。以顯慶年內奉勅與使人相隨禮覲西國到大覺寺。於金剛座廣興供設。七日七夜然燈續明獻大法會。又於菩提院內無憂樹下。彫刻佛㉜形及觀自在菩薩像。盛興慶讚時人歎希。後還唐國。又奉勅令往交阯採藥。于時交州時屬大儉人物飢饑。於日日中營辦飲食救濟孤苦。悲心內結涕泣外流。時人號為常啼菩薩也。纔染微疾㉝奄爾而終。春秋六十餘矣

彼岸法師。智岸法師。並是高昌人也。少長京師傳燈在念。既而歸心勝理。遂乃觀化中天。與使人王玄廓相隨汎舶。海中遇疾俱卒。所將漢本瑜伽及餘經論。咸在室利佛逝國矣

曇*潤法師。洛陽人也。善呪術學玄理。探律

四

①屣＝履(三)(宮) ②志＝忍(三)(宮) ③仗＝杖(三)(宮) ④汎＝泛(元) ⑤觀＝視(三)(宮) ⑥〔表〕ー(三)(宮) ⑦期＝斯(宋)(宮) ⑧詣＝詣(三)(宮) ⑨曰＝日(宋)，乎(元)(明) ⑩期＝斯(三)(宮) ⑪權＝據(三)(宮) ⑫潤＝閏(三)(宮)* ⑬逝＝遊(三)(宮) ⑭四＝三(三)(宮) ⑮耳＝矣(三)，〔耳〕ー(宮) ⑯〔城〕ー(宮) ⑰(法)十師(三)(宮)* ⑱辯＝辨(宋)(元)(宮) ⑲許＝所(三)(宮) ⑳喇＝嚩(三)(宮) ㉑五十(矣)(三)(宮) ㉒〔右三十人〕ー(明) ㉓慧＝惠(三)(宮) ㉔社＝杜(三)(宮) ㉕鄭＝劉(宋)(元) ㉖託＝記(三)(宮) ㉗復＝複(三)(宮) ㉘兼十(脩)(三)(宮) ㉙〔知〕ー(三)(宮) ㉚成＝我(三)(宮) ㉛空＝室(三)(宮) ㉜〔形〕ー(三)(宮) ㉝奄＝掩(宋)(宮)

典誥醫明。善容儀極詳審。❶振錫江表拯物爲懷。漸次南行達于交阯。住經載稔緇素欽風。❷汎舶南上期西印度。至訶陵北渤盆國遇疾而終。年三十矣

義輝論師。洛陽人也。受性聰敏。理思鉤深。博學爲懷尋眞是務。聽攝論俱舍等頗亦有功。但以義有異同情生舛互。而欲❸思觀梵本親聽微言。遂指掌中天還望東夏。惜哉苗而不實壯志先秋。到郎迦戍國嬰疾而亡。年三十餘矣

復有大唐三僧。從北道到烏長那國。傳聞向佛頂骨處禮拜。今亦❹弗委存亡。烏長僧至傳說之矣

❺右四十人

慧輪師者。新羅人也。梵名般若跋摩(*唐云慧❻甲)自本國出家翹心聖迹。汎舶而陵閩越。涉步而屆長安。奉勅隨玄照*師西行以充侍者。旣之西國遍禮聖蹤。居菴摩羅❼跛國在信者寺住經十載。近住次東邊北方覩貨羅僧寺。元是覩貨羅人爲本國僧所造。其寺巨富❽貲產豐饒供養飡設餘莫加也。寺名健陀羅山❾荼。慧輪住此。❿旣善梵言薄閑俱舍。來日尚⓫在年向四十矣。其北方僧來者。皆住此寺爲主人耳。大覺寺西有迦畢⓬試國寺。寺亦巨富多諸碩德。普學小乘。北方僧來亦住此寺。名窶⓭挐折里⓮多(*唐云德行)大覺東北兩驛許有寺名屈錄迦。卽是南方屈錄迦國王昔所造也。寺雖貧素而戒行清嚴。近者日軍王復於故寺之側更造一⓯寺。今始新成。南國僧來多住於此。諸方皆悉有寺。所以本國通流。神州獨無一處。致令往⓰還艱苦⓱耳。那爛陀寺東四十驛許。尋弶伽河⓲而下至蜜栗伽悉⓳他鉢娜寺(*唐云鹿⓴園寺也)去此寺不遠有一故寺。但有塼基。厥號支那寺。古老相傳云。是昔室利笈多大王爲支那國僧所造(支那卽廣州也。莫訶支那卽京師也。亦云提婆㉑弗呾羅。*唐云天子也)于時有唐僧二十許人。從蜀川牂㉒牁道而出(蜀川㉓去此寺有五百餘驛)向莫訶菩提禮拜。王見敬重。遂施此地以充停息。給大村封二十四所。於後唐僧亡沒。村乃割屬餘人。現有三村㉔入鹿園寺矣。准量支那寺至今可五百餘年矣。現今地屬東印度王。其王名提婆跋摩。每言曰。若有大唐天子處數僧來者。我爲重興此寺。還其村封令不絕也。誠可歎。曰雖有鵲巢之易。而樂福者難逢。必若心存濟益。奏請弘此誠非小事也。金剛座大覺寺卽僧訶羅國王所造。師子洲僧舊住於此。大覺寺東北行七驛許至那爛陀寺。乃是古王室利鑠羯羅昳底。爲㉕北天菼羯曷羅社㉖槃所造。此寺初基纔餘方堵。其後代國王苗裔相承造製宏壯。則贍部洲中當今無以加也。軌模不可具述。但且略敘區寰耳。然其寺形疉方如域。四面直簷長廊遍匝。皆是塼室。重疊三層層高丈餘。橫梁板闐本無椽瓦。用塼平㉗覆。寺㉘背正直隨意旋往。其房後壁卽爲外面也。㉙壘塼峻㉚峭高三四丈。上作人頭高共人等。其僧房也面有九焉。一一房中可方丈許。後面通窓戶向簷矣。其門旣高唯安一扇。皆相瞻望不許安簾。出外平觀四面皆覩。互相檢察寧容片私。於一角頭作。閣道還往。寺上四角各爲塼堂。多聞大德而住於此。寺門西向飛閣凌虛。雕刻奇形妙盡工飾。其門乃與房相連。元不別作。但前出兩步齊安四柱。其門雖非過大㉛實乃裝架彌堅。每至食時重關返閉。旣是聖教意在防私。寺內之地方三十步許。皆以塼砌。小者或㉜七步或五步耳。凡所覆屋脊上簷前房內之地。並㉝用塼㉞屑如桃棗大。和雜粘泥以杵平築。*用疆石灰。雜以麻筋幷油及麻滓爛皮之屬。浸漬多日泥於塼地㉟之上。覆以青草經三數日。看其欲乾重以滑石揩。拭拂赤土汁或丹朱之類。後以油塗鮮澄若鏡。其堂殿階陛悉皆如此。一作已後縱人踐蹋。動經一二十載曾不圮㊱礫。不同石灰水沾便脫。如斯等類乃有八寺。上皆平通規矩相似。於寺東面㊲西取房。或一或三。用安尊像。或可卽於此面前出多少。別起臺觀爲佛殿矣。㊳此寺西㊴南大院之外。方列大窣覩波(舊云塔者訛略)及諸制底(舊云支提者㊵訛)數乃盈百。聖跡相連不可稱㊶記。金寶瑩飾實成希有。其間僧徒綱軌出納之儀。具如中方錄及寄歸傳所述。寺內但以最老上座而爲尊主。不論其德。諸有門鑰每宵封印。將付上座。更無別置寺主維那。但造寺之人名爲寺主。梵云毘訶羅莎弭。若作番直典掌寺門及和僧白事者。名毘訶羅波羅。譯爲護寺。若鳴㊷健稚及監食者。名爲羯磨陀那。譯爲授事。言維那者略也。衆僧有事集衆平章令其護寺。巡行告白一一人前。皆須合掌各伸其事。若一人不許則事不得成。

❶振＝杖【元】【明】 ❷汎＝附【元】【明】 ❸思＝異【三】【宮】 ❹弗＝不【三】【宮】 ❺〔右四十人〕－【明】 ❻甲＝申【三】 ❼跛＝跋【三】 ❽貲＝資【三】【宮】 ❾荼＝茶【三】【宮】 ❿旣＝卽【宮】 ⓫在＝存【三】【宮】 ⓬試＝施【三】【宮】 ⓭挐＝拏【三】【宮】 ⓮多＝夕【宋】【元】 ⓯〔寺〕－【元】 ⓰〔還〕－【元】 ⓱耳＝苦【元】 ⓲〔而〕－【元】 ⓳他＝伽【三】【宮】 ⓴〔園〕－【三】【宮】 ㉑弗＝佛【三】【宮】 ㉒牁＝牱【三】【宮】 ㉓去＝寺【三】【宮】 ㉔入＝人屬【三】【宮】 ㉕北＝比【宮】 ㉖槃＋(社)【三】【宮】 ㉗覆＝履【元】 ㉘背＝皆【三】【宮】 ㉙壘＝疊【三】【宮】* ㉚〔峭〕－【三】【宮】 ㉛實＝寶【元】 ㉜七＝十【三】【宮】 ㉝用＝周【三】【宮】* ㉞屑＝糲【三】【宮】 ㉟〔之〕－【宮】 ㊱礫＝坼【三】【宮】 ㊲〔西〕－【三】【宮】 ㊳此＝於【三】【宮】 ㊴南＝而【三】【宮】 ㊵訛＋(也)【三】【宮】 ㊶記＝說【三】 ㊷健＝犍【三】【宮】

全無衆前打槌秉白之法。若見不許以理喩之。未有挾强便加壓伏。其守庫當莊之流。雖三二人亦遣典庫家人合掌爲白。若和方可費用誠無獨任之咎。[1]不白而獨用者。下至半升之粟。即交被驅擯。若一人稱豪獨用僧物處斷。[2]綱務不白大衆者。名爲俱攞鉢底。譯爲家主。斯乃佛法之大疣人神所共怨。雖復於寺有益。而終獲罪彌深。智者必不爲也。又諸外道先有九十六部。今但十餘。若有齋會聚集。各各自居一處。並與僧尼無競先後。既其法別理不同行。各習所宗坐無交雜。此之寺制理極嚴峻。每半月令典事佐史巡房讀制。衆僧名字不貫王籍。其有犯者衆自治罰。爲此僧徒咸相敬懼。其寺受用雖迮而益利彌寬。曾憶在京見人畫出祇洹寺樣。咸是憑虛。爲廣異聞略陳梗概云爾

又五天之地但是大寺。君王悉皆令置漏水。爲此晝夜。期候不難。准如律教。夜分三分。初後制令禪誦。中[3]間隨意消息。其漏水法廣如寄歸傳中所述。雖復言陳寺樣。終恐在事還迷。爲此畫出其圖。冀令目擊無滯。如能奏請依樣造之。即王舍支那理成無別耳。[4]此下宜畫寺樣也

此是室利那爛陀莫訶毘訶羅樣唐譯云吉祥神龍大住處也。西國凡喚君王及大官屬幷大寺舍。皆先云室利。意取吉祥尊貴之義。那爛陀乃是龍名。近此有龍名那伽爛陀。故以爲號。毘訶羅是住處義。[5]比云寺者不是正翻。如觀一寺餘七同然背上平直通人還往。

凡觀寺樣者須[6]南面看之。欲使西出其門方得[7]直勢。於門南畔可二十步有窣堵波。高百[8]尺許。是世尊昔日夏三月安居處。梵名慕攞健陀俱胝。唐云根本香殿矣。門北畔五十步許。復有大窣堵波。更高於此。是幼日王所造。皆並塼作。裝飾精妙。金床寶地。供養希有。中有如來轉法輪像。次此西南有小制底。高一丈餘。是婆羅門執雀請問處。唐云雀離浮圖。此即是也。根本殿西有佛齒木樹非是楊柳。其次西畔[9]有戒壇。方可大尺一丈餘。即於平地周*壘塼[10]牆[11]子。高二尺許。牆內坐基可高五寸。中有小制底。壇東殿角有佛經行之基。*壘塼爲之。寬可二肘。長十四五肘。高可二肘餘。上乃石灰[12]塑作蓮華開勢。高可二[13]寸。闊一尺許。有十四五表佛足跡。此寺則南望王城。纔三十里。鷲峯竹苑皆在城傍。西南向大覺。正南尊足山。並可七驛。[14]北向薜舍離。乃二十五驛。西瞻鹿苑。二十餘驛。東向耽摩立底國。有六七十驛。即是海口昇舶歸唐之處。此寺內僧衆有三千五百人。屬寺村莊二百一所。並是積代君王給其人戶永充供養一言驛者即當[15]踰繕那也重曰。龍池龜[16]洛地隔天津。途遙去馬道絕來人。致[17]令傳說罕得其眞。模形別匠軌製殊陳依俙。[18]畫古勞撫鷲新。庶觀者之虔想。若佛在而翹神

大唐西域求法高僧傳卷上

大唐西域求法高僧傳卷下[19]幷重歸南海傳

[20]三藏法師義[21]淨撰

道琳法師者。荊州江陵人也。梵名尸羅鉢頗[22]唐云戒光弱冠之年披緇離俗。成人之歲訪友尋眞。搜律藏而戒珠瑩啓。禪門而定水清。稟性虛潔雅操廉貞。濯靑溪以恬志漱玉泉而養感。既常坐不臥一食全誠。後復慨大教東流時經多載。定門[23]鮮入律典[24]頗虧。遂欲尋流討源遠遊西國。乃杖錫遐逝鼓舶南溟。越銅柱而屆郎迦。歷訶陵而經裸國。所在國王禮待極致慇厚。經乎數載到東印度耽摩立底國。住經三年學梵語。於是捨戒重受。學習一切有部。律非唯學兼定慧。蓋亦情耽呪藏。後乃觀化中天頂禮金剛御座菩提聖儀。復至那爛陀寺。搜覽大乘經論。[25]注情俱舍。經於數年。至於鷲嶺杖林山園鵠樹。備盡翹仰並展精誠。乃遊南天竺國搜訪玄謨。向西印度於羅[26]荼國住經年稔。更立靈壇重稟明呪。嘗試論之曰。夫明呪者梵云毘睇陀羅必得[27]丁澤反家。毘睇譯爲明呪。陀羅是持。必得家是藏。應云持明呪藏。然相承云此呪藏。梵本有十萬頌。唐譯可成三百卷。現今求覓多失少全。而大聖沒後阿離野那伽曷樹那。即龍樹菩薩。特精斯要。時彼弟子厥號難陀。聰明博識漬意斯典。在西印度經十二年。專心持呪遂便感應。每至食時食從空下。[28]又誦呪求如

[1] (若)+不(三)(宮) [2] 綱=網(宋)(宮) [3] 間=閒(元) [4] 此下宜畫寺樣也=乃數日衆美仍羅列群英已吉今也知生死分那得不傷心寺樣(三)(宮)
[5] 比=此(明) [6] 南面=南西(宋)(宮), 南西(元)(明) [7] 直=眞(三)(宮) [8] 尺許=許尺(三)(宮) [9] 有+十(莖)(三)(宮) [10] 牆=墻(宮) [11] 子=可(明) [12] 塑=素(三)(宮) [13] 寸=肘(元)(明)(宮) [14] 北=比(宋)(元)(宮) [15] 踰=瑜(三) [16] 洛=浴(三)(宮) [17] 令=今(三)(宮) [18] 畫=盡(宋)(元)(宮) [19] (此卷十五人)夾注+幷(宋)(元), [幷重歸南海傳]－(明) [20] (唐)+三(明) [21] 淨+(奉詔)(明) [22] 唐云戒光宋元二本倶作本文, 唐=此(明)* [23] 鮮=尠(三) [24] 虧=窺(三) [25] 注=漬(三)(宮) [26] 荼=茶(三)(宮)* [27] [丁澤反]－(明) [28] [又]－(宮)

意瓶。不久便獲。乃於瓶中得經歡喜。不以呪結其瓶遂去。於是難陀法師恐[1]呪明散失。遂便撮集可十二千頌。成一家之言。每於一頌之內。離合呪印之文。雖復言同字同實乃義別用別。自非口相傳授而實解悟無因。後陳那論師見其製作[2]功殊人智思極情端。撫經歎曰。嚮使此賢致意因明者。我復何顏之有乎。是知智士識己之度量。愚者闇他之淺深矣。斯之呪藏東夏未流。所以道琳意[3]存斯妙。故呪藏云。升天乘龍役使百神。利生之道唯呪是親。淨於那爛陀。亦屢入壇場希心此要。而爲功不並就。遂泯斯懷爲廣異聽。粗題綱目云爾。道琳遂從西境轉向北天。觀化羯濕彌羅。便入烏長那國。詢訪定門搜求般若。次往迦畢試國禮烏率膩沙 (佛頂骨也) 自爾之後不委何託。淨迴至南海羯*茶國。有北方胡至云。有兩僧胡國逢見。說其狀跡應是其人。與智弘相隨擬歸故國。聞爲途賊斯擁還乃覆向北天。年應五十餘矣

曇光律師者。荊州江陵人也。旣其出俗遠適京師。卽誠律師之室灑善談論有文情學兼內外戒行淸謹。南遊溟渤望禮西天承已至訶利鷄羅國在東天之東。年在盛壯不委何之中[4]訪寂無消息。應是擯落江山耳。又見訶利鷄羅國僧。說有一唐僧年餘五十。得王敬重乘檝一寺。多齎經像好行楚撻。卽於此國遇疾[5]而終他鄉矣

慧命[6]師者。荊州江陵人也。戒行疎通有懷節操。學兼內外逸志雲表。仰祥河而[7]牒想。念竹苑[8]以翹心。汎舶[9]而行至占波遭風。而屢遘艱苦。適馬援之銅柱。息上景而歸唐

玄逵律師者。潤州江寧人也。俗姓胡。令族高宗。兼文兼[10]史。尚仁貴義。敬法敬僧。枝葉蟬聯。嘉聲靡墜。律師則童子出家長而欽德。及其進具卓爾不群。遍閑律部偏務禪寂。戒行嚴峻誠[11]罕共流。聽諸大經頗究玄義。博翫文什草隸尤精。空有三衣祖。髆爲飾。不披覆膊衣角搭肩。入寺徒跣行途著[12]屨。縱使時人見笑高節曾不問然。不臥長坐。詎脇安眠之席。杜多乞食。寧過酒肆之門。善人皆愛草鞋巧知。皮[13]亦無過[14]鑒者。足不履地能閑露脚。是儀嗟乎。此子闇與理諧。激揚清波。恥汨[15]泥而從俗。獨醒在旦。豈共醉而居昏。[16]繞於丹[17]陽一[18]而遂卽同契。南上毘季留連愴矣。三荊之析友于攀絕。傷哉八翼之離。以爲傳法在懷無抑高節。行至廣州遂[19]染風疾。以斯嬰帶弗遂遠懷。於是悵恨而歸返錫吳楚。年二十五六。後僧哲師至西國云。其人已亡有[20]疚于懷。嗟乎不幸。勝途多難驗非虛矣。實冀還以法資空有欝藍之望。復欲旋歸遺鍔。徒懷[21]隴樹之心。乃歎曰。淑人斯去。誰[22]當繼來。不幸短命。嗚呼哀哉。九仞希岳。一簣便摧。秀而不實。嗚呼哀哉。解乎易得。行也難求。嗟爾幼年。業德俱修。傳燈念往。嬰痾情收。慨乎壯志。哀哉去留庶傳爾之令節。秉輝曜[23]于長秋。于時逵師言離廣府還望[24]桂林。去留愴然自述贈懷云爾 [25]五言

標心之梵宇。運想入仙洲。嬰痾乖同好。沈情阻若抽。葉落乍難聚。情離不可收。何日乘杯至。詳觀演法流

淨以咸亨元年在西京尋聽。于時與并部處一法師。萊州弘禕論師。更有[26]二三諸德。同契鷲峯標心覺樹。然而一公屬母親之年老。遂懷戀於并川。禕師遇玄瞻於江寧。乃敦情於安養。玄逵旣到廣府復阻先心。唯與晉州小僧善行同去。神州故友索爾分飛。印度新知冥焉未會。此時躑躅難以爲懷。戲擬四愁聊題兩絕而已 五言

我行之數萬。愁緒百重思。那教六尺影。獨步五天陲 五言 (重自解憂曰)

上將可[27]凌師。疋士志難移。如論惜短命。何得滿長祇

于時咸亨三年坐夏揚府。初秋忽遇龔州使君馮孝詮。[28]隨至廣府。與波斯舶主期會南行。復蒙使君命往崗州。重爲檀主及弟孝誕使君孝軫使君郡君寧氏郡君彭氏等。合門眷屬。咸見資贈。爭抽上賄各捨奇飡。庶無乏於海途。恐有勞於險[29]地。篤如親之[30]惠。順給孤之心。共作歸依同緣勝境。所以[31]得成禮謁者。蓋馮家之力也。又嶺南法俗。共鯁去留之心。北土英儒。俱懷生別之恨。至十一月。遂乃面翼軫背番禺。指鹿園而遐想。望鷄峯而太息。于時廣莫初飈。向朱方而百丈雙[32]挂。離箕創節。棄玄朔而五兩單飛。長截洪溟。似山之濤橫海。斜通巨壑。如雲之浪滔天。未隔兩旬果之佛逝。經停六月漸學聲明。王贈支持送[33]往末羅瑜國 (今改爲室利佛逝[34]也) 復停兩月轉向

[1] 呪明＝明呪〔三〕，恐明〔宮〕 [2] 功＝巧〔三〕〔宮〕 [3] 存＝非〔元〕 [4] 訪＝方〔三〕〔宮〕 [5]〔而〕－〔宮〕 [6]（禪）＋師〔三〕〔宮〕 [7] 牒＝諜〔元〕〔明〕 [8] 以＝而〔三〕 [9]〔而〕－〔三〕〔宮〕 [10] 史＝武〔三〕 [11] 罕＝空〔宮〕 [12] 屨＝履〔三〕〔宮〕 [13] 亦＝赤〔三〕〔宮〕 [14] 鑒＝鑑〔三〕〔宮〕 [15] 泥＝沒〔宋〕〔宮〕 [16] 繞＝纔〔三〕〔宮〕 [17] 陽＝楊〔三〕〔宮〕 [18] 而＝面〔三〕〔宮〕 [19] 染＝沈〔宮〕 [20] 疚＝疾〔三〕〔宮〕 [21] 隴＝朧〔宋〕〔宮〕 [22] 當繼＝復當〔宋〕〔宮〕 [23] 于＝於〔宋〕〔宮〕 [24] 桂＝柱〔三〕〔宮〕 [25]〔五言〕－〔三〕〔宮〕 [26] 二三＝三二〔三〕〔宮〕 [27] 凌＝陵〔三〕〔宮〕 [28]〔隨〕－〔三〕〔宮〕 [29] 地＝阻〔宋〕〔宮〕 [30] 惠＝慧〔宋〕〔宮〕 [31]〔得〕－〔宮〕 [32] 挂＝桂〔三〕〔宮〕 [33]〔往〕－〔三〕〔宮〕 [34]〔也〕－〔明〕〔宮〕

羯*茶。至十二月舉帆還乘王舶漸向東天矣。從羯*茶北行十日餘至裸❶人國向東望岸可一二里許。但見❷鄁子樹檳榔林森然可愛。彼見舶至爭乘小艇有盈百數。皆將鄁子芭蕉及❸籐竹器來求市易。其所愛者但唯鐵焉大如兩指。得鄁子或五或十。丈夫悉皆露體。婦女以片葉遮形。商人戲授其衣。卽便搖手不用。傳聞斯國當蜀川西南界矣。此國旣不出鐵亦寡金銀。但食*鄁子藷根無多稻穀。是以盧❹呵最爲珍貴(此國名鐵爲盧*呵)其人容色不黑量等中形。巧織團藤箱餘處莫能及。若不共交易便放毒箭。一中之者無復再生。從茲更半月許望西北行。遂達耽摩立底國。卽東印度之南界也。去莫訶菩提及那爛陀可六十餘驛。於此創與大乘❺燈師相見。留住一載。學梵語習聲❻論。遂與燈師同行取正西路。商人數百詣中天矣。去莫訶菩提有十日在。過大山澤路險難通。要藉多人必無孤進。于時淨染時患身體疲羸。求趁商❼旅因不❽能❾進。雖可勵己求進五里終須百息。其時有那爛陀寺二十許僧。幷燈上人並皆前去。唯餘單己孤步險隘。日晚晡時山賊便至。援弓大喚來見相陵。先撮上衣次抽下服。空有條帶亦並奪將。當是❿時也。實謂長辭人代。無諧禮謁之心。體散鋒端。不遂本求之望。又彼國相傳。若得白色之人殺充⓫天祭。旣思此說更軫于懷。乃入泥坑遍塗形體。以葉遮蔽扶杖徐行。日云暮矣營處尙遙。至夜兩更方及徒侶。聞燈上人村外長叫。旣其相見⓬令授一衣。池內洗身方入村矣。從⓭此行數日。先到那爛陀敬根本塔。次上耆闍崛見⓮氎衣處。後往大覺寺禮眞容像。山東道俗所贈絁絹。持作如來等量袈裟。親奉披服。濮州玄律師附羅蓋數萬爲持奉上曹州安道禪師寄拜禮菩提像亦爲禮訖。于時五體布地一想虔誠。先爲東夏四恩。普及法界含識。願龍華⓯初會遇慈氏尊。並契眞宗獲無生智。次乃遍禮聖跡過方丈。而屆拘尸。所在欽誠。入鹿園而跨鷄嶺。住那爛陀寺十載求經。方始旋踵言歸還耽摩立底。未至之間遭大劫賊。僅免⓰剸刃之禍。得存朝夕之命。於此升舶過羯*茶國。所將梵本三藏五十萬餘頌。唐譯可成千卷。⓱權居佛逝矣

善行師者。晉州人也。少辭桑梓訪道東山。長習律儀寄情明呪。溫恭儉素利物是心。則淨之門人也。隨至室利佛逝有懷中土。旣⓲染痼疾返棹而歸。年⓳四十許

靈運師者。襄陽人也。梵名般若提婆。志懷耿介情存出俗。追尋聖跡與僧哲同遊⓴戲南溟達西國。極閑梵語利物㉑存懷。所在至處君王禮敬。遂於那爛陀畫慈氏眞容菩提樹像。一同尺量妙簡工人。齎以歸㉒唐廣興佛事。翻譯聖教實有堪能矣

僧哲禪師者。澧州人也。幼敦高節早託玄門。而解悟之機實有灌瓶之妙。談論之銳。固當重席之美。沈深律苑控總禪畦。中百兩門久提綱目。莊劉二籍亟盡樞關。思慕聖蹤泛舶西域。旣至西土適化隨緣。巡禮略周歸東印度到三摩呾吒國。國王名曷羅社跋㉓毛。其王旣深敬三寶爲大鄔波索迦。深誠徹信光絕前後。每於日日造拓模泥像十萬軀。讀大般若十萬頌。用鮮華十萬㉔尋親自供養所呈薦設積與人齊。整駕將行觀音先發。旛旗鼓樂漲日彌空。佛像僧徒並㉕居前引。王乃後從。於王城內僧尼有四千許人。皆受王供養。每於晨朝令使入寺合掌房前急行疾問。大王奉問法師等宿夜得安和不。僧答曰。願大王無病長壽國祚安寧。使返報已方論國事。五天所有聰明大德廣慧才人博學十八部經通解五明大論者。並集茲國矣。良以其王仁聲普洎駿骨遐收之所致也。其僧哲住此王寺。尤蒙別禮。存情梵本頗有日新矣。來時不與相見。承聞尙在年可四十許。僧哲弟子玄遊者。高麗國人也。隨師於師子國出家。因住彼矣

㉖右五十人

智弘律師者。洛陽人也。卽聘西域㉗大使王玄策之姪也。年纔弱歲早狎冲虛。志蔑輕肥㉘情。懷棲遁。遂往少林山飡㉙和服餌。樂誦經典頗工文筆。旣而悟朝市之諠譁。尙法門之澄寂。遂背八水而去三吳。捨素禔而擐緇服。搴瑳禪師爲師稟承㉚思慧而未經多載卽髣髴玄關。復往蘄州忍禪師處重修定慮。而芳根雖植崇條未聳。遂濟湘川跨衡嶺。入桂林而託想。遁幽泉以息心。頗經年載。仗寂禪師爲依止。㉛觀山水之秀麗。翫林薄之清虛。揮翰寫衷㉜製幽泉山賦申遠遊之㉝懷。旣覽三吳之

八.

❶人=入(宮) ❷鄁=鄭(三)(宮)* ❸籐=藤(三)(宮) ❹呵=阿(明)* ❺[燈]—(宮) ❻[聞]—(三)(宮) ❼旅因=徒旋困(三)(宮) ❽[能]—(宋)(宮) ❾進=及(三)(宮) ❿[時]—(宮) ⓫天=大(宋) ⓬令=念(三) ⓭此+(北)(三) ⓮氎=疊(三)(宮) ⓯初=總(三)(宮) ⓰剸=專(三)、車(宮) ⓱權=擁(三) ⓲染=沈(三)(宮) ⓳四=三(三)(宮) ⓴戲=越(三)(宮) ㉑存=在(三)(宮) ㉒唐=國(三)(宮) ㉓毛=吒(三)(宮) ㉔尋=朵(三)(宮) ㉕[居]—(宮) ㉖[右五十人]—(明) ㉗大使=太史(三)(宮) ㉘情懷=懷情(三)(宮) ㉙和=松(三)(宮) ㉚思慧=恩惠(宋)(宮) ㉛觀山=斯(宮) ㉜製=裂(三)(宮) ㉝懷=壞(宋)(元)(宮)

法匠。頗盡芳筵。歷九江之勝友。幾閑妙理。然而宿植善根匪由人獎。出①日中府欲觀禮西天。幸遇無行禪師與之同契。至合浦升舶長②泛滄溟。風便不通漂居上景。覆向交州住經一夏。既至冬末復往海濱神灣。隨舶南遊到室利佛逝國。自餘經歷具在行禪師傳內。到大覺寺住經二載。瞻仰尊容傾誠勵想。諷誦梵本月故日新。閑聲論能梵書。學律儀習對法。既解俱舍復善因明。於那爛陀寺③則披覽大乘。在信者道場。乃專功小教。復就名德重洗律儀。懇④懇懃懃無忘寸影。習德光律師所製律經。隨聽隨譯實有功夫。善護浮囊無虧片檢。常坐不臥知足清廉。奉上謙下久而彌敬。至於王城鷲嶺僊苑鹿林。⑤祇樹天階菴園山穴。備申翹想。⑥東契幽心。每撥衣鉢之餘。常懷供益之念。於那爛陀寺則上湌普設在王舍城中乃器供常住。在中印度近有八年。後向北天羯濕彌羅。擬之鄉國矣。聞與琳公為伴。不知今在何所。然而翻譯之功其人已就矣

無行禪師者。荊州江陵人也。梵名般若提婆（*唐云慧天）叶性虛融稟質溫雅。意存仁德志重烟霞。而竹馬之年。投足石渠之署。暨乎弱冠。有懷金馬之門。頗已漁獵百氏流睇三經。州望推奇鄉曲排俊。于時則絢彩霞開。鏡三江而挺秀。芳思泉涌。灌七澤而流津。然宿因感會今果現前。希慕法門有窺玄⑦苑。幸遇五人之度。爰居等⑧界道場。既而創染⑨諦門初霑法侶。事大福田寺慧英法師為鄔波馱耶（*唐云親教師和⑩上者訛也）斯乃吉藏法師之上足。可謂蟬聯碩德。固乃世不乏賢。於是標心般若棲志禪居。屏棄人間往來山水。每因談玄講肆擊關微言。雖年在後生⑪而望逾先進。及乎受具同壇乃二十餘人。誦戒契心再辰便了。咸稱上首餘莫能加。次隱幽巖誦法華妙典。不盈一月七軸言終。乃歎曰。夫尋筌者意在得魚。求言者本希趣理。宜可訪名匠鏡心神啓定門斷煩惑。遂乃杖錫九江移步三越。遊衡岳處金陵。逸想嵩華長吟少室。濯足八水界袂三川。求善知識即其志也。或携定門而北上。獵智者禪匠之精微。屣戒巘而東歸。究道宣律師之淳粹。聽新舊經論。討古今儀則。洋洋焉波瀾萬頃嶷嶷也。崖岸千尋。與智弘為伴。東風汎舶一月到室利佛逝國。國王厚禮特異常倫。布金華散金粟。四事供養。五對呈心。見從大唐天子處來倍加欽上。後乘王舶經十五日達末羅瑜洲。又十五日到羯*茶國。至冬末轉舶西行。經三十日到那伽鉢亶那。從此*泛海二日到師子洲。觀禮佛牙。從師子州復東北*泛舶一月到訶利鷄羅國。此國乃是東天之東界也。即贍部州之地也。停⑫在一年。漸之東印度。恒與智弘相隨。此去那爛陀途有百驛。既停息已便之大覺。蒙⑬國安置入寺俱為主人。西國主人稍難得也。若其得主則衆事皆同如也。為客但食而已。禪師後向那爛陀。聽瑜伽習中觀。研味俱舍探求律典。復往羝羅茶寺。去斯兩驛。彼有法匠善解因明。屢在芳筵習陳那法稱之⑭作。莫不漸入玄關頗開幽鍵。每唯杖錫乞食全軀。少欲自居情超物外。曾因閑隙譯出阿笈摩經。述如來涅槃之事。略為三卷。已附歸唐。是一切有部律中所出。論其進不乃與會寧所譯同矣。行禪⑮師既言欲居西國。復道有意神州。⑯疑取北天歸乎故里。淨來日從那爛陀相送。東行六驛各懷生別之恨。俱希重會之心業也。茫茫流泗交袂矣。春秋五十六。又禪師稟性好⑰尙欽禮。每以覺樹初⑱綠。觀洗沐於龍池。竹苑新黃。奉折華於鷲嶺（此二時⑲者春中也。皆是大節會。無⑳問㉑遠近。道俗咸觀。洗菩提樹也。又鷲峯山此時有㉒華大如手許。實同金色。人皆折㉓以上呈。當此之時。彌覆山野名春女華㉔也）曾於一時與行禪師同遊鷲嶺。瞻奉既訖遐眺鄉關無任殷憂。淨乃聊述所懷云爾　雜㉕言。

觀化祇山頂。流睇古王城。萬載池猶潔。千年苑尙清。髣髴影堅路。摧殘廣脇壘。七寶仙臺亡舊迹。四彩天華絕雨聲。聲華遠。自恨生何晚。既傷火宅眩中門。還嗟寶渚迷長坂。步陟平郊望。心遊七海上。擾擾三界溺邪津。渾渾萬品亡眞匠。唯有能仁獨圓悟。廓塵靜浪開玄路。創逢飢命棄身城。更為求人崩意樹（施也）持囊㉖畢契戒珠淨（戒也）被甲要心忍衣固（忍也）三祇不倦陵二車。一足忘勞超九數（勤也）定瀲江清沐久結（定也）智㉗釼霜凝斬新霧（慧也）無邊大劫無不修。六時㉘愍生遵六度。度有流化㉙功收。金河示滅歸常住。鷄林權唱演功周。聖徒㉚往㉛傳餘響。龍宮祕典海中探。石室眞言山處仰。流教在茲辰。傳芳代有人。沙河雪嶺迷朝徑。巨海鴻崖亂夜津。入萬死。求一生。投針偶㉜穴非同喻。㉝東馬懸車豈等程。不徇今身樂。

①日＝自【三】【宮】　②泛＝汎【三】*　③〔則〕－【宮】　④懇＝志【三】【宮】　⑤祇＝低【宮】　⑥東＝並【三】【宮】　⑦苑＝化【三】【宮】　⑧界＝戒【三】　⑨諦＝課【三】　⑩上＝尙【明】　⑪〔而〕－【三】【宮】　⑫在＝住【三】【宮】　⑬國＋（家）【三】　⑭作＋（者）【三】【宮】　⑮師＋（說）【三】【宮】　⑯疑＝擬【三】【宮】　⑰尙＝上【三】【宮】*　⑱綠＝菉【三】【宮】　⑲者＝也【三】【宮】　⑳問＝間【三】【宮】　㉑遠＝連【宮】　㉒（黃）＋華【三】【宮】　㉓以＝情【宋】【元】　㉔也＝耳【三】【宮】　㉕言＋（詩曰）【三】　㉖畢＝異【宮】　㉗釼＝劍【三】，歛【宮】　㉘愍生遵＝改心遵【宮】　㉙功＋（德）【三】　㉚往＝佳【宋】【元】　㉛（昔）＋傳【三】　㉜穴＝伉【宋】【宮】　㉝東＝速【三】【宮】

無祈後代榮。誓捨危軀追勝義。咸希畢契傳燈情。勞歌勿復陳。延眺且周巡東。睇女雞留二迹。西馳鹿苑去三輪。北睨舍城池尚在。南睎尊嶺❶穴猶❷聳。五峯秀。百池分。粲粲鮮華明四曜。輝輝道樹鏡三春。揚錫指山阿。攜步上祇陀。既覩如來疊衣石。復觀天授迸餘蛾。佇靈鎮凝思遍生河。金華逸掌儀前奉。芳蓋。陵虛殿後過。旋繞經行砌。目想如神契。廻❸斯少福❹潤❺津梁。❻共會龍華捨塵翳

❼在西國❽王舍城懷舊之作❾一三五七九❿言

遊愁赤縣遠。丹思抽。鷲嶺寒風駛。龍河激水流。既喜朝聞日復日。不覺頹年秋更秋。已畢⓫祇山本願誠難遇終望。持經振錫往神州

法振禪師者。荊州人也。景行高尚唯福是修。濯足禪波棲心戒海。法侶欽肅爲導爲歸。諷誦律經居山居水。而思禮聖迹有意西遄。遂共同⓬州僧乘悟禪師梁州乘如律師。學窮內外智思鉤深。其德不孤結契⓭由蹊。於是攜二友出三江。整帆上景之前。鼓浪訶陵之北。巡歷諸島漸至羯*茶。未久之間法振遇疾而殞。年可三十五六。既而一人斯委彼二情疑。遂附舶東歸。有望交阯。覆至瞻波⓮(即林邑國也)乘悟又卒。瞻波人至傳說如此。而未的委。獨有乘如言歸故里。雖不結實仍嘉⓯令秀爾。獨何爲三無一⓰就

大⓱津⓲師者。澧州人也。幼染法門長敦節儉。有懷省欲以乞食爲務。希禮聖跡啓望王城。每歎曰。釋迦悲父既其不遇。天宮慈氏[illegible]曷我心。自非覩覺樹之眞容謁祥河之勝躅。豈能收情六境。致想三祇者哉。遂以永淳二年振錫南海。爰初結旅頗有多人。及其角立唯斯一進。乃齎經像與唐使相逐。汎舶月餘達尸利佛逝洲。停斯多載。解崑崙語頗習梵書潔行齊心更受圓具。淨於此見。遂遣歸唐望請天恩。於西方造寺。既覩利益之弘廣。乃輕命而復滄溟。遂以天授⓳二年五月十五日附舶而向長安矣。今附⓴新譯雜經論十卷。南海寄歸內㉑法傳四卷。西域求法高㉒僧兩卷

讚曰。嘉爾幼年。慕法情堅。既㉓虔誠於東夏。復請益於西天。重指神州。爲物淹流傳十法之弘法。竟千秋而不秋

㉔右總五十六人

又重歸南海傳有師資四人

苾芻貞固律師者。梵名娑羅笈多(譯爲貞固)即鄭地㉕祭川人也。俗姓孟。粵以驅烏之歲。早蘊慈門。總角之秋。棲心慧苑。年甫十四遂丁荼蓼。眷流俗之難保。知法門之可尚。爰興正念企步勝場。遂於汜水等慈寺遠法師處。申侍席之業。意存教網便誦大經。經三兩歲師遂淪化。後㉖往相州林慮諸寺尋師訪道。欲致想禪局。自念教檢未窮難㉗辯眞僞。即往東魏聽覽唯識。復往安州大欲禪師處習學方等。數旬未隔即妙相現前。復往荊州歷諸山㉘寺。求善知識希覓未聞。復往襄州遇善導禪師受彌陀勝行。當爾之時。交望棄索訶之穢土。即欲趣安養之芳林。霍思獨善傷大士行。唯識所變何非淨方。遂往峴山恢覺寺澄禪師處。創蒙半字之訓漸通完器之言。 禪師則沈研律典。荷世尊五德之重寄。轄轢經論。當末代四依之住持。定澈波深。㉙濯八解而流派。戒峯岳峻。聳六度而疏㉚巖。五塵無雜。九惱非驚。外跨四流內澄三定。法俗欽望推爲導首。特蒙綸旨召入神都。在魏國東寺。居多聞之數。固師年餘二十。即於禪師足下而進圓具。纔經一載總涉律綱。覆向安州秀律師處三載。端心讀宣律師文抄。可謂問絕鄔波離。貫五篇之表裏。受諸毘舍女。洞七聚之幽關。律云。五歲得遊方。未至歲而早契。十年離依止。不屆年而㉛預合。其秀律師即蜀郡與律師之上足。既進圓具仍居蜀川。於和*尙處學律四載。後往長安宣律師處。爲依止㉜之客。投心乳器。若飲鵝之善識精麁。竭智水瓶。等歎喜之妙持。先後經十六年不離函丈。㉝研窮諸部㉞淘鍊數家。將㉟首律師疏以爲宗本。然後去三㊱陽之八水。復向黃州報所生地。次往安州大興律教。諸王刺史咸共遵承。故律云若有律師處與我身不殊。居十力寺。年七十餘。方始寂化。戒行清素耳目詳知。嗟乎代有其人棟梁佛日。蟬聯靡絕繼踵相承。實謂漢㊲珠荊玉。雖別川而俱媚。桂枝蘭葉。縱㊳異節而同芳。固師既得律典斯通。更披經論。又復誦法華維摩向一千遍。心心當續念念恒持。三業相驅四儀無廢。覆往襄州在和㊴上處。重聽蘇呾羅披尋對法藏。頗通㊵纖處薄撿衣珠。化城是息終期寶渚。遂乃濯足襄水顧步廬山。仰上德之清塵。住東林而散志。有意欲向師子洲頂禮佛牙觀禮聖迹。以垂拱之歲

❶穴＝窟【宋】【宮】 ❷聳＝存【三】，遊【宮】 ❸斯＝向【宮】 ❹潤＝澗【元】 ❺津梁＝生津【三】【宮】 ❻共＝於【宮】 ❼❾〔在西…作〕十字∞〔一三五七九言〕【三】，宋元明三本俱在乃至作十字作夾註，同一三五七九言作本文 ❽王舍城懷＝懷王舍城【三】【宮】 ❿〔言〕－【宮】 ⓫祇＝耆【三】 ⓬州＝炯【宮】 ⓭由＝遊【三】【宮】 ⓮即＝弗【三】【宮】 ⓯令＝合【宋】【宮】 ⓰就＋(耳)【三】 ⓱津＝律【宋】【宮】 ⓲師者＝法師【三】【宮】 ⓳二＝三【三】【宮】 ⓴〔新〕－【宮】 ㉑〔法〕－【三】【宮】 ㉒僧＋(傳)【三】【宮】 ㉓虔＝度【宮】 ㉔〔右總五十六人〕－【明】 ㉕祭＝榮【元】【明】 ㉖往＝後【元】 ㉗辯＝辨【宋】【元】【宮】 ㉘寺＝木【三】 ㉙濯＝灌【三】【宮】 ㉚巖＝巘【三】【宮】 ㉛預＝豫【宋】【宮】 ㉜〔之〕－【三】【宮】，之＝有【元】【明】 ㉝研＝幽【三】【宮】 ㉞淘＝濤【宋】【元】【宮】 ㉟首＝守【三】【宮】 ㊱陽＝楊【三】【宮】 ㊲珠＝珍【三】【宮】 ㊳異＝易【三】【宮】 ㊴上＝尙【明】 ㊵〔纖〕－【宮】

移錫桂林適化遊方。漸之淸遠峽谷。同緣赴感。後屆番禺廣府。法徒請開律典。時屬大唐聖主天下普置三師。欲令佛日再明法舟長汎。既而威儀者律也。固亦衆所欽❶情。三藏道場講毘奈耶敎。經乎九夏。究竟七篇。善敎法徒汎誘時俗。于時制旨寺恭闍梨。每於講席親自提獎。可謂恂恂善誘弘濟忘倦。闍梨則童眞出家高行貞節。年餘七十。而恒敬五篇。有福之人可逢上智。實乃禪池淼漫引法海而通波。思嶺崔嵬❷聳慧嶽而騰峭。深明幻本巧悟心源。雖閑諸法體空。而利物之用❸盛集構有爲之福業。作無上之津梁。而屢寫藏經常營衆食。實亦衆所知識應物❹感生。勸悟諸人共敦律敎。固師既法侶言散還向峽山。冀託松林之下。用畢幽棲之志。蒙謙寺主❺等特見賓迎寺主乃道冠生知體含仁恕。供承四海靡倦三朝。屈己申他卑辭是務。固師意欲息想山門。有懷營構傾廊通直道脫階正邪基。曲❻製山池。希流八解之淸潤。傍開壇界。冀闡七聚之芳規。復欲於戒壇後面造一禪龕立方等道場修法華三昧。功雖未就而情已決然。布薩軌儀已紹綱目。又每歎曰。前不遭釋父。後未遇慈尊。末代時中如何起行。既沈吟於空有之際。復躑躅於多師之門矣。淨於佛逝江口❼升舶附書還信廣州。見求墨紙抄寫梵經。幷雇手直。于時商人風便擧帆高張。遂被載來求住無路。是知業能裝飾非人所圖。遂以永昌元年七月二十日達于廣府。與諸法俗重得相見。于時在制旨寺處衆嗟曰。本行西國有望流通。迴住海南經本尙闕。所將三藏五十餘萬❽頌。並在佛逝❾終須覆往。既而年餘五十。重越❿滄波。隙駟不留身城難保。朝露溘至何所囑焉。經典既是要門。誰能共往收取。隨譯隨受須得其人。衆僉告曰。去斯不遠有僧貞固。久探律敎早蘊精誠。儻得其人斯爲善伴。亦既纔聞此告髣髴雅合求心。於是裁封山扃啓陳行李。固乃啓封暫觀。卽有同行之念。譬乎⓫聊城一發下三將之雄心。雪山小偈亦大隱之深志。遂乃喜辭幽澗歎去松林。攘臂石⓬門之前。褰衣制旨之內。始傾一蓋合襟情於撫塵。既投五體。契虛懷於囊日。雖則平生未面而實冥符宿心。共在良宵頗論行事。固乃答曰。道欲合不介而自親。時將至求抑而不可。謹卽共弘三藏助燭千燈者歟。於是重往峽山。與謙寺主等言別。寺主乃照機而作。曾不留連。見述所懷咸助隨喜。己闕無念他濟是心。並爲資裝令無少乏。及廣府法俗悉贈資糧。卽以其年十一月一日附商舶去番禺。望占波而陵帆。指佛逝以長驅。作含生之梯⓭橙。爲欲海之舟艫。⓮慶有懷於⓯從志。庶無廢於長途。固師年四十矣。讚曰

智者植業。稟自先因。童年潔想。唯福是親。情求勝己。意仗明仁。非馨香於事利。固⓰寶愛於賢珍。(其一)受持妙⓱典。貞明固意。大善敦心。小瑕興畏。有懷脫屣。無望榮貴。若住犛之毛尾弗虧。等遊蜂之色香靡費。(其二) 孤辭⓲衆澤。隻步漢陰。哲人務本。律敎是尋。既知綱領。更進幽深。致遠懷於覺樹。遂⓳仗藜於桂林。(其三)怡神峽谷。匠物廣川。既而追舊聞於東夏。復欲請新教以南遄。希⓴揚布於未布。冀㉑流傳於未傳。慶斯人之壯志。能爲物而身捐。(其四)爲我良伴。㉒其屆金洲。能㉓堅梵行善友之由。船車遞濟。手足相求。儻得契傳燈之一望。亦是不慚生於百秋。(其五)既至佛逝宿心是契。得聽未聞之法。還觀不覩之例。隨譯隨受。詳檢通滯。新見新知。巧明開制。博識多智。每勵朝聞之心。恭儉勤懷。無憂夕死之計。恐衆多而事撓。且逐靜而兼濟。縱一焰之隨風。庶㉔十登而罔翳。(其六) 又貞固弟子一人。俗姓孟。名懷業。梵號僧伽提婆。祖父本是北人。因官遂居嶺外。家屬權停廣府。慕法遣奉師門。雖可年在弱冠。而實志逾㉕强。仕見師主。懷弘法之念。卽有隨行之心。割愛抽悲。投命溟渤。至佛逝國。解骨崙語。頗學梵書。誦俱舍論偈。雖事遷於一獵。冀有望於千途。儻㉖策勤於熟思。希比迹於生鍔。且爲侍者現供翻譯。年㉗十七耳

苾芻道宏者。梵名佛陀提婆(*唐云覺天) 汴州雍丘人也。俗姓靳。其父早因商侶移步南遊。遠歷三江遐登五嶺。遂過韶部後屆峽山。覩巖谷之淸虛。翫川源之澄寂。逢善知識披緇釋素。于時道宏其年尙小。任業風而萍轉。隨父師而遊涉。入桂林以翹想。步幽泉而疊息。父名大感禪師。遂於寂禪師處學祕心關。頗經年載薄知要義。還之峽谷。道宏隨父亦復出家。年滿二十此焉進具。往來廣府出入山門。雖可年望未高。而頗懷節槪。既聞淨至走赴莊

❶情＝請(三)(宮) ❷聳＝竦(三)(宮) ❸盛＝成(元)(明) ❹感＝成(宮) ❺〔等〕－(宮) ❻製＝制(宋)(宮) ❼升＝昇(宋)(元) ❽頌＝言(三)(宮) ❾終＝國事(三)(宮) ❿滄＝流(三)(宮) ⓫聊＝遼(三)(宮) ⓬門＝簷(宮) ⓭橙＝隥(三)(宮) ⓮慶＝愛(宋)(宮) ⓯從＝促(元)(明) ⓰寶＝實(三)(宮) ⓱典＝册(三)(宮) ⓲衆＝榮(三)(宮) ⓳仗＝杖(明) ⓴揚布＝敷揚(宋)(宮)，布揚(元)(明) ㉑流＝傳芳(宋)(宮)，傳流(元)(明) ㉒其＝[illegible] ㉓堅＝持(三)(宮) ㉔十登＝千燈(三)(宮) ㉕强＝弘(元)(明) ㉖策＝[illegible](三)(宮) ㉗十七＝七十(三)

嚴。詢訪[illegible]居云停制旨。一申禮事。卽有契於行心。再[illegible]生津。實無論於性命。聞說滔天之浪。蔑若小池。觀橫海之鯨。意同鮪鱓。尋卽重之清[illegible]言別山庭。與貞固師同歸府下。於是乎畢[illegible]南海共赴金❶洲。擬寫三藏德被千秋。識[illegible]聰敏叶性溫柔。頗❷功草隸復翫莊周。體[illegible]物之篇虛誕。知指馬之說❸悠悠。不憚河而徒涉。能臨懼而善籌。雖功未厠於移照。終有慶於英猷。英猷何陳求法輕身。不計樂而爲樂。不將親而作親。欲希等生靈於己體。豈若媿㹀狗而行仁。既至佛逝敦心律藏。隨譯隨寫傳燈是望。重瑩戒珠極所欽尚。求寂滅之圓成。棄❹迷津之重障。畢我大業由斯小匠。慶爾拔擢於有流。庶福資於無量。年二十❺一矣

苾芻法朗者。梵名達❻摩❼提婆*唐云法天襄州襄陽人也。住靈集寺。俗姓安實。乃家傳禮義門襲冠纓。童年出家欽修是務。遂離桑梓遊涉嶺南。淨至番❽禺報知行李。雖復學悟非遠而實希尚情深。❾意喜相隨同越滄海。❿未經一月屆乎佛逝。亦既至此業行是修。曉夜端心。習因明之祕⓫冊。晨昏勵想。聽俱舍之幽宗。既而一簣已傾。庶罔隤於九仞。三藏虔念。擬剋成乎五篇。弗憚劬勞性有聰識。復能志託弘益抄寫忘疲。乞食自濟但有三衣。祖膊塗跣。⓬遵修上儀。雖未成於角立。終有慕於囊錐。凡百徒侶咸希自樂。爾獨標心利生是恪。恪勤何始專思至理。若能弘廣願於悲生。冀大明於慈氏。年二十四矣

共僧貞固等四人。既而附舶俱至佛逝。學經三載梵漢漸通。法朗⓭須往訶陵國。在彼經夏遇疾而卒。懷業戀居佛逝不返番*禺。唯有貞固道宏相隨。俱還廣府。各並淹留且住更待後追。貞固遂於三藏道場敷揚律教。未終三載染患身亡。道宏獨在嶺南。爾來迥絕消息。雖每顧問音信不通。嗟乎四子俱汎滄⓮波。竭力盡誠思然法炬。誰知業有長短各阻去留。每一念來傷歎無⓯及。是知麟喻難就危命易虧。所有福田共相資濟。龍華初會俱出塵勞耳

大唐西域求法高僧傳卷下

❶洲＝州【三】【宮】 ❷功＝攻【三】【宮】 ❸悠悠＝攸攸【宋】【宮】 ❹迷＝生【宮】 ❺二＝三【三】【宮】 ❻摩＝磨【三】 ❼提＝得【宋】【元】 ❽禺＝隅【宋】【元】【宮】* ❾意＋(存)【宋】【宮】 ❿未經＝經歲【三】【宮】 ⓫冊＝典【三】 ⓬遵＝尊【三】【宮】 ⓭須＝頃【三】【宮】 ⓮波＝海【三】【宮】 ⓯及＝極【三】【宮】

BIBLIOGRAPHY

Arnold, Sir Edwin : *The Light of Asia,* edited by Lin Yu Tang, Wisdom of India and China (New York, 1942).

Bagchi, P. C. : *India and China,* 2nd revised edition, (Calcutta, 1981).

——— : *India and Central Asia* (Calcutta, 1955).

Banerjee, A. C. : *Sarvāstivāda Literature* (Calcutta, 1979).

Bapat, P. V. : ed., *2500 Years of Buddhism* (Delhi, 1959).

Barua, Beni Madhab : *Gayā and Buddha Gayā* I, II (Calcutta, 1931, 1934).

——— : *History of Pre-Buddhistic Indian Philosophy* (Delhi, 1970).

Beal, Samuel : *Travel of Fa-hian and Sung-yun, Buddhist Pilgrims from China to India, 400 A.D. and 518 A.D.* (London, 1869).

——— : *The Life of Hiuen-Tsiang* by the Shamanas Hwui-Li and Yen-Tsung (London, 1888).

——— *Buddhist Records of the Western World* (Si-yü-ki by Huien-Tsang), I and II (London, 1885).

: *Indian Travels of Chinese Buddhists,* The Indian Antiquary Vol. 10, 1881.

Bhattacharya, Binoytosh : *The Indian Buddhist Iconography*, 2nd ed. (Calcutta, 1958).

Bose, Phanindra Nath · *Indian Teachers of Buddhist Universities* (Madras, 1923).

Boulnois, Luce : *The Silk Road,* tr. by Dennis Chamberlain (New York, 1966).

Broadley, A. M. : *Ruins of the Nālandā Monasteries at Burgaon* (Calcutta, 1872).

Brown, Percy : *Indian Architecture (Buddhist and Hindu Periods)*, 4th ed. (Bombay, 1959).

Chandra, G.C. : *Excavation at Nālandā,* Annual Report, Archaeological Survey of India, 1934-35 (Delhi 1937), 1935-36 (Delhi 1938).

Chattopadhyaya, Sudhakar : *Early History of Northern India: From the Fall of the Maurya to the Death of Harsha C.* 200 *B.C.—A.D.* 650. (Calcutta, 1958, Reprint 1968).

Chao Pu-chu: Buddhism in China (Peking, 1960).

Ch'en, K. S. Kenneth : The Chinese Transformation of Buddhism (Princeton University Press, 1973).

——— : *Buddhism in China* (Princeton University Press, New Jersey, 1964)

Chou Hsiang-Kuang : *Indo-China Relation* : *A History of Chinese Buddhism* (Allahabad, 1955).

Clyde, Paul H. and Burton F. Beers : *The Far East* 1830-1964, 4th ed. (New Jersey 1966).

Cressey, George B. : *Land of 500 Million* (New York 1955).

: *Asia's Lands and Peoples*: *A Geography of One-third the Earth and Two-thirds Its People* (New York 1951).

Cunningham, A. : *Ancient Geography of India*, ed. by Surendranath Mazumdar Shastri (Calcutta 1924).

: *Mahābodhi or The Great Buddhist Temple Under the Bodhi Tree at Buddha-Gayā* (London, 1892).

Das Gupta, S. N. : *A History of Indian Philosophy* (Motilal Banarsidass, Delhi, 1975).

Das Gupta, Nalini Nath : *Banglaya Bauddhadharma* (Bengali, Calcutta).

De Bary, Wm. Theodore : *Sources of Chinese Tradition* (New York, 1960).

Dey, N. L. : *A Geographic Dictionary of Ancient and Mediaeval India* (London, 1927).

Dobbins, K. Walton : *The Stūpa and Vihāra of Kanishka I* (The Asiatic Society, Calcutta, 1971).

Durga Prasad : *Rājataraṅgiṇi* Ed. (Bombay, 1872).

Dutt, Nalinaksha : *Aspects of Mahāyāna Buddhism and Its Relation To Hīnayāna* (London, 1930).

: *Early Monastic Buddhism*, 2 Vols. (Calcutta, 1941, 1945).

Dutt, Sukumar : *Buddhist Monks and Monasteries of India* (London, 1962).

: *The Buddha And Five After-Centuries* (Calcutta 1957, 1978).

: *The Early Buddhist Monachism* (600 *B. C.*—100 *B.C.*) (London, 1924).

Eitel, E. J. : *A Handbook of Chinese Buddhism, being A Sanskrit-Chinese Dictionary with Vocabularies of Buddhist Terms* (Tokyo, 1904).

Eliot, Sir Charles : *Hinduism and Buddhism : An Historical Sketch* 3 Vols. (London, 1921, Reprint, 1954, 1957, 1962, 1968).

Fairbank, John K. : *Chinese Thoughts and Institution* (Chicago University Press, 1957).

Feng Ch'en-chün : *The Geographical Names of the West* (Hsi-yü-ti-ming (Peking 1955).

Fenn, C. H. : *The Five Thousand Dictionary*, Chinese-English (Cambridge Massachusettes, 1963).

Fitzgerald, C. P.: *China—A Short Cultural History* (London, 1942).
: *The Southern Expansion of Chinese People* (Vikas Publication, New Delhi, 1972).

Fung Yu-lan: *A History of Chinese Philosophy* Vols. I, II. English tr. by Derk Bodde (Princeton University Press, 1952).

Ghosh, A. : *Nālandā* 5th ed. (New Delhi, 1965).

Giles, Herbert A. : *The Travel of Fa-hsien* (Cambridge, 1887, 1923).

——— : *Chinese Biography Dictionary*, (Taipei, 1898).

——— : *Chuang-tze* tr. (Reprinted London 1961).

Gokhale, B. G. : *Buddhism and Aśoka* (Baroda, 1948).

Goodrich, L. C. : *A Short History of Chinese People* (New York, 1959).

——— . *A Syllabus of the History of Chinese Civilisation and Culture* (New York 1958).

Grousset, René : *In the Footsteps of Buddha* (London, 1932).

——— · *The Rise and Splendour of the Chinese Empire* (University of California, 1953).

Gullik, R. H. Van : *Siddham* edited by Prof. Raghuvira Vol. 36 (Saraswati Vihar, New Delhi).

Hajime, Nakamura : *The Influence of Confucian Ethics on Chinese Translation of Buddhist Sutra, Sino-Indian Studies* (Shantiniketan, Viswa Bharati, 1957).

Hirth, Frederich : *Ancient History of China to the end of the Chou Dynasty* (New York 1923, Reprint 1975).

Horner, I. B., tr. : *Cullavagga* : Sacred Books of the Buddhist XX (London, 1952).

Hu-Shih : *The Indianisation of China* : *A Study in Cultural Borrowing* (Cambridge, Massachuset, 1937).

Kern, H. : *Manual of Indian Buddhism* (Strassburg, 1896).

——— : *The Lotus Sūtra* tr. Sacred Books of the East, 21 (Oxford. 1884).

Kosambi, D. D. : *The Culture and Civilisation of Ancient India* (Bombay, 1975).

Kuraishi, M. H. and Ghosh, A. : *Rājgir* 5th ed. (New Delhi, 1958).

Lady John, F. : *South East Asia* : *Its Historical Development* (New York, 1964).

Law, B.C. : *Geography of Early Buddhism* (Reprint, New Delhi, 1978).

Legge, James : *A Record of the Buddhist Kingdoms* (Oxford, 1886)

——— : *Four Books* (Taipei)

——— : *Five Classics* (Hongkong, 1960).

Liebenthal, Walter : *On Trends in Chinese Thoughts*, Silver Jubilee Vol. (Kyoto University, 1954).

Lin Yu-tang : *The Wisdom of India and China* (New York, 1942).

Malalasekera, G. P. : *A Dictionary of Pali Proper Names* (London, 1960).

——— : *Encyclopaedia of Buddhism* (Ceylon, 1965).

Manuel, Komoroff : *The Travels of Marco-Polo* : The Venetial, ed. (New York, 1926).

Marshal, J. H. : '*Rājagṛha and Its Remains*', Annual Report, Archaeological Survey of India, 1905-6 (Calcutta, 1909).

Matsumoto, J. : *Prajñā Pāramitā Sūtra* (J.R.A.S., 1933).

Mathews, R. H. : *Chinese-English Dictionary* (Harvard University Press, 1956).

Mayers Frederic William : *Chinese Readers' Manual* (Shanghai, 1874, Reprint 1964).

Minayeff, J.P. ed. : *Mahāvyutpatti*, Bibliotheca Buddhica.

Mazumdar, R. C. : *Hindu Colonies in the East* (Calcutta, 1973).

——— : *The History of Bengal* (Dacca, 1942).

Mazumdar, R. C. and Pusalkar, A. D., ed.: *The Age of Imperial Kanauj*, Bharatiya Vidya Bhavan's History and Culture of the Indian People, IV (Bombay, 1955).

——— : *The Age Of Imperial Unity*, Bharatiya Vidya Bhavan's

——— : *History and Culture of Indian People*, II (Bombay, 1960).

Mitra, Debala : *Buddhist Monuments* (Calcutta, 1971).

Mitra, Rajendra Lal : *Buddha Gayā* (Calcutta, 1878).

Murti, T.R.V. : The *Central Philosophy* of *Buddhism* (London, 1955).

Nanjio, Bunyiu : *A Catalogue of the Chinese Translation of the Buddhist Tripiṭaka* (Oxford, 1882, Reprint with Additions and Corrections by Dr. Lokesh Chandra, New Delhi, 1980).

Nazim, M. : *Excavation at Nālandā*, Annual Report, Archaeological Survey of India 1936-37 (Delhi, 1940).

Playfair, G. M. M. : *The Cities and Towns of China* : *A Geographical Dictionary* (Taipei, 1965).

Reichelt, (Dr.) K. L. : *Truth and Tradition in Chinese Buddhism* (Sanghai, 1927).

Reischauer, Edwin O. : *Ennin's Travel in T'ang China* (New York, 1955).

— and Fairbank, Jonh K. : '*East Asia*': *The Great Tradition* Vol. I (Harvard University, 1960).

Rhys Davids, T.W. : *The Sects of Buddhists*, J.R.A.S., 1891, pp. 409-22.

———— : *Different Buddhist Schools*, J.R.A.S., 1892.

Ray, Nihar Ranjan : *Bangalir Itihas* (Bengali) (Calcutta Bengali year 1356, 1359).

Sastri, Hira Nanda: *Annual Report of the Director General of Archaeology in India for 1919-20* (Calcutta, 1922).

Sen, Narayan Chandra : *Accounts of India and Kashmir in the Dynastic Histories of the T'ang Dynasty* (Viswa Bharati, Shantiniketan, 1968).

Scott, Latourette Kenneth : *The Chinese* : *Their History and Culture* (New York, 3rd ed. revised, 2 vols 1946).

Smith, D. Howard, Li-chi : *Chinese Religion from 1000 B.C. to the Present Day.*

Soothhill, Edward William : *Lotus of the Wonderful Law* (Oxford, 1930).

——— : *Three Religions of China*, 3rd ed. (London 1929).

—and Houdous Lewis : *A Dictionary of Chinese Buddhist Terms with Sanskrit and English Equivalents and a Sanskrit Pali Index* (London, 1937, Taipei 1968).

Stcherbatsky, T. : *The Central Conception of Buddhism*, 2nd ed. (Calcutta, 1956).

Stein, Sir Aurel : *On Ancient Central-Asian Tracks : Brief narrative of three expeditions in Innermost Asia and North Western China*, (Reprinted in China, 1941).

——— : *Innermost Asia*, Geographical Journal, Vols. I-IV, 1925.

Suzuki, (Dr.) D. T. : *Impression of Chinese Buddhism* (1935)

Takakusu, J. : *A Record of the Buddhist Religion as Practised in India and Malay Archipelago.* (tr. Reprint, Munshiram Manoharlal, 1966).

—and Watanabe, K.: *The Tripiṭaka in Chinese*, Revised, Collated, Added, Rearranged and Edited (The Taishō Issai-kyo, Tokyo).

Waddel, L. Austine : *Buddhism and Lamaism in Tibet* (Reprint) (New Delhi, 1979)

Walay, Arthur : *The Book of Songs* tr. (London, 1937).

——— : *The Way and Its Power* (London, 1934).

——— : *The Analects of Confucius* (London, 1938).

——— : *The Real Tripiṭaka* (New York, 1952).

——— : *The Three Ways of Thought In Ancient China* (London, 1936, New York, 1956).

Wang Chun-heng : *Simple Geography of China* (Peking, 1958).

Ware, J. R. : "*Wei-shu on Buddhism*", T'ong Pao, 30, 1933.

Watson, Burton : *Ssu-ma Ch'ien*, tr. *Record of the Grand Historians of China* (New York, 1961).

Watters, Thomas : *On Yuan Chwang's Travel in India*, 629 *A.D.*—645 *A.D.*, tr. Vol. I and II (London 1904, Peking 1941).

Weber, Max. : *The Religion of China : Confucianism and Taoism.* tr. Gerth, H. H. (Illinois, 1951).

Wieger, Leo : *A History of Religious Beliefs and Philosophical opinions in China*, tr. by Edward Chalmers Werner (Shanghai, 1927).

Williams, Monier : *A Sanskrit-English Dictionary* (Motilal Banarsidass, Delhi).

Winternitz, Maurice : *A History of Indian Literature* Vol. II (Calcutta University, 1933, 1972).

Wright, Arthur, F. : *Buddhism in Chinese History* (Stanford University, 1959).

——— : *Biography and Hagiography : Hui-Chiao's Lives of Eminent Monks* (Silver Jubilee Vol. Kyoto University, 1954).

——— : *Studies in Chinese Thought*, American Anthropological Association Memoir No. 75 (Chicago University Press, 1957).

Zürcher, E. : *Buddhist Conquest of China* (Leiden, 1959).

CHINESE

A—Yü Wang-ching (Aśoka rāja Sūtra) Taishō 50 p. 99 No. 2042.
Chang Hsing-lang, Chung-hsi Chiao-t'ung Shih-liao (Historical materials of Mutual Exchange between China and Western region, Vol. 6.

Ch'iu-fa Kao-seng chuan Taishō 51, 1a-12-b.

Fa-hsien chuan—Taisho 51, 857 C.

Hung-ming chi—Taisho 52, No. 3002.

KSC—Taishō 50, 357c—361b (on Hui-Yuan)

KSC—Taishō 50, 366b—367a (On Tao sheng)

KSC—Taishō 50, 425 (On Tao-Hsuang)

KSC—Taishō 51, No.2089 (On Wu-K'ong).

Nan-hai Chi-kuei nei-fa chuan, Taishō 51, 204c—234a.

SKSC—Taishō 50, 710b—711b (On I-Ching).

Seng-Yü—Ch'u-san tsang-chi-chi, Chapter 13-15.

Ta-T'ang Hsi-yü chi Taishō—51, 868—947c.

Tao-Hsüan, Kuang-hung-ming-chi, (Further collection of Essays on Buddhism)—Taishō 52, No. 3003.

T'zu-hai (Śabda Sāgar) (Shanghai, 1932).

Yang Hsüan-chih. Lo-yang Chia-lanchi (Record of the Monasteries in Lo-yang)—Taishō 51, No.2092, p. 999.

PALI AND SANSKRIT

Bhikkhu Jagadish Kasyapa : *Mahāvagga* edited. (Nava Nālandā Mahāvihāra, 1956), *Cullavagga* 12 ed. (Nava Nālandā Mahāvihāra).

Konow, Sten : *Rājataraṅgiṇī*

Vaidya, P. L. : *Daśabhūmika Sūtra* ed. (Darbhanga, 1967).

INDEX